PROFESSIONAL
SKI INSTRUCTOR
OF AMERICA

CROSS-COUNTRY
SKIING
RIGHT

BY WILLIAM HALL

THE PROFESSIONAL SKI INSTRUCTORS OF AMERICA PRESENT

CROSS-COUNTRY SKIING RIGHT

BY WILLIAM HALL

FOREWORDS BY HORST ABRAHAM AND SVEN WIIK

PRODUCED BY DANIEL PRODUCTIONS

1817

Harper & Row, Publishers, San Francisco

Cambridge, Hagerstown, New York, Philadelphia
London, Mexico City, Sao Paulo, Sydney

ART DIRECTOR/DESIGNER: **JOSEPH DANIEL**

EDITORS: **LINDA BEVARD, TERI TITCHENAL**

EDITORIAL & PRODUCTION STAFF: **VALERIE JACK, JOAN WOOD, CHRISTINA THOMAS, SUSAN EASTMAN, WENDY ROTHMAN**

TYPESETTING & CAMERA WORK: **HORIZON GRAPHICS & TYPE CO.**

PRINTING: **JOHNSON PUBLISHING**

P.S.I.A. ADVISOR: **MIKE DOLAND**

ISBN: 0-06-250170-4

LCCN: 84-47724

Copyright © 1985 by Professional Ski Instructors of America, Inc.

COVER PHOTO/DESIGN: **JOSEPH DANIEL**

ILLUSTRATION CREDITS: **P.S.I.A.**—History etchings
TOM ZILIS—Line drawings   **JOSEPH DANIEL**—ATM graphics

PHOTO CREDITS: **ASPEN SKIING CO./MICHAEL KENNEDY**—93, 94, 206
BEAVER CREEK/BRUCE BENEDICT—155   **COLORADO DAILY**—134, 178   **DOUG CONARROE**—58,
88, 124, 126, 201   **COPPER MOUNTAIN**—90, 166   **JOSEPH DANIEL**—23, 26, 36, 41, 50,
53, 54, 64, 68, 71, 72, 130, 170   **BILL GLUDE**—24   **RICK GODIN**—196
SCOTT McCREA—48   **MONTANA HIGHWAYS**—209   **KEN REDDING**—186
SCANDINAVIAN LODGE—156   **BILL SCOTT**—8

The author gratefully acknowledges permission to reprint Charles C. Bradley's field notes
on avalanche safety (page 197); Bradford Washburn's notes on frostbite—Boston
Museum of Science (page 193); Mike Gallager's quotes in "Learning Right," "Bob
Anderson's "Stretching for Cross-Country"—*Cross-Country Skier;* Cindy Hammond's quote
in the "Introduction"—*Ski;* and Michael Brady's quote in the "Skis" section—Doubleday & Co.

PRINTED IN THE UNITED STATES

FIRST EDITION

Dedicated to my wife Collette—a source of constant inspiration and motivation to persist.

I would like to express my thanks to my teacher, Sven Wiik, who gave me the background, understanding, and knowledge of cross-country skiing; to Horst Abraham, who laid the foundation of ATM; and to the P.S.I.A. Nordic Demonstration Team for their insights and direction in technical matters.

This book would not have been possible without the help of Linda Bevard and Teri Titchenal for editing it, and Joe Daniel for masterfully putting all the pieces together.

TABLE OF CONTENTS

FOREWORDS

PREFACE 11
FOREWORD: *HORST ABRAHAM* 12
FOREWORD: *SVEN WIIK* 13
AN INTRODUCTION 14

PART I – A HISTORY OF SKIING

HOW SKIING EVOLVED 18

PART II – EQUIPMENT

TECHNIQUE & TECHNOLOGY 24
SKIS 26
BOOTS & BINDINGS 36
POLES 41
CLOTHING FOR ACTION 44
CARRY IT! 50

PART III – SKI PREP

THE ART OF WAXING 54
CARE & REPAIR 64
MOUNTING BINDINGS 68

PART IV – PRE-SKI CONDITIONING

PHYSICAL TRAINING 72
THE SKI SCHOOL & YOU 88
CROSS-COUNTRY ETIQUETTE 90

PART V – LEARNING RIGHT

AMERICAN TEACHING METHOD 94
BEGINNING FLAT TRACK 100
UPHILL 108
BEGINNING DOWNHILL 112
ADVANCED DOWNHILL 118
POLE IMPORTANCE 124
TELEMARK TURNS 126

PART VI – DESCENTE STAR TEST

GO FOR THE GOLD 134
BRONZE TEST DESCRIPTION 136
SILVER TEST DESCRIPTION 142
GOLD TEST DESCRIPTION 148

PART VII – COMPETITION

HOW THE RACERS SKI 156
THE NORDIC EVENTS 170

PART VIII – SKI TOURING

THE ALL-DAY TOUR 178
THE OVERNIGHT TOUR 186
AVALANCHE! 196

PART IX – CROSS-COUNTRY KIDS

CHILDREN & SKIING 202
IN TERMS OF SKIING 206

PART X – SKIING DIRECTORY

CANADA 210
UNITED STATES 214

SOURCE DEVELOPMENT 237

PREFACE

Cross-country skiing is a subject I have grown to know in its many varieties. My involvement has taken me through the recreational and competitive sides of the sport.

When I was a child growing up in Denver, I was fortunate that my parents started us skiing at a young age. My brother, sister, and I began our skiing careers on the alpine slopes, learning how to negotiate snowpacked downhill runs. It was not long before we started racing and competing all over the state.

The cross-country bug hit during my years at Western State College in Gunnison, Colorado. The Western State ski team, coached by Kenneth McLennan, provided an excellent opportunity to learn the sport. I used an old pair of wood Bonnas, and my first few times on skis showed me that cross-country really had something to offer. Trying to master the techniques provided challenge enough to capture my interest and total dedication. Since then, I have been enthralled by the constant discovery of new skills to use in a sport that has meant so much to me. The sport is much more than simply sliding around on "skinny" skis. It is a fulfilling exercise for mind and body.

Medical experts continually prescribe exercise to maintain health. Racewalkers and joggers on the streets today are evidence of this trend. Cross-country skiing offers increased cardiovascular efficiency, greater lung capacity, and lower blood pressure. The tension-free environment of the back woods, the slow stride after a fresh powder morning puts the mind at ease, free to think and ramble its way through the day.

This book is set up as an experience in cross-country skiing—from the beginning strides around the park to an extended overnight tour. The technique chapters are designed for the ski teacher, as well as to offer a student the smooth acquisition of skills. Equipment, clothing, waxing, and touring chapters are also included.

The philosophical influence of this book was Horst Abraham, PSIA's Research and Development Chairman. He wrote PSIA's popular book *Skiing Right*, which addresses the subject of how people learn. This basic question has been overlooked in most educational systems. Today, ski teachers throughout PSIA's nine divisions are dealing with this question through varying methods of instruction. Each method is student oriented, attempting to develop each individual's innate potential to move on skis. This book, too, is concerned with allowing each student to discover his or her own most efficient way to learn cross-country skiing.

Use this book to guide you through the many facets of cross-country skiing, and put yourself on the road to self-discovery and enjoyment.

BILL HALL, 1984

FOREWORD

Nordic skiing has come into its own. More and more winter resorts are sporting cross-country trails to augment their skiing menu; some alpine ski schools are starting beginning skiers on cross-country equipment to facilitate the transition from sneakers to ski boots; nordic skiers telemark through mogul fields, formerly the exclusive domain of alpine skiers. The melding of alpine and nordic skiing is rapidly accelerating.

Sensing the importance of nordic skiing in alpine stations, ski areas have given increasing attention to building their nordic centers, as well as providing out-of-bound skiing for touring. Telemark lessons in alpine schools are beginning to gain in popularity.

The slow start of nordic skiing in this country can perhaps be attributed to a strong bias for alpine skiing, as well as poor promotion of nordic skiing. While the image of nordic skiers is beginning to be more colorful, the winter customer is simultaneously looking for quiet alternatives as a means to recreate.

This book is written for teachers and learners alike. Learning this sport needs to be mingled with the courage to think of cross-country skiing not as a mechanical activity, but as a symphony of flowing, interdependent movements. In seeking and finding this harmony lies the challenge of any sport—nordic skiing specifically.

Reflecting upon my own finest moments in sports and skiing, I think of a dance, a game of rhythm, flow and transcendence . . . I find myself describing peak performance in emotional terms, analogies, and metaphors, rather than in terms of technical description or discipline.

I therefore suggest that all of you who are learners (and what good teacher is not also a good student?) allow yourselves to explore skiing as if it were something you were very familiar with—a dance, a symphony in motion. Those of you who are teachers, find methods that are play and experience oriented; such teaching will bring a sense of flow and contextual clarity to learners; such teaching will allow students to learn to learn, grow toward optimum performance levels, but also beyond the skill of being a good skier. When teaching and learning become one, the essence of it all becomes clear!

"THE WHOLE IS UNPREDICTED BY ANY OF ITS PARTS TAKEN SEPARATELY."

Buckminster Fuller

HORST ABRAHAM

FOREWORD

The legendary Jackrabbit Johannsen, aged 107, was once asked the secret to his longevity. "Moderation in everything," he answered, ". . . and ski."

Yes, skiing is a way of life and the "total skier" enjoys the sport to its fullest, skiing both nordic and alpine styles. Cross-country skiing, which is a part of nordic skiing, is the foundation to all skiing.

Anybody taking up skiing is well advised to start on cross-country equipment, for many reasons. Let me mention just a few:

• Cross-country skiing can be enjoyed on a few inches of snow in one's own back yard, the city park, or golf course.
• One or two lessons are sufficient—and

important—and will teach you all phases of skiing: skiing uphill and downhill, turning, and, yes, even ski jumping.
• Become a cross-country skier first and the transition to the thrilling, exciting and fast sport of alpine (slope) skiing becomes easier.

This book by Bill Hall—author, PSIA Nordic Demonstration Team Member, and PSIA-RM Nordic Chief Examiner—is a must to all entry-level skiers. It also provides invaluable information and suggestions to the more avid tour skier, the ski mountaineer, and the serious cross-country ski racer.

SVEN WIIK

AN INTRODUCTION

"Evolution is not a force but a process; not a cause but a law."

Viscount Morley of Blackburn

The first step into the world of skiing is on cross-country skis. With their loose heels, they enable the cross-country enthusiast to ski uphill *or* down, unlike alpine skiers.

Nordic skiing, of which cross-country is a part, includes all loose-heel events such as the biathlon (a combined skiing and shooting event), ski jumping, and citizen racing. Alpine skiing includes events during which the heel is fixed to the ski: downhill, giant slalom, and slalom.

With the concepts presented in this book, you will be able to develop your cross-country skills on your way toward becoming a total skier. Skiing, whether alpine or nordic, is based upon the same principles. There is no one way to ski. The important thing is to discover what brings you the most personal satisfaction.

What has been overlooked in the rush to the slopes is the contribution cross-country skiing provides for improving and developing your overall physical prowess. Ease of movement, lightweight equipment, and familiar movements make cross-country skiing a natural introduction to standing and sliding on skis. After the first lesson on cross-country skis, the possibilities available in the skiing world increase. They multiply when you include prepared track skiing, backyard exploring, touring, telemarking, slope skiing, and mountaineering. The variety of choices abound—you're limited only by your energy level.

Several alpine ski schools have been experimenting with programs that let novice skiers experience cross-country skiing first, before moving on to the slopes. The shoe-like boots and lightweight skis allow easy, less restricted movement. After the initial attempts at sliding around on the flat and on gradual hills, the student has developed a feeling for balancing on the skis. The sensations of these early attempts at cross-country skiing are ingrained into the basic skiing stance. Through repetition of a skill—done the proper way—the student develops muscular movements or patterns that stay with him (a skier's "muscle memory") during future learning attempts. The muscles used to balance over the feet are strengthened and the student carries that ability to balance over a gliding or sliding ski into other, and more demanding, skiing endeavors. The cross-country stance is the fundamental position basic to continued success and enjoyment on skis.

Horst Abraham, technical advisor to the Professional Ski Instructors of America, technical director of the Vail Ski School and creator of the ATM (American Teaching Method), has experimented with the "nordic intro" to skiing. "The growth in ability of those who started on nordic skis was phenomenal," he says. "They were much more aggressive and willing to try new maneuvers."

Cindy Hammond, co-director of the ski school at Sugarloaf, Maine, says, "Sugarloaf 'never-evers' progress faster when they spend their first day on nordic equipment. They learn to sense more quickly when they go off balance, in plenty of time to recover instead of falling or staggering. Stiff alpine boots and fixed bindings tend to mask the sensation of losing your balance."

Cross-country skiing, whether enjoyed solely on its own merits (and they are many) or as an introduction to other forms of skiing, involves skills intrinsic to all skiing. In summary, in the words of Sven Wiik, owner-operator of the Scandinavian Lodge in Steamboat Springs, Colorado: "It's a well-rounded skier who knows the benefits of both alpine and nordic skiing, enhancing their overall enjoyment of this wintertime recreation called skiing."

Use this book as a stepping stone, to start you off on the right track. The benefits cross-country skiing has to offer will be self-evident as you continue reading. I personally hope you use this book as the first step in your skiing career. And whatever path you take after reading and practicing the contents herein, be assured you will have developed the basics of all good skiing: balance and *fun*.

A HISTORY OF SKIING

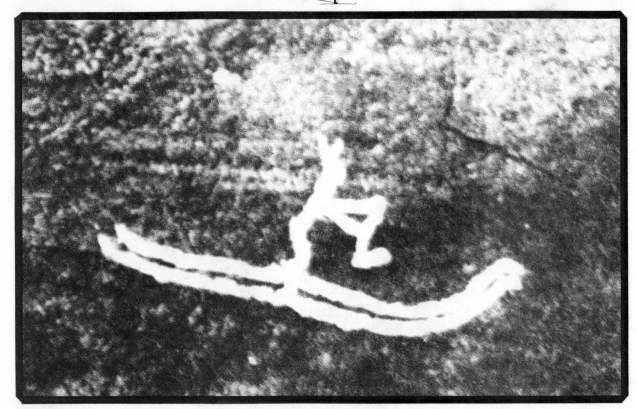

HOW SKIING EVOLVED

"History is bunk."

Henry Ford

When historians and researchers explore the origins of skiing, their journey begins in Scandinavian countries, where 4,500-year-old remains of skis have been found. The Laplanders of Sweden, Norway, and Finland, and also the people of the Ural Mountains of Russia, have always been snowbound during winter. To survive, they have learned to adapt to the realities of winter. The ski was an integral part of their development. The earliest known skis were discovered through petroglyphs found on an island in Northern Norway which archaeologists date at about 2,000 B.C. Norsemen used skis to travel and to hunt. They even had a mythological god, "Ullr," the protector of skiing and hunting, and a ski goddess, "Skade." Hunting large game on skis gave man an advantage. The faster moving skis allowed hunters to slide up on elk or reindeer in deep snow, making their capture imminent. Eventually an early Norwegian "Code of Law" (dating back to 1274) was needed to restrict hunting on skis, because it was too easy. Herds were being wiped out.

Chronicles exist of hunting trips during which the hunters' spears served not only to kill their prey, but to help climb uphill and steer downhill. At the time skis were long (from eight to fifteen feet in length), cut from a single piece of wood (usually a softer fir or spruce). Skis sometimes varied in length—one long, one short. The shorter ski had reindeer or sealskin on its bottom to facilitate climbing. The tips were curved up; sometimes even the tails were curved, too, for quick escapes! The ski was a fast means for early man to move on top of the deep snowpack.

The first military use of skis was reported in the Norwegian Civil War (1140-1210), when ski troopers were used to scout enemy troop positions. An early historian, Snorre Sturalson (1179-1241), writes, "The Viking Kings were skillfull skiers." In the war between Sweden and Norway in 1716 both sides utilized ski patrols, along with winter strategies, to scout the enemy. Since then skis have remained a part of military training. During World War II the Tenth Mountain Division was the toughest group of men on skis. Their dramatic exploits in battling the Germans on skis were due to their extensive winter training in the mountains outside of Leadville, Colorado. The men of the Tenth Mountain Division are still honored as the best-prepared ski troops of the war.

War, hunting and family scenes from Norway in 1555. Stone Age ski touring shown in petroglyph (opposite page) found on Norwegian island.

Cross-country ski technique itself had an early beginning. In 1765, the Norwegian Army put together the first instructional manual on skiing, and it was not long before the public became interested. The first organized cross-country race took place in northern Norway in the city of Tromsoe in 1843. The following excerpt from the book, *The Flying Norseman* (published by the National Ski Hall of Fame Press, Ishpening, MI, 1983) is Carl Howelson's account of the competition: "The Tromsoe Times of March 19, 1843, published the following invitation to a ski race: 'At 4:00 p.m., Tuesday, March 21, certain persons intend, weather and skiing conditions permitting, to test the speed of their skis and their own staying power in a race from Town Hall to the well at Merchant Ebeltoft's house on the other side of the island, and back. They expect to complete the course in 40 minutes. Assemble in the marketplace at 3:45. All skiers, including those who use ordinary skis and those who use short ones—in a word, all who are interested in a genuine Norwegian contest—are invited to take part. NB: Those who think they can complete the course in a shorter time on short skis are welcome to try.'" Later the paper commented about the race: "On returning, all were red in the face as lobsters. The crowd was also greatly amused when various competitors, skiing downhill at full speed, lost their balance and bathed their tired bodies in the cold snow."

The race was an apparent success. A few days later, the same newspaper could report, "Skiing has become a real national recreation, inasmuch as most youth of the town and some of the older citizens have recently tried this brisk and very beneficial physical exercise."

Although skiing had been around for hundreds of years, it wasn't until the middle of the nineteenth century that it was popularized as a recreational sport. The growing interest and enthusiasm for this winter mode of exhilaration brought about the first ski school in Telemark, Norway, in 1881. The beginning of this new era in skiing's development was sparked by an inventive young man named Sondre Nordheim, born in 1825 in Telemark, one of the eighteen provinces of Norway.

Nordheim experimented with ways of obtaining more control on descents. To complement the standard leather toe strap used to hold the foot on the ski, he devised a heel strap made out of birch rope that wrapped around the back of the boot and kept the heel from sliding off the ski. In the process, the added lateral control over the ski prompted the use of shorter skis that had a little side cut. It was through Nordheim's new binding support and ski design that steep hillsides could be maneuvered by turning the ski in long arcs. The one long pole gave way to two short poles, one for each hand.

During this period long-radius turns became known as "telemark turns." The word spread about Nordheim's amazing ability to turn down mountainsides with such ease and grace; soon instruction was given to others on how to make *their* skis turn downhill. Eventually another type of turn developed as a result of Nordheim's binding. The "christie" was created by turning with both feet held together instead of one in front of the other. Named for the capital of Norway, Christiana (Oslo), the "christie" is still a common turn today.

What Thomas Edison did for electricity, Sondre Nordheim did for skiing. The avenues of development were opened up for such pioneers as Fridtof Nansen who, in 1881, crossed Greenland on skis. Also a great writer, Nansen detailed his experiences cross-country skiing and its benefits for body and mind.

Snowshoe Thompson

Skiing came to America with the early European immigrants. One of the first such adventurous individuals was John Thompson, a man they called "Snowshoe Thompson." Born in Telemark, Norway, in 1836, he emigrated to the United States at the age of ten. He eventually moved West and became

known for his exploits in the Sierra Nevada Mountains of California, where he carried mail on skis, up and over the divide from Placerville to Carson Valley, a distance of ninety miles or more. His career began in 1856 and spanned the next twenty years. He developed a ski wax during that time called "Lightning Dope" or, in some areas of the Sierras, "Sierra Dope." The recipe was never the same and each batch differed. I'm sure it held on the uphills, but the glide had to be questionable! Inhabitants relied on John Thompson's mail delivery until his death in 1876 at the age of forty-nine.

Under the Norwegian influence, people were skiing on long boards from the Atlantic to the Pacific. It was in 1904, following a ski competition in Ishpening, Michigan, that a group of Norwegian ski leaders got together to discuss the future of skiing in the United States. At that meeting the "National Ski Association of America" was formed; it elected Carl Tellefsen as president. Ski clubs sprang up around the country. The Steamboat Springs (Colorado) Winter Sports Club was started by a Norwegian immigrant, Carl Howelson, in 1913. Like many others, he left his mark on skiing history.

An Englishman, Sir Arnold Lunn, contributed the first rule book for competition skiing. His motive was to organize the British University skiers for their first competition in the United States in 1911. They raced against the Dartmouth team led by Otto "Skiing Is A Way Of Life" Schneib.

In the 1930s, ski and binding designs began to change again. Skis evolved from a single piece of wood to laminated layers of wood, glued and molded together to form a stronger, more responsive tool. This process of gluing and pressing pieces of wood together under heat allowed ski manufacturers to shape camber into skis, giving the ski the bowlike bend that helps distribute weight evenly over the ski. Strength was increased by the gluing process and the six to seven laminations of different densities of wood. Eventually manufacturers laminated ten to twenty different layers of material. Ski construction was becoming industrialized.

Austrian Hannes Schneider worked on perfecting the ski binding, going to metal for strength, rigidity, and lateral support. He published a book on the different types of turns in use at the time, such as the snowplow, stem christie, and parallel christie. The "arlberg technique" was added to developing schools of instruction. Skiing began to take a new direction; the downhill mode became increasingly popular.

A new era in skiing began when the first ski lift was devised on a farm near Woodstock, Vermont, in 1934. The long, time-consuming climbs to the top of the slope were cut in half by a contraption of ropes and pulleys hooked up to an old tractor engine. Skiing began to develop in two directions: skiers who enjoyed skiing primarily downhill and those who enjoyed skiing across the countryside, uphill and down. To denote this difference it became necessary to use terms to describe these two types of skiing. Hence the term "alpine," taken from the European skiers who climbed up into the steep rugged Alpine terrain and skied down., In some areas of the United States the term "alpine skiing" has been shortened to just "skiing."

An individual who did not enjoy the lifts and the heavy, more physically restrictive equipment of alpine skiing soon was viewed by the public as a different type of skier. The trend in the United States was certainly toward lift riding. Skiing with a loose heel and the ability to traverse a variety of terrains was now becoming separated from the mainstream. Developing in the late 1930s, the term "cross-country skiing" was used to acknowledge this difference. Taken from the American term for running over varied terrain, "cross-country" perfectly described the same

activity performed on skis. It was chosen to represent all recreational and competitive aspects of loose-heel skiing, classified as "nordic skiing."

Today alpine and nordic skiing are merging, opening up a new interest in these once similar sports. The chance to experience the benefits of both is becoming a popular way to approach skiing. For the first-time skier, the benefits of learning to ski on cross-country equipment, then gradually switching to alpine equipment, makes the process much easier. Cross-country's lightweight skis, flexible boots and unintimidating terrain make the novice's initial attempts at sliding on skis much less traumatic, but much more satisfying than the "bunny slopes" he would have to resign himself to on alpine equipment. Once the feeling of standing on slippery skis is experienced, the whole wide world of skiing opens up. Nowadays, skiers enjoy not just one type of skiing, but both. They divide their vacations between the unique experiences of nordic skiing and the thrill of alpine skiing.

The sublimities and peculiarities of cross-country skiing are the topic of this book. It is hoped that the information covered in these pages will be but a stepping stone for your continued growth and development in the fun-filled, physically exciting, stimulating activity of skiing.

EQUIPMENT

TECHNIQUE & TECHNOLOGY

"All the means of action — the shapeless masses — the materials — lie everywhere about us."

Henry Wadsworth Longfellow

Cross-country equipment is versatile, and the kind of skiing you plan to do will determine the type of equipment you use. Do you plan to ski in the back country, climbing tall peaks, skiing the steep-and-deep—or would you rather ski in prepared tracks? How about a little of both? Why a whole chapter devoted to equipment? There are *many* different makes and models of skis, boots, bindings, and poles on the market, and this chapter will help you sort out the facts and fancy.

Walking into a ski shop and looking at a wall full of skis can be disheartening. Don't pick your equipment by color or fancy cosmetics. A reputable ski shop or touring center will help you select the appropriate equipment to your needs. A knowledgeable salesperson (or your ski instructor) can help you decide.

First, ask yourself what kind of skiing you will be doing the most. To help you decide, here are four common categories of skiing that correspond to the four categories of equipment. See which group you fall into.

CITIZEN RACING

"I plan to ski entirely in prepared tracks, working on technique." "I've been skiing for a couple of years now, but I'd like to try some lighter equipment and really practice on my cross-country technique. I want to try a citizens' race in the future." "I enjoy running in the summer and want to continue my running in the winter, but on cross-country skis."

A growing number of foot runners are discovering the benefits of cross-country skiing. It is not exercise for the legs alone, but a total conditioner, working the entire body—the legs, arms, shoulders, stomach and back. In addition, cross-country skiing ranks at the top, along with swimming, in caloric expenditure per hour. So, if you want some good wholesome exercise to strengthen you and consume calories, the racing category is for you.

How do you know if you are ready for racing equipment? You'll know. Once you have learned how to move on the flats, uphills and downhills with ease, the heavier light touring skis will have served their purpose. You'll require lighter, more responsive, racing equipment.

LIGHT-TOUR SKIER

I am just starting and plan to ski on packed, prepared trails." "I want an all-around ski, something I can use on prepared tracks, maybe even ski a citizens' race, but I also want to ski in the back country."

Approximately sixty percent of all cross-country skiers fall into this category. Versatility is the main advantage of light touring equipment. With it you are not restricting yourself to only one kind of skiing; you have the option to experience both prepared track skiing and back country tours. This equipment is a real plus for the first-time skier, as well as for weekend rompers.

GENERAL TOURING

I like to tour a lot, skiing in the back country through deep powder, spending the whole day exploring, especially skiing into my favorite summer hiking spots." "I like to get away away and ski where nobody else is, sometimes spending the night and skiing out the next day." "I'm always skiing in the back country. I never ski on prepared tracks."

About twenty-five percent of all cross-country enthusiasts fall into this group, but you can expect an increase when more people discover the solitude of a quiet, peaceful day on cross-country skis. Away from the hustle and bustle of city life, the easy pace of a long ski tour relaxes the mind and body. By the end of the day, you will feel pleasantly tired and relaxed, ready for a good night's sleep.

MOUNTAIN SKIING

I enjoy climbing above timberline and then skiing down in the powder." "I enjoy skiing at alpine ski areas on metal-edge nordic skis. Telemark turns have added a new dimension to my skiing. They have really helped my alpine skiing."

This category of skier is expanding to include not only back country mountaineers, but telemark skiers as well. The groomed slopes of alpine ski areas provide lift service and plenty of continuous practice. Many skiers relish the all-day tour to a far-off peak where waist-deep powder awaits; they savor every run in the untracked snow. These skiers, when asked where they skied all day, will not tell you. Approximately ten percent of all cross-country skiers fall into this group. Don't tell anybody, OK!!

SKIS

"This is the short and the long of it."

William Shakespeare

Skis have come a long way since those early attempts to stand on top of the snow. Developments have emphasized form and function. Ski manufacturers have developed equipment for different types of skiing, as well as for individual differences among enthusiasts.

Each ski has certain distinguishing characteristics, its own personality. You might ask, "Aren't all skis the same, nothing but a piece of wood with the tip curved up?" Not quite. Michael Brady, author of many books on cross-country skiing, writes, "If you were to go into a well-stocked ski shop cold, with no prior knowledge of the sport, you probably would find selecting cross-country supplies incredibly confusing, because they are made with a greater variety of characteristics than any other item of sports gear, including jogging shoes."

Ski construction has advanced a long way from the early days when they were one piece of wood with the tip steamed and bent a little. Modern ski technology has developed through three stages.

Each new era in ski construction has not only made equipment better, but has brought changes in the way people ski. Skiing on an eight- to nine-foot ski made it difficult to really push and glide. It took a lot of effort to slide along, singing a song. The early ski pioneers probably could foresee lighter, faster skis, but knew it would take time.

During the 1930s, ski manufacturing was industrialized and skis become lighter and stronger. Recreational skiers and racers truly appreciated this new development in ski construction and design. Ski construction went from one piece of wood to several layers laminated together. Layering six to nine different types of wood, then gluing, compressing, and shaping, formed a stronger, lighter ski that slid better.

Each type of wood had different attributes. Hickory and birch (dense, tough woods that do not wear out easily) were used for the ski's bottoms. These woods were porous enough to accept pine tar when sealing and waxing.

Some models began sporting specialized edges. Hickory was not durable enough to withstand constant turning on ice and crust; the ski's edges tended to round off. Therefore, the lignistone edge began to appear. Made by compressing beech wood under extreme heat to harden the wood, this produced a durable edge to bite into the snow. It is not uncommon to see older skis with the lignistone edge still intact but the bottoms badly worn.

Splitken was one of the early companies to use nine laminated layers to make their skis. There was hardwood on the bottom, usually hickory, and birch or cherry wood on top. These skis were finely crafted tools for recreation or sport.

By the end of this era in ski construction, it was not uncommon to see skis with sixteen to thirty-two layers, all glued and pressed together. Now you know where skiers coined the phrase, "Oh, darn, my skis are starting to delaminate."

At the opening of the 1974 World Championships in Falun, Sweden, the weather played an important role. Conditions were excellent for the newer fiberglass ski. The Russians surprised the world, using a ski that would revolutionize ski construction. Fiberglass had been used in ski construction on a limited basis ever since the early 1970s when Jarvenen put a plastic base on wooden skis. The fact that a skier won a major race on a synthetic-based ski brought national attention to the sport and sparked the continued production and use of this faster-gliding material. Cross-country ski manufacturers began to use the successful polyurethane bottoms, sandwiching layers of fiberglass above and below a wood core that alpine skiers had enjoyed since the early sixties.

The major advantage of a synthetic bottom over a wooden one is that it can be waxed on the tip and tail for glide and waxed for hold in the middle of the ski. The strength-to-weight ratio of fiberglass makes it an ideal material to combine with the wood of the past. With it, skis could be made stronger to withstand more abuse without breaking. The skis' camber (the bow in each ski) could be strengthened, keeping the cross-country wax off the snow when gliding—an important consideration for performance-minded skiers. This was the main reason the Russians surprised the world in 1974. Today's skis have taken on a new reliability and speed, two characteristics that the pioneers knew were coming. Today's equipment allows human movement to become a natural extension of the body's source of locomotion.

SKI SELECTION

Skis, like cars, are an investment (usually a depreciating one) you have to live with. When selecting a car, you must first determine what type of driving you will be doing—mostly inner city jaunts, with a lot of stop-and-go and parking in tight spots, or do you plan to cruise the country on the interstate? Will you need a car big enough to sleep in, maybe even a truck?

The same holds true when selecting skis. Consider first what type of skiing you will be doing the most. Then choose a pair of skis from one of the four major categories (racing, light touring, touring, or mountaineering), which will set the stage for selecting boots, bindings and poles as well. Now the selection process is narrowed to specific characteristics within that category. Here is where a reputable ski shop can fit your equipment to your skiing personality.

You would not buy a car without first driving it. If possible, rent or borrow skis at first, experimenting with equipment until you decide on a particular ski that is best for you and that you want to buy.

If you are planning to ski every weekend, buying your own skis is easier on the pocketbook. Once-a-month skiers may prefer to rent and continue trying different skis until a decision is reached based on experience.

SKI LENGTH

The proper ski for you depends on your height, weight and ability. The length of your skis determines how you will be supported above the snow. A general guideline in ski length selection is to raise one arm straight over your head and choose a ski whose tip reaches to the wrist of the outstretched hand.

Your weight determines whether you will go slightly longer or shorter for your height. An extremely light skier may choose a slightly shorter ski, whereas a heavier skier may choose a slightly longer ski. Keeping your weight in mind, move up or down, five to ten centimeters, in length to tailor the ski to your needs.

Ski length is measured in centimeters from the tip to the tail. If you are six feet tall, a 210-

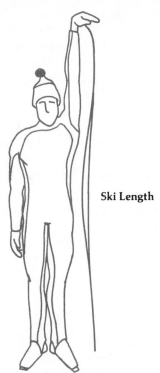

Ski Length

Racers or performance skiers who are concerned with speed choose skis that apportion weight equally between both feet. Distributing weight evenly over the entire ski facilitates speed. A 230-pound racer may find the normal-length ski too short for his weight; going 10 centimeters longer helps support his weight better. In theory, the more surface area contacting the snow, the less pressure per square inch, thus allowing the ski to slide faster. In general, when talking ski length, go shorter for less experience, then work toward the standard length ski.

SKI WIDTH

The ski's width varies from category to category depending on use. The scale below will help you understand ski width as it relates to use.

Tail   Waist   Tip

RACING—Narrowest   The racer wants lightweight skis that do not drag in the tracks. The racer always skis in prepared tracks so support is not a concern. **Common Width Measurement:** Tip—45 mm, Waist—44 mm, Tail—45 mm.

LIGHT TOURING—Narrow to Medium   The light tour skier wants skis suited to racing, but they must be wide enough to support his weight in the powder and for off-track skiing. **Common Width Measurement:** Tip—49 mm, Waist—46 mm, Tail—48 mm.

TOURING—Medium to Wide   The tour skier wants support when breaking trail and skiing the powder. In the back country a wider ski is a must. **Common Width Measurement:** Tip—55 mm, Waist—50 mm, Tail—53 mm.

MOUNTAINEERING—Widest   The mountain skier wants skis for support and turning. A wider ski is made to turn more easily and the increased width supports better on the trail. **Common Width Measurement:** Tip—65 mm, Waist—58 mm, Tail—63 mm.

SIDE CUT

The difference in width measurements from tip to tail is referred to as the ski's side cut. Side cut makes the ski easier to turn.

centimeter ski would be appropriate. A five-foot six-inch skier may choose a 185 to 195-centimeter ski. Depending on your weight and ability, you may select a shorter or longer ski. A common size for ladies is 185 to 200 centimeters for the big woman or racer. For the taller woman and man, sizes range from 205 to 220 centimeters unless longer skis are specially ordered.

Although the skis' length is 210 centimeters, the actual number of centimeters that touch the snow when skiing is somewhat less. This measurement of the actual surface in contact with the snow is called "contact length." The contact length of a 210-centimeter ski is approximately 190 to 195 centimeters, depending on tip and tail design. This measurement is the crucial one, but the more common reference is to overall length.

Contact Length

A less skilled skier will benefit from a slightly shorter ski. They are easier to turn on the hill and maneuver on the flat. As you become more proficient, a longer ski will provide more control and stability.

Tour skiers who are always in the back country breaking trail might use longer skis than normal. In deep snow, a longer ski stays afloat more easily. If you plan long day trips or overnights, you can add twenty to forty pounds for your pack. Longer skis help distribute your weight evenly over the entire ski.

Side cut was first introduced in 1870 by Sondre Norheim. He used side cut to increase the mobility and versatility of skis, and literally revolutionized ski construction. Side cut paved the way for metal edges and the christiana turn. The christiana was the first parallel skidded turn, similar to today's parallel turn. The use of side cut was a step in the right direction and opened the door to further advancements and changes in how people skied, particularly downhill.

Side cut works when pressure is applied on a ski at an angle to the snow surface. The tip and tail dig into the snow more vigorously than the middle of the ski, thus turning the ski. The ski follows the tip around the corner. When a ski is on edge and pressured, resistance of tip and tail to twisting (its torsional rigidity) determines how well it holds on edge. A soft tip will deflect and slip sideways; a stiffer tip will hold better in hard-packed conditions.

How does this relate to our different categories of skiing? The mountain skier makes turns coming downhill. Therefore, mountain skis have more side cut than racing skis. Light touring and touring skis function better with side cut, increasing turning ability and control.

A racing ski is designed to be used only in tracks, the tracks turn the ski. Racing skis sometimes have a straight cut, meaning that the measurements at the shovel, waist and tail are the same (44mm, 44mm, 44mm). International standards have set 44mm at the waist as the narrowest width ski manufacturers can design. A javelin cut refers to narrower measurements at the tip and tail becoming widest at the waist. For example, 35mm, 44mm, 36mm is a great cut for track skiing but not the best ski for turning. When a javelin ski is placed on edge, it has what is called a "reverse side cut" and instead of turning into the turn, it turns away from the intended turning direction.

The wider the ski, the more support it provides and the stronger it becomes. It is also heavier, which can be tiring when skiing fast, and which slows the response time of the ski when turning. The narrower the ski (as in racing), the more responsive and lighter it is. That is why performance skiers prefer skinny skis. They are light, and a straight or javelin cut lessens the drag created by a wider ski. Racing skis follow the tracks better and eliminate excessive friction when hitting the sides. Wider skis may not even fit into prepared tracks and, if they do, will always rub the sidewalls, reducing speed.

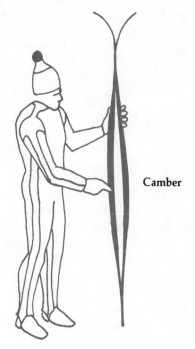

Camber

THE SKI'S BOW: CAMBER

If you look at a pair of skis, you will notice they're not totally flat. Each has a bow in it—what ski manufacturers call "camber." If you were to put that pair of skis on the ground and stand with one foot in the middle of each ski, the bow would flatten out. The amount of weight needed to flatten this bow affects how the ski handles.

Picture the bottom of a ski. The cross-country wax is in the middle third. In order for the wax to contact the snow, enough pressure must be applied to flatten the ski's bottom to the snow. Think of how cross-country wax works. The wax must be of a hardness to allow the snow to penetrate it and give hold. Skis glide faster when the cross-country wax is off the snow. Pressuring the ski comes during the push-off from one ski onto the other. This is when the most force is exerted down onto the ski, flattening it onto the snow. The amount of pressure necessary to flatten the ski depends on the skier's weight and ability.

A ski of proper length is one way to distribute weight; camber is another. A 200-pound man standing on a short, soft-cambered ski would flatten the ski to the snow easily; the ski's bottom would always be running on the snow. The stiffer-cambered ski requires more weight or pressure to become flattened. In order to push off the ski, the cross-country wax must touch the snow for a brief moment to give hold and prevent the ski from slipping backward. Therefore, selection of the right camber is an important consideration for your skiing enjoyment. Select too stiff a ski for your weight and you will never be able to flatten the ski to get hold. Choose too soft a ski and you will always be wearing your cross-country wax off the middle of the ski. Refer to the section on Camber Selection for a further discussion on testing methods.

SKI CONSTRUCTION VS. CAMBER

With the developments of synthetic material, ski manufacturers have been able to strengthen the bow in skis—something wooden skis always had, but which lasted only as long as the wood held its shape. Wood skis *do* have other attributes, though as a wood ski holds a certain aesthetic appeal for some skiers. The smell of pine tar used to preserve and seal wooden ski bottoms is mystifying. The feel of wood skis is like the feel of a solid wooden-hulled sailboat. It's something that cannot be described. A good pair of wood skis is hard to part with.

Some synthetic skis still use wood at the core, but now are covered and reinforced with fiberglass or other exotic materials (foam, carbon/graphite), like a wood frame house that is insulated and covered with paneling or brick. The wood core provides the structure, the fiberglass provides the strength.

With a combination of the old and new, cross-country skis have advanced, becoming stronger, faster, more durable and increasingly versatile to benefit all four major categories of skiers. The racers have enjoyed a synthetic ski's stiff camber. Increased speed has been a result of stiffer camber and polyurethane bottoms, with glide wax used on the tip and tail and cross-country wax only in the middle of the ski. The stiff camber does not flatten to the snow until all the skier's weight is on one ski—and then only when he/she pushes hard, down and forward off the ski, does the middle of the ski touch the snow.

"Double camber" is a term that has been used to describe the stiffer-cambered skis made today, although it is a misnomer. All skis have *one* camber, but it is the camber stiffness in the middle of the ski that dictates the amount of force required to flatten the ski, the stiffer the camber, the more the ski can be said to have a gliding camber *and* a grip wax camber—hence the term "double camber."

On wood skis, the cross-country wax always touched the snow a little when gliding on both skis and especially when balancing on one ski. The

result was a much slower ski than today's synthetic skis. Cross-country wax does not have the gliding properties of the petroleum-based glide waxes used now. Specifically, the cross-country glide waxes that can be ironed on the ski have contributed to the synthetic ski's success. Therefore, wood or synthetic skis with a very soft camber are referred to as "single cambered." The bow in the ski is not strong enough to support a skier's weight without the entire ski bottom contacting the snow.

How does this relate to your ability and the proper ski for you? It is easier to ski on a soft or single-cambered ski than a stiff or double cambered ski.

SELECTING THE RIGHT CAMBER FOR YOU

Selecting a pair of skis with the right camber is an individual process. Consider three factors when choosing the right camber for you: (1) body weight, (2) ability, and (3) intended use.

The ski's bow or camber is directly affected by your weight. Downward pressure when standing with feet equally weighted should distribute weight over the entire ski. The ski's camber should be proportionate to your weight; a heavy skier needs stiff camber and a light skier, soft camber.

Ability also determines whether the ski's camber should be stiffer or softer. Generally the stiffer the camber, the more refined the technique. A soft-cambered ski is good for a novice, because the cross-country wax is always touching the snow. A stiff-cambered ski for the performance skier or racer glides faster, but takes a more powerful push-off (or kick) to flatten the ski to the snow and get hold.

The intended use of the skis further determines camber selection. Will you be skiing in prepared tracks where the snow is groomed to a smooth, compacted consistency, or touring in the back country where the snow is soft and powdery? In general, follow this rule of thumb: in hard, icy snow conditions, a stiff-cambered ski works best; soft, powdery snow conditions require a softer cambered ski. Racers may take this to the extreme, owning not just two pairs of skis but several, each with its individual flex (camber) pattern.

Keep in mind that light touring or touring skis are made to withstand the undulating terrain of touring trails, through dips, over bumps and in varying snow conditions. Wider, heavier skis are built stronger to withstand this kind of punishment. Racing skis, at the other extreme, will not withstand the abuse of touring trails. They are at home in firm, hard tracks. Determine your needs and select a ski and camber to suit them. Some methods for selecting camber follow.

SQUEEZE TEST

The squeeze test is one way to develop a feel for camber stiffness. Hold a pair of skis together with the bottoms facing each other, squeeze them together just behind the balance point, and feel whether the skis come together easily or with difficulty. If you can flatten the skis together easily with one hand, they are too soft for high-performance skiing. It might be a good ski, if it is your first time out, but not if you have skied before. If you can almost press the ski bottoms together with one hand but need both hands to close the gap, then they are right for recreational skiing. The skis are too stiff when you cannot bring the bottoms together with both hands. The racer may enjoy a ski this stiff, but for the intermediate to advanced skier, the force needed to flatten the ski to the snow and get the cross-country wax to hold is too great.

PAPER TEST

The paper test is done indoors with a partner. Place both skis to be tested on a perfectly flat, smooth surface (the flatter the surface, the more accurate the test). Slide a piece of 8½ by 11 paper under the midsection of each ski. Now, put a foot on each ski in the binding. If it is a new ski, the toe of your shoe should be at the ski's balance point. Stand equally weighted over both skis and have your partner slide the paper under the midsection of the skis. If it won't slide under the ski, the skis are too soft. If it slides back and forth with a little resistance in front of the toes about four to six inches, and behind the heels two to four inches, the skis are about right for your weight.

If you stand with all your weight on one foot, the ski should clamp the paper to the floor; your partner shouldn't be able to move it at all. If your partner can still move the paper back and forth, the ski is too stiff for recreational skiing. Racers may even mark how far forward and backward the paper is slid when all their weight in on one

foot. Making a black or white slash on the skis' side wall helps when waxing. Knowing where the stiffest part of the ski (or wax pocket) is will help when applying a softer wax for added grip and less drag when gliding.

"Camber testers" are another means to determine camber stiffness. These are mechanical pressure gauges that are clamped onto the skis while the bottoms are together and tightened until bottoms touch. The pressure gauge is calibrated to determine the force necessary to flatten one ski against the snow. By transferring the gauge reading to equivalent weight charts, skis can be matched to individual weights.

Similar to the ski camber test gauge, "first touch," is a measurement used to test the number of pounds of direct pressure on the balance point of the ski required to cause the wax pocket to make initial contact (first touch) with the snow (*Cross-country Skier*, November 1984, Jax Pierce). This reading is used in relation to body weight, which corresponds to the pressure exerted on the ski when pushing off. For example, a skier weighing 150 pounds would select a ski with a first touch reading of 75 (half the body weight)—meaning any skier up to 150 pounds could use that ski without flattening the ski out and slowing down.

This test is helpful for racers who need to select skis to fit their weight, but don't depend on it for recreational skiing. Racing skis are much stiffer cambered than recreational skis and the pressure readings differ.

These camber tests are worth trying, but don't rely totally on them for ski selection. There is no better test than experiencing different skis. Ski a few times on rented or borrowed skis before you decide to buy. After actual skiing experience, these tests on the ski shop floor will have more meaning to you. Experience will give you an understanding of your needs, likes, and dislikes. A day skiing on a stiff ski will quickly tell you, if in doubt, to select the softer cambered ski. The extra energy expeded to flatten the ski to the snow is exhausting.

If you think you have trouble selecting skis, listen to what Mike Gallagher, coach of the 1980 and 1984 Winter Olympic cross-country teams, says: "Frankly, we don't have an awful lot of faith in mechanical methods of selecting skis. You have to see the skis, ski 'em if it is at all possible, and make your own selection. Skis are just too individualized, too personal to let some machines do the picking for you."

Olympic medalist Bill Koch says, "I ski on them;

that is really the only way to tell—get out and try them, see how they work." Ski selection is an individual process, even for the best. Use the aforementioned tests and your good judgment to select the right ski for you.

the answer; that will only weaken the ski. Now might be the time to splurge on a new pair of skis. The change would be good—and who knows what it might do for your skiing?

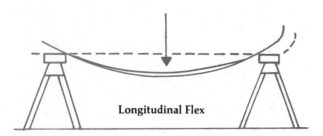

Longitudinal Flex

LONGITUDINAL FLEX

Ski flex can be measured over the whole length of the ski. A ski's longitudinal flex is most important, because of the variety of terrain the skis will be used on. An even flex or bend, forming a smooth arc from tip to tail, indicates that body weight will be distributed evenly over the entire ski. Test for an even flex by applying pressure to the ski's midsection, sighting down the ski's edge and looking for an even curve. Wider touring and telemark skis with an even flex will turn more easily than a double-cambered racing ski.

Another test related to longitudinal flex is to place skis bottom to bottom and pull the tip of one back. It should become stiffer as you approach the binding area. Any unevenness or hinge spots will be noticeable while skiing by uneven wax wear. The tail should be slightly stiffer than the tip, but neither tip nor tail should exert excessive pressure (which will slow glide) on the track when skiing.

WARP

Check for warp by placing skis bottom to bottom and closing them together. One thing to watch for is uneven side matching at the waist. The four bottom edges should match. With skis in the same position, sight straight down from the tip; the bottoms should be flush. If there is a high point or light showing, try switching the tip to the tail and resight. If the gap is still present, try another pair of skis, because the ones you chose may be twisted or warped already. Trying to remedy the problem after buying a pair of warped skis is usually more of a headache than it's worth. On used skis, particularly wooden ones, sanding isn't

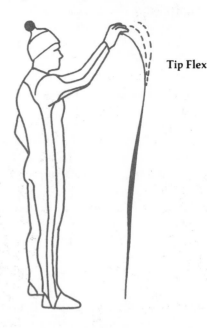

Tip Flex

TIP FLEX

How the tip bends upward is measured by feeling the ease with which the tip is pulled toward you with one hand. Test several pairs, comparing different brand names and models, using the following guidelines to help direct your decision.

Soft tips follow the terrain easily, flowing over bumps, dips, and irregularities in the snow. Racing skis usually have soft tips to follow tracks better without hitting the side walls trying to climb out. If the tip is too soft, the skis tend to wander, becoming difficult to control in turns. Check to see that the tip flexes evenly into the forebody of the ski. A tip that flexes evenly down to a point below the shovel, then stops, is preferable for track skiing, as it tends to be more responsive and quicker. If the tip flexes far back toward the waist of the ski, it will be easier to follow the irregularities in the snow and to ski in the back country.

Softer tip flex is desirable for back country touring and mountain skiing. These skis provide better flotation in powder and adequate control when turning. A stiff tip, on the other hand, holds turns better on hard-packed slopes, but tends to plow through powder and doesn't ride up and over the snow.

Tail Flex

TAIL FLEX

Flex the tail by placing it on the floor and pressing down the ski's midsection. Tail flex is similar to tip flex in its response to the snow and turning. A soft tail flows easily over the terrain. If it's too soft it may wash out of turns or not hold an edge while turning. A heavier person may consider a stiff tail for added support. Most skis have a slightly stiffer tail than tip. How well the ski will perform is not related to any one characteristic of tip or tail flex, but is combination of the two in conjunction with the overall longitudinal flex and our next characteristic, torsional flex.

TORSIONAL FLEXIBILITY

Torsional flexibility refers to the twisting action, side to side, that a ski goes through while in a turn or track. Grab the ski tip and twist it to each side. The ease with which the tip section can be twisted from an even plane relates to the skis' torsional flexibility.

For track skiing, a torsionally soft tip will give slightly when hitting the track side walls and will run with less resistance to irregularities in the terrain. But that same ski off the track may not hold when turning. A good touring or mountain ski has a torsionally stiffer tip. It gives the ski more holding power and better edge control when turning. When placed on edge the tip and tail tend to hold that edge angle better without slipping, compared to a softer ski.

FLAT BASES

How flat is the ski's base? There are three types of bases: (1) convex (bowed), (2) concave (railed), or (3) flat (square). Check the base flatness by sliding a metal scraper on the base and sighting for light sneaking through. Light showing through in the center of the ski indicates a concave ski base; light showing from under the metal scraper at the edges indicates a convex ski. Look for another pair.

If the base angles change from use, such as wear or warp, a belt sander does wonders. But don't take too much base off or you might lose the groove. A sanding block may be all it takes to flatten the high points. On metal-edged skis, flat filing will take off a railed edge, usually necessary on new skis. But check before you buy.

GROOVE

Why a groove anyway? If you look at the bottom of almost every cross-country ski, you will see a u-shaped or l-shaped cut called a groove going from just below the tip to the tail. This groove in the bottom of each ski is not a cosmetic feature that some ski designer thought would look good. No, not quite. It is specifically designed to help cross-country skis run over the snow in a straight line. Without the groove, the skis would tend to wobble or move sideways, especially on long downhills. Where speed is increased, the groove provides stability.

The groove's stabilizing effect is further realized on jumping skis. It is not uncommon to find three to five grooves on the bottom of a nordic jumping ski. The longer ski length plus the numerous grooves helps stabilize the ski at the high speeds jumpers reach at takeoff and landing. That is why cleaning wax from the groove will help any skis run straighter.

WAXABLE OR NO-WAX?

To thoroughly cover ski selection and the options available to all types of skiers, the following section on waxable and no-wax skis discusses the advantages and disadvantages of each.

Cross-country skis are different from alpine skis, jumping skis, snow sleds, or ice skates in that they must both glide on *and* grip the snow. Glide is the feeling of sliding effortlessly over the snow. Grip, on the other hand, is the feeling of hold when you step on the ski and push off. The ski shouldn't slip back. Cross-country skis are at home going downhill, uphill, or across the flat.

Your next decision will be whether to use a no-wax ski or a ski that has to be waxed for grip. No-wax skis were developed as a result of customer demand. In the 1960s and 1970s, the public wanted a ski that didn't have to be waxed every time. They wanted to avoid the decision of which wax to use, because they found waxing difficult and frustrating. Lately, the manufacturers and industry people have begun to ease the consumer's mind by tackling the waxing stigma two ways.

First, ski manufacturers got into the act by making skis that did not need wax. Second, the waxing chemists began to devise waxes that covered a broader range of snow conditions. What did the consumer gain by these actions? For one, the whole sport of cross-country skiing became easier to understand. For the first time, the skier didn't feel overwhelmed by the array of waxes or the many different kinds of skis. There was now a choice, waxable or no-wax skis—one required wax, the other did not.

The main difference between these two types of skis is how they run on the snow. A waxable ski has the potential to be the best performance ski. Adjusting the wax to suit the day's snow adds to the versatility of a waxable base. If the temperature changes or new snow is falling, the wax may be adjusted to fit the existing conditions.

No-wax skis have a set pattern molded into the bottom of the ski. They allow no adjustment for different snow conditions. The pattern is always there, whether gliding or gripping. Therefore, optimum performance in all types of snow conditions is maximized.

To give you a thorough understanding of the difference, let me make one point. There is no better feeling than moving over the terrain on a well-waxed ski, which holds when pushing off and yet slides easily and efficiently when gliding. It is not too difficult when temperatures are cold (22° F. to 0° F.) or, at the other end of the spectrum, very warm. It is when the temperature ranges around 32° F., give or take a few, that waxing can present a problem.

Rather than becoming frustrated with sticky skis that won't slide or slick skis that won't hold, the no-wax ski is ideal. This is when they perform best. When the temperature is around freezing, even the best skiers have been known to use no-wax skis; they ease the mind (which is always wondering if the snow will change from the shade to the sun). But when the snow is consistently cold, watch out for your friends on their waxable skis. You may find keeping up with them an arduous task!

WHO SHOULD USE A NO-WAX SKI?

- If you are just beginning or plan on skiing infrequently (once a month).
- If you want the convenience of doing less waxing and more skiing during the time you are out.
- If you are not concerned with how fast you go on the downhills and flats.
- If you want a ski that holds well and does not slip back, especially on the uphills.
- If you want a carefree ski that requires little maintenance.
- If you ski in geographic areas where snow conditions change constantly.
- If you are a racer and have several pairs of skis, then a conversion for those tricky waxing days might fit your needs.

Generally, no-wax skis mean convenience and fewer waxing foul-ups in changeable snow conditions, but it is a convenience not without some tradeoffs.

There are three main types of no-wax ski bottoms: (1) hair, (2) pattern, and (3) smooth.

Hair. - These bottoms developed from the fur-based skis of early pioneers. The fur would slide forward, but wouldn't slide backward; therefore, climbing uphill was made easier. The concept is just like petting a cat or dog from head to tail. Your hand moves easily to the tail, but move the hand from the tail to the head and there is more resistance. Placing strips of specially designed hair into the ski on each side of the groove acts the same way. Hair-type skis work best on icy, hard-packed conditions. Their main disadvantage is moisture absorption. Once the hair becomes wet and freezes, the skis won't slide. Silicone sprays help to repel water and prevent the hair from icing.

Pattern. - Patterned bases are by far the most reliable no-wax skis. They work best in wet, changeable snow conditions. For a pattern base to hold, the ski's bottom must be compressed into the snow, allowing the snow to build up behind each raised irregularity so it won't slip back when pressure is applied. Therefore, performance is reduced on hard or icy tracks, because there is no snow buildup to grip onto. Patterns such as fish-scale, step, crown, diamond or radial can be either stamped flush into the base (called "negative" pattern) or raised up from the base (called "positive" pattern). The exact spacing of the many angular shapes affects how far back the ski will slide before it catches. The more small angles and irregularities, the better the hold. All no-wax skis slide back a little when pressure is applied, until enough snow builds up behind the pattern to hold.

Noise is a sure giveaway as to who is on the patterned no-wax skis. A soft-cambered pair of patterned skis on the trails becomes a virtual music box—there is a whizzing sound accompanying them in certain snow conditions. But don't laugh, it might be those same no-wax skis that zip past you on the next uphill!

Smooth. - Bases that are, by feel, relatively smooth compared to a pattern or hair base may be the future of no-wax skis. Presently skis may feel smooth yet have microscopic irregularities in the base. As they would in wax, snow crystals become embedded in the bottoms. If no-wax skis are to improve, it will be by refining bottoms like these.

Individual testing of the different types of no-wax skis is a learning experience in itself. You will appreciate the different patterns for what and where they perform best. Consult with friends and experienced shop personnel to help guide your decision. Choose a no-wax ski according to the previously defined parameters. The length of the waxless section affects glide and hold. If the waxless pattern extends eight to twelve inches behind the heel plate, the ski will be slow. If the camber is too soft, the no-wax pattern drags and slows glide. Test and try before selecting a no-wax ski. The time will be paid back on the trail.

Almost all no-wax skis glide more slowly than a properly waxed ski. Therefore you work a little harder to slide the skis forward. As Sven Wiik of the Scandinavian Lodge in Steamboat Springs, Colorado, says, "No-wax skis don't slip backward, but they don't slide very well forward, either."

Manufacturers of no-wax skis have not given up the ship on equalizing their product's performance with that of waxable skis. They have worked hard to develop just the right bottom to glide without resistance and grip like wax. New designs boast smooth bottoms with microscopic striations that bind with the snow crystals to give that momentary hold when compressed into the snow.

The United States Cross Country Ski Team, particularly two-time Nordic World Cup champion Bill Koch, have been experimenting with with no-wax skis. In the 1976 Winter Olympics in Seefeld, Austria, Bill used a no-wax ski to post the fastest time for the 3 x 10 km relay. In certain snow conditions, when the temperature is hovering around 32° F. and it's snowing, waxing is difficult even for the expert.

A type of no-wax skis built to fit these tough waxing conditions called the "hairy" has been developed by the United States Cross-Country Ski Team. The "hairy" is nothing more than a waxable ski bottom, roughed up in the midsection from the heel plate forward, about nine to twelve inches in front of the binding. Using a specially designed sander, or #100- to #180- grit sandpaper, this area is sanded, raising the P-Tex on the ski's bottom. The "hairy" effect of roughed-up plastic bottoms provides just enough bind between snow and ski to grip and not slip back. A skier's technique and the snow conditions influence how much of an area needs to be roughed for the necessary grip.

Looking into the future, Bill Danner of Trak Skis declares, "There's too much emphasis on the bases themselves. In the future, we'll see adjustability of the ski and of the pattern as major breakthroughs in waxless technology." Adjustable camber to fit different snow conditions will add versatility. The same ski could be used in powder snow *and* hard tracks.

Patterned bases still remain the most reliable no-wax skis. Their performance has been proven over the years. There will always be new innovations in this highly competitive market, so give the new skis a year or two to prove themselves.

WAXING THE WAXLESS

It may seem redundant to talk about waxing a no-wax ski. Yet this is just what we do to prepare a new no-wax ski. Glide wax is applied to the tail to seal the base and improve glide. Using a parafin-based wax and an iron, the wax is melted and smoothed over the tip and tail of the ski only. Leave the no-wax pattern uncovered. After the wax has cooled for at least twenty minutes, scrape the excess thin. Rubbing a bar of glide wax on the pattern itself helps repel water and prevents icing. Silicone-based sprays accomplish the same thing.

So when you say "no-wax," remember it means no cross-country wax, but it *does* mean glide wax.

BOOTS & BINDINGS

"With all appliances and means to boot."

William Shakespeare

Cross-country boots and bindings go together like tennis balls and racquets. The game is not complete without both parts. Boots and bindings provide the bond between foot and ski. Once you have chosen a ski category, select appropriate boots and bindings. For example, you would not use a lightweight racing boot with a pair of mountain skis or a heavy, high-topped mountain boot with racing skis. The combination just doesn't fit.

The boot/binding combinations differ in size at the toe of each boot. Width at the front part of the sole is measured in millimeters. Most of these measurements have been standardized by manufacturers to eliminate customer confusion, and boots and bindings are now interchangeable. Some manufacturers, though, have experimented with specially designed systems that preclude any other boot being used in their binding. The nordic norms have been set up to make your decision less muddled.

Essentially, the system works like this. The binding attaches the boot's toe to the ski, using a simple system like the safety pin which allows complete movement of the heel and control of the ski. The system you select is based on the type of skiing you plan to do.

There are three main internationally standardized boot/binding systems that are interchangeable within that grouping: (1) nordic norm—75 mm, (2) touring norm—50/12, and (3) racing norm—50/7. Note: Other racing-oriented bindings are available under specific company names. They are not adaptable to other systems and therefore remain as individual systems of exclusive boot/binding companies. Consult your local ski school or ski shop for more information.

Nordic Norm — 75 mm: This is the most familiar and commonly used system. The 75-mm-wide toe and binding is seen on more touring trails than any other system. This system matches well with light touring, touring and mountain skiing. The oldest binding system, developed in the 1920s, this 3-pin system has been the starting point for all boot/binding design. The binding works very simply. Three metal pins extend from the front of the binding and sink into corresponding holes in the toe of the boot. A metal or wire bale is clamped over the boot's sole, holding it firmly to the ski. The toe should fit snugly in the binding with virtually no side-to-side movement. The binding is sturdy and durable for use with lightweight touring boots or heavy mountain boots. There is also junior sizing (71 mm) for smaller boots and an extra large (79 mm) for oversized boots.

Touring Norm — 50/12: This is the manufacturer's answer to lightweight, durable boots that support the foot and ankle, providing optimal ski control. Using a 50-mm toe and a 12-mm-thick sole, manufacturers were able to lighten the load and reduce the drag from the wider 75-mm style. The boot was made for tourers, combining the warmth and security of the 75-mm width with a 12-mm thick sole for off-snow walking or hiking. Check the bindings; make sure they will clamp down on the toe. The 50/12 bindings look very similar to the 50/7 racing norm.

Racing Norm — 50/7: Similar to the 50/12's but with a 7-mm thick sole, this is used for racing when weight is always a concern. Like a finely tuned racing bike is best suited for speed, so lightweight boots are appropriate for cross-country ski racing. The major drawbacks are lack of warmth and traction. The thinner sole material, usually made of hardened nylon such as Hytrel, is colder and does not provide the best walking sole. Improvements, including insulated liners and rubber inserts on the soles for traction, have kept these boots on ski shop shelves. They are ideal for racing and track skiing, but on longer tours or day trips, they lack the necessary insulation and ankle support.

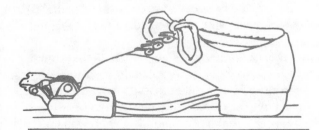

BOOTS

Boots are the most important pieces of your ski equipment. Cross-country boots are your link to performance and enjoyment. Comfort and warmth are prime concerns in boot fit. Like a good hiking boot, cross-country boots should fit snugly in the heel and should be roomy in the toes. If you have ever hiked in street shoes or boots that were too big or too tight, you know how easily blisters form. When trying boots on, use two pair of socks (one light nylon or cotton blend and one heavier wool). In socks, your toes should have room to wiggle without touching the end of the boot. A good test is to slide your foot into an unlaced boot. There should be room enough to slip two fingers behind your heel. Another test is to lace both boots up and simulate your cross-country stride on the floor. The toes should not feel pinched or cramped as you push off. The boots' upper material should break or fold evenly over the instep and toes. If you feel any discomfort, ask the salesperson whether the material will stretch when broken in. Most leather boots feel stiff at first, but will soften with use. Wearing too many socks will also stretch boots.

Don't rush into buying a pair of boots. Take time to try different kinds and makes. Boot sizes vary depending on which part of the world they come from. Boots are made by shaping the sole and upper material over and around a "last" or an average foot mold from the particular country of origin. Americans' feet characteristically are larger than Europeans'; therefore, the boot that fits may not be the size you usually wear. Ladies, especially, may have width problems, but don't take up the extra room with another layer of socks. You will just be compounding the problem. The boots feel good in the store, but once they are worn for a day and get wet, they will stretch. Leather tends to stretch more than synthetic boots.

LEATHER OR SYNTHETIC

Boots are made with leather or synthetic uppers. The upper part of a boot extends from the sole upward. The uppers can either be high or low cut. Low-cut boots resemble street shoes, while high-cut boots extend above the ankle and provide more support, like a hiking boot. The material uppers are made of should be durable, waterproof, breathable and warm—quite a tall order for any one material.

Quality leather is just such a material to meet all these criteria. That is why tanned cowhide is used more often in boot uppers than any other material. Leather boots have a certain quality about them just like wooden skis. Because the cow's hide is so thick, once dried, it is split into layers, making it more manageable for boot construction. The outside layer, which has been exposed to the elements, creates the best split of the hide. It will last and protect through cold winter days and wet spring weather. Not only are leather boots waterproof when treated, but they "breathe." Remember, your foot perspires while skiing and even before, while driving *to* the snow. Leather allows water vapor to be dissipated out, away from the foot, something rubber or synthetic boots cannot do. Rubber boots are great for keeping moisture out, but they keep it in, too. The feet will still get wet by the end of the day.

Early cross-country boots imitated the hiking boot design. They were good boots to wear all year. Many skiers spent the summer months hiking in them. The square toe was the only real difference. Therefore, boot uppers in the 1950s and 1960s were stitched to the sole, like leather hiking boots.

Stitched, top-grain leather boots are finely crafted pieces of equipment. As material and labor costs went up, bootmakers had to find less time consuming and expensive ways to make boots. Using the thinner splits from the cow's hide, cost of material went down. These thinner leather splits went through a chrome tanning process to increase durability, but the leather lost its natural waterproofing properties. It was made more porous, and sealants were required to make the boots waterproof. Instead of stitching uppers to soles, which took time, cementing or vulcanizing began in the 1960s. Bonding between the upper and the sole produced a watertight seal—one plus for the system.

Your leather boots need to be dried carefully after each trip. Let them dry naturally, away from direct heat, to prevent cracking and stiffening. Rubbing compounds help to preserve the natural oils of the leather and should be used before summer storage.

Running shoe companies began to experiment with nylon cross-country uppers, and at the 1976 Winter Olympics in Seefeld, Austria, nylon uppers made their appearance before the media. U.S. Cross-Country Ski Team member, Bill Koch, wearing the boots with the 38-mm knobby toe protrusion, skied to a third-place victory in the thirty-kilometer special event. Nylon is definitely lighter than leather. It is breathable, water repellent, and for short trips around the track, relatively warm. Nylon dries quickly and requires little maintenance. But it is not an insulating material. Without an inner lining or overboot, nylon boots can be cold. Use them for short tours or track skiing, not for the long haul or overnight trips.

The use of Gore-Tex in boot uppers is another attempt to duplicate leather while making the boot lighter, waterproof, and breathable. Gore-Tex uppers, like nylon, are reinforced with leather strips to provide shape and support in crucial areas such as the toe and sides of the boot. To prolong the life of a Gore-Tex boot (or any clothing item made of Gore-Tex), keep it clean. Dirt, body oils, waterproofing compounds, etc. can literally plug the microscopic holes in the material, reducing its breathability.

The choice between lined or unlined boots depends on need. For mountaineers and telemark skiers, the added warmth and support make lined boots a good decision. Even heavy, double boots are available for expedition skiers. Skiers who need warmth and don't intend to be skiing fast, and consequently ending up with sweaty feet, should choose a lined boot. When fitting boots with a fleece lining or similar material, be sure the boot is snug, because the fleece lining will mat down with use, enlarging the boot size by at least half a size.

Unlined boots are particularly suited to performance and light touring skiers who need to dissipate moisture from the foot. These boots dry quickly (overnight) and are ready to go again the next morning. Unlined boots are easier on the pocketbook.

SOLE TALK

The material used on the soles of cross-country boots is worth a closer look. With street shoes, the material of the sole is less important, although you wouldn't want to wear slick leather soles on ice. Think back to your winter school days when a smooth-soled shoe won the run and slide contest. Cross-country boots, on the other hand, need a rougher sole, something that *won't* slip on ice when walking. The 75-mm boot usually has lugged, vibram, or rubber-patterned soles for traction when walking. The touring norms, 50/12s, have a thicker sole than the thin racing norm soles. The racing norm's 7-mm-thick sole is very slick on snow and ice. Check to see if there are rubber insets on the sole for grip on icy walkways like from the car to the trail. More people have slipped walking this short distance than on the whole ski tour put together.

The overall warmth of cross-country boots depends on the boots' upper material and sole thickness. Generally, the thicker the sole, the warmer the boot, provided it has some kind of foot bed or insulated liner. Specially designed materials or air pocket insoles have been designed for foot warmth. Ask around and find out what is the latest in foot bed protection.

Cross-country boots are the foot's link to the ski. Ski control reflects back to the boot and foot. If the foot is making the right moves to control the ski and yet doesn't have total control, it may not be the fault of your technique. The boot's sole is a big part of ski control, especially when turning.

When pressure and torque are applied to the boot as in turning, it will either transmit that force to the ski or it will lose it in the process. A stiff sole that resists lateral side to side twisting, but still flexes forward, is a characteristic of a good all-around boot. The stiffer soled, high-top boot is preferred by telemark skiers, because it transfers foot forces directly to the ski. High-speed turning on hard-packed slopes requires sole strength to resist the forces applied by the foot and leg. A softer sole may move slightly to the side or even off the ski when forces increase. Boot makers use different shank material to provide this torsional rigidity. Ask what type of shank material the boot has before buying.

Another reinforcing agent on the better 75-mm boots are toe plates. Where the binding connects with the sole, there can be wear from constant use. The pins may eventually wear bigger holes in the sole. Quality boots have toe inserts or metal reinforcing plates to maintain the hole size.

Check boots for torsional rigidity by grabbing the toe with one hand and the heel with the other and twisting. Boots that can be twisted like a popsicle stick to the point of the heel turning upside down are very soft soled. If you test another boot and find it difficult even to *twist* the sole, but it still has good forward flex, this boot would be a good choice for all-around skiing use.

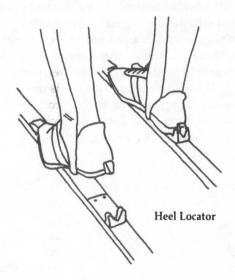

Heel Locator

HEEL PLATES

Heel plates work with the boots' soles to stabilize the heels. If your sole is soft, the heel plate helps keep it on the ski. Heel plates are small discs about the size of half dollars with tiny metal or plastic ridges. The boot's heel will more easily stay on this plate when the ski is weighted. In turning, pressure on the heel plate will keep the heel from sliding off the ski.

Boot and binding companies have devised various types of heel plates—wedges, stars, "V's,"—but the most popular for light touring are metal ridges or plastic points. Heel plates are attached to the ski with either a screw or small nails. To retard heel plate icing, make sure the screw is covered, either with a plastic cap or something like silver duct tape from the local hardware store. An iced heel plate is irritating. The same is true of snow buildup under the ball of the foot from skiing in powder snow. Instead of always picking at those with your ski poles, place that same silver tape on the ski, from the binding back to the heel plate. (A little trick of the trade to calm your mind. When you are out skiing, it is the trivial things that work on your patience.)

Cross-country skiing offers the opportunity for physical and mental self-expression. Don't let little irritants creep into the sport. Feel the entire experience as an emotional high.

Along the same lines as heel plates to keep the heel firm on the ski, some manufacturers have developed a slotted ridge system under the ball of the foot for added control. A "V" ridge extends straight from the binding for about four to five inches, matching with a slot in the boot's sole. The increased stability of the front ridge and heel plate creates better lateral ski control when turning. This system is primarily used on light touring and racing equipment.

Another type of heel plate is called a "heel locator." This works by attaching a plastic protrusion—about one-half to three-fourths of an inch long to the outer heel of the boot. The protrusion slides into a plastic wedge to keep the heel centered on the ski. Heel locators can be awkward when the heel misses the slot and, on the other hand, may reduce the heel's lateral movement in a fall. They are not really necessary if the sole is stiff.

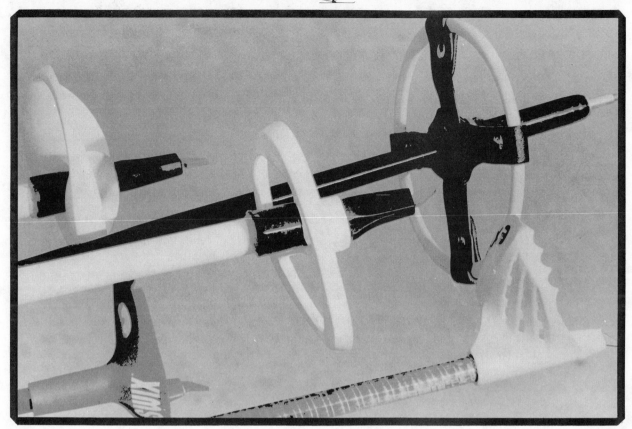

POLES

"Man is a tool-using animal . . . without his tools he is nothing, with tools he is all."
Thomas Carlyle

Ski poles have a fit, just like ski boots. You wouldn't ski twenty kilometers in boots that are too small, nor should you ski twenty kilometers in boots that are too small, nor should you ski twenty kilometers with short poles. Think of a gondolier on the canals of Venice, using his long pole to push off from the bottom and move the boat forward. Sometimes you hear him singing a song as he sticks the pole down in the water and, hand over hand, he climbs the pole as he moves the boat through the canals of this watery city. If he used short poles, he could still push, but he would have to push more frequently. He would lose the elongated poling strokes of the longer pole.

Like the gondolier, the cross-country skier benefits by poles that can be pushed from over a greater distance. Since cross-country skiers provide their own momentum, the ability to pull and push off a lightweight pole is vital. Have you ever tried to cross-country ski with alpine length poles?

Alpine skiers rely on gravity for their motion. Consequently, their poles are shorter and are used for turning and maintaining body position, as well as to give their hands something to do in lift lines (just kidding).

SELECTION

Proper pole length is determined by standing flat in your street shoes or cross-country boots. With the tip on the floor, the top of the pole should reach to a snug fit under the armpit—not so snug that the shoulder is raised up, but a tight fit. The same measurement is achieved by a pole that extends to a point halfway between the top of the shoulder and armpit with arms at your sides.

This method is appropriate for choosing most recreational skiing and racing poles. Individual strength, especially in the upper body, may dictate a slightly longer pole for performance skiing. Poles, like skis, are measured in centimeters. For

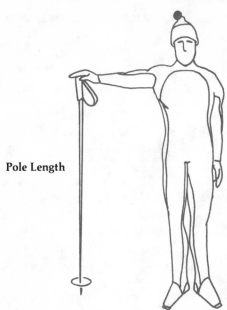

Pole Length

the hand plays a much larger role in efficient skiing than it is given credit for, and the strap is important to this fit. Next time you go out skiing, look around at the way people hold their poles. Some will grab the pole well below the handle grip, others grip the top of the pole, and still others won't even wear the strap! Little do they know how much extra work this makes for them!

The pole strap should be adjustable to fit whatever gloves or mitten are worn. It should come out of the pole about one inch below the top, leaving a small knob. When the strap is adjusted properly, pressure is applied to the strap by the hand as the hand extends to the rear and the arm straightens. The small knob should catch in the web of the glove (between the thumb and forefinger), allowing the skier to release his grip on the pole and recover forward. Therefore, proper strap adjustment will even let you relax your arm at the extension and recovery. Be sure the pole strap is adjustable and that there is a knob at the top.

performance skiers or racers, a slightly longer pole (two to four centimeters over optimum) for use on predominantly flat courses may be an advantage. If a skier's strength permits, he/she will have more pole length to push with. Remember our gondolier! However, a longer than standard pole on uphills is tiring. The hand and arm have to be raised too high before the pole is planted. Racers may even choose short poles for hilly courses and longer poles for flat courses.

For mountain skiers and tourers who are always skiing in off-track conditions such as powder and side hills, a slightly shorter pole (five to eight centimeters) makes less work. The tour skier breaking trail through two feet of new powder using a regular length pole may find it tiring. It becomes too much work to raise the hand and arm each time. In conditions like this, gripping the poles lower or dragging them in the snow without planting them saves energy.

Racers have devised a mathematical formula for determining pole length: height (inches) x 2.54 - 35 cm = individual pole length. For example: a six-foot skier would multiply 72 inches x 2.54 = 182 - 35 cm = 147 cm pole. This formula can be used to help guide your decision but should not become your only criteria. There may be a variance of a few centimeters due to individual differences such as arm strength and body build.

STRAPS

An adjustable strap at the handle of the pole enhances a firm fit with the hand. Here is some equipment that all skiers could devote more time to. How the pole fits in

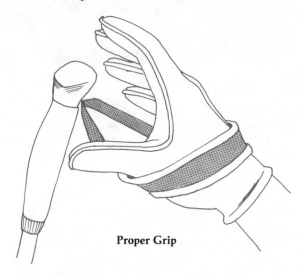

Proper Grip

Leather or nylon straps are really a matter of preference and availability. The nylon straps offered are slightly lighter and last longer. Leather straps may stretch slightly, but like a good leather boot, have a pleasing feel.

SHAFTS

Pole shafts transmit your muscular energy to the snow and result in forward momentum. New technology has made pole shaft materials less resistant to bending. The older tonkin cane (bamboo) poles did the job, and still do. They are reliable and aesthetically appealing to some. With the advances in ski construction, poles have undergone a similar change.

Pole shaft material ranges from bamboo to carbon graphite (the same material used in golf club shafts). However, graphite is expensive and brittle, at times. When hit just right, the pole may break clean. I've seen racers using their poles to knock snow off their boots and snap their poles in half. The shaft material adds strength and durability to the pole's life. Metal alloys, particularly aluminum and fiberglass, are strong and lightweight. Fiberglass, epoxy, graphite and boron are enabling manufacturers to cut the pole's weight dramatically and make them stiffer. Racers know this has a time and energy relationship.

When poles bend too much as force is applied, power is lost and energy wasted in bending the pole shaft. A stiffer pole may not bend as much when force is applied and will transfer the skier's poling energy directly to forward momentum.

The biggest difference among shaft materials, though, is price. The lighter you go, the higher the price. If you're speed conscious, then the lightweights are for you. If you just want an all-around track and touring pole, stick with the fiberglass or aluminum ones. The price is right!

POLE BASKETS

Pole baskets keep the pole from disappearing in the snow. There are different types of baskets for various uses and snow

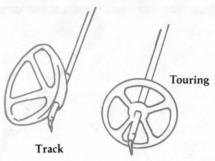

Touring

Track

conditions. The common round basket is a good choice for light tour skiers and tourers. These provide enough support in deep snow and are fine for prepared track skiing. They are usually four to six inches in diameter. For the tour skier who wants more support, a powder basket (seven to nine inches diameter) provides a larger area of support. A clip-on addition to your regular basket gives you the best of both worlds on one pole.

The drawback with round baskets when track skiing is that the basket tends to pop the tip out of the snow before the final push and arm extension. The half basket, developed in the 1970s, has eliminated this quirk. Full power is applied all the way through the poling motion. Half baskets are great for packed trails, but these asymmetrical baskets for off-track skiing are useless.

Even though poles seem like such insignificant sticks, you can see that it is worth your time to select good ones.

CLOTHING FOR ACTION

"Rags they may be, but I love my rags."

Moliere

"You are what you wear." This phrase, heard often in the business world, is applicable when dressing for the outdoors as well. The clothes you don for a stroll through the park or a day of skiing can work to complement your movements—to go with you, not against you.

Think back. Remember how your mother used to dress you for school and how she bundled you up for playing in the snow? The clothes may not have felt very comfortable. As you left the house, off came the tie. You loosened your collar to breathe and removed your hat because you couldn't hear. Mother was well intentioned, but you were miserable. The clothes you wear each day, whether for work, a summer hike, or a Sunday buffet, require thought and planning.

This is especially important in cross-country skiing.

Dressing for outdoor activities varies depending on physical exertion. The scientific researcher taking outdoor measurements in subzero temperatures has different needs than a skier in the same environment. The activity levels of these two individuals require different clothing.

Dressing for cross-country skiing involves a principle called "functional warmth." Functional clothes allow unrestricted movement, while insulating the body from heat loss.

The body, like a woodburning stove, produces heat. Instead of wood, the body burns food. Because your body will produce heat, gear your clothing needs to the intensity of your efforts. Speaking strictly physically, a cross-country skier moving at five miles per hour burns 500 to 700 calories per hour. The heat generated while skiing can warm the entire body. Your clothing should take advantage of your body's own heat, maintaining it when cold and dissipating it when warm.

The body burns fuel constantly at rest or when moving. One's muscular activity level determines how fast calories are used up. The body continues to burn calories until the stove runs out of fuel. An adult burns sixty to seventy-five calories per hour at rest. If you are moving and engaging nearly every muscle, 2,500 calories a day will not last long. It's a good idea to snack frequently while skiing on day trips. Eating at intervals eliminates the bloated stomach from one big meal. When the stomach is full, the blood spends too much time there, digesting food, rather than circulating throughout the body and keeping you warm.

The body releases its spent energy through perspiration. Perspiring is one way the body cools itself. How we dress helps prevent clothes from becoming too wet and lessens heat loss through evaporation.

For example, a cross-country ski tour group has reached their destination by lunch, only to find they are soaking wet from sweat. Adding a layer of clothing won't help much to prevent further evaporation and cooling. The best cure for this problem is prevention.

LAYERING

Clothing should provide protection from the wind, insulating from cold weather, and "wicking" moisture away from the skin. These objectives are best accomplished by dressing in layers, adding or removing clothing to maintain a comfortable temperature. Like a thermostat in a car we can regulate our own inner temperature.

Wind is our biggest annoyance. Wind blows heat away from our bodies faster than we can produce it. That is one reason we get cold. The 'wind chill" index combines wind speed with air temperature, calculating increased heat loss from the wind. The effects of wind chill are easily felt when skiing across an open meadow in a thirty-mile-per-hour wind at –5° Fahrenheit. You quickly realize that wind is something to avoid. Moisture, another concern, is generated from both external and internal sources. How we protect ourselves from external moisture—rain,

snow, etc.—is easily handled by our outer layer of clothing. Protection from internal moisture—perspiration—is of prime importance. No single piece of clothing has been invented to meet all our winter needs.

Dressing for a day of skiing is best accomplished using three layers: (1) the inner layer, next to the skin, dissipates perspiration; (2) the middle layers insulate, and (3) the outer layer protects us from the elements.

From the inner to the outer, here are some guidelines to help you choose your winter attire. Start with cotton or cotton blend undergarments. Comfort and support are important considerations at this level. Next come "long johns" or long underwear. Both above and below the waist, long johns dissipate or wick body moisture away from the skin. Depending on the weather and the day's intended activity level, the material may vary. If you are an active tourer or racer, synthetic long underwear will wick moisture away, leaving a tiny air pocket encircling the entire body. Active skiers, perspiring heavily, appreciate the trade name Polyprophylene, a synthetic that works like "fishnet" underwear. Imagine a small-weave net creating individual air spaces or pockets of warm, dry air next to the body. Like a wet suit, polyprophylene keeps a thin layer of perspiration next to the skin for insulation.

In severe weather or for less active skiers, heavier underwear of a tighter weave provides more insulation. Even down-insulated undergarments may be appropriate for extended winter expeditions. Without increasing physical activity and, consequently, burning more calories, the use of snug-fitting insulating layers retains heat.

After the inner layer, it is the middle layer that insulates and keeps body heat from escaping. Have you ever noticed that cold is a subjective term? Each of us has our own idea of cold. For example, when the radio reports that "a mass of cold air engulfs Florida, threatening the citrus crop," the temperature might have dipped to 30°F. Relatively speaking, that is extremely cold weather for Floridians. Each of us determines what cold is, based on our own comfort zone. Use the middle layer of clothing to maintain your own personal comfort.

If the turtles ever knew what they started with their long retractable necks, they could have made a fortune on a patent. The "turtleneck," with its tight-fitting, elastic, extendable neck is an ideal second layer. A cotton or cotton blend turtleneck helps absorb any upper body perspiration that has been wicked away from the body by the first layer. The high neck keeps heat in and, when pulled up, protects against the wind.

A wool sweater or lightweight jacket creates additional insulation as another middle layer. Depending on your ability level, the type of skiing you'll be doing and the expected weather, choose more or less insulation.

The final layer is our protection from the elements—not an insulating layer, but a lightweight, tightly woven shell, preventing wind and moisture from entering our protective cocoon. The poplins, polyester and Gore-Tex are popular materials for outer garments. Gore-Tex is the trade name for a synthetic fabric which is waterproof, yet allows moisture droplets to escape. A Gore-Tex pore is 1/20,000 the size of a droplet of water, and water can't penetrate it. Yet, because there are about nine million pores per square inch, each about seven hundred times larger than a water vapor molecule, Gore-Tex allows perspiration to pass freely.

On colder days with less skiing, your outer layer needs to be thicker. Use a coat with more insulation to create "dead air" spaces that keep heat in.

Rounding off our layer system are socks, gloves, and hat. Keeping the extremities warm on cold days plays an important role in preventative maintenance. On cold days, the farther the blood travels from the heart (or body's core), the less heat it retains. Naturally, your feet and hands may suffer. Thick insulation surrounding these sensitive body parts is a definite advantage.

On cold days, skiers need to constantly monitor their hands, making adjustments in clothing or even stopping to warm them. The kind of glove or mitten used depends on the individual. Some people never wear gloves or a hat, insisting, "I'm so warm blooded; I don't need those!" It was at the 1980 Winter Olympics that the Russian Alexander Zavjalov skied the thirty-kilometer event bare-handed in subzero temperatures. Most of us are not quite that warm-blooded.

Mittens provide the best safeguard against heat loss. Skin against skin surrounded by insulation (as in mittens) is heat-maintaining. Some skiers contend that gloves allow more control and a

better feel of the pole handle. But if warmth is your concern, opt for the mitten. A nylon or poplin water-repellent shell with a wool liner is an ideal setup for those cold days.

Gloves, in varying thicknesses and amounts of insulation, are chosen with your activity level in mind. If you plan to ski hard and fast in prepared tracks, then a thin leather glove will work fine. These protect the skin from elements and blisters and provide good pole contact. For warmth, select more insulation and a thicker glove. After trying these different combinations, you'll discover what works best for you.

The feet, like the rest of the body, do perspire. Moisture develops around the feet even at rest. Have you ever noticed that after you dress, put on your boots, and drive to your favorite skiing area, your socks are already wet before you begin skiing? Carry another pair of socks for just this reason. Take off your traveling socks and put on a dry pair of nylon or synthetic weave socks. They work in a manner similar to long johns to wick moisture away from the foot and leave a dry layer next to the skin. Then slip a wool sock on for comfort and insulation, preferably a high knicker sock if you are wearing knickers, or a short wool sock if you are wearing a one-piece outfit. Two socks will cushion the feet and protect them from any rubbing, and will insulate for warmth. The activity level from skiing, coupled with a warm inner core temperature, helps alleviate cold feet.

ACCESSORIES

Boot muffs, for extremely cold conditions or overnight trips, provide additional insulation. There are excellent commercial products on the market. When buying muffs, it is a good idea to take along your boots and skis to see how the muffs fit in the binding. If a fancy boot muff isn't in the budget, try an old sock. Either pull the whole sock over the boot (if it is big enough) or sculpture the end to fit over the toes and into the binding. It is surprising the difference this extra layer makes on cold days.

An accessory on the other end of the temperature spectrum is the rubber booty. For the wet snows of spring or for rainy days, a thin rubber shell can be slipped over the whole boot, like a rubber glove. This prevents the boots and socks from becoming saturated with water. In this case, we sacrifice the wicking away of perspiration for keeping excess water out.

Boot Muff

The hat tops off our outfit, like a lid to a teapot. Hats prevent heat from escaping from the head. Skiing without a hat is like boiling an egg without water. The heat is there, we just have no way to maintain it. Without a hat, we lose almost sixty percent of our body heat through our head. You may have heard the saying, "If your hands or feet are cold, put on a hat." For skiers, that is sound advice. Hats that pull way down over the ears are best. Racers have also found that thin, snugly fitting earmuffs protect the lower ear from exposure. The lower earlobe needs protection, too!

OUTFITS

Don't let anyone tell you cross-country skiing isn't fashionable! Each year, clothing manufacturers produce an array of glamorous outfits. Bright colors and form-fitting stretch nylons give cross-country skiers the look of experience even as they wax their skis. Two-piece and one-piece suits are popular with racers and recreational skiers alike.

For recreational skiing, the two-piece suit is ideal, either with knickers and a separate top or with the high bib knickers. Knickers are pants that end just below the knee. Their use in cross-country skiing permits complete freedom of movement. The stiffer, thicker material of an alpine stretch pant, when stretched continuously for a fifteen-kilometer ski tour, requires needless energy expenditure. A knicker pant made of poplin or a nylon/polyester blend will repel snow and allow unrestricted movement. Bib knickers extend above the waist with suspenders, and are comfortable even when bending over. The clothes stay in and the snow stays out.

To fill the gap between the end of the knicker and the boot, a long knicker sock is the ticket. Made of one hundred percent wool or a mixture, the knicker sock insulates even when wet.

Often called the miracle fabric, wool is ideal for winter clothing and insulates even when wet. Of all the natural and man-made insulating materials, it remains the leader. Snow may encrust the entire garment, yet because of the natural qualities of wool, you will still be warm and dry.

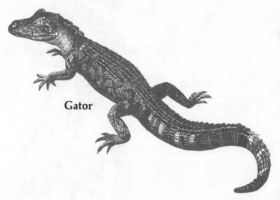

Gator

GAITERS

No, not the Florida variety. Gaiters are the snow cuffs used for off-track skiing to keep snow from getting down into the boot. Several types are available, from short anklets to long below-the-knee styles. Besides keeping the snow out of the boot, some cover the shoelaces. This may not seem like such a big deal, but I've been touring in boots without gaiters when my shoelaces have iced and frozen so badly that I had to thaw them before I could untie my boots. And at the end of a long day of skiing, slipping your boots off easily is worth plenty! The long gaiter also adds to leg warmth on cold, windy days.

Keep watching the new fashions and see what happens to the gaiter. With an emphasis on sleek all-inclusive one-and two-piece suits, gaiters may

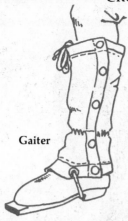

Gaiter

be banished to the closet in the name of progress. The built-in gaiter is already being used, eliminating the process of putting on those sometimes-hard-to-figure-out contraptions.

ONE-PIECE SUITS

I f you want the look and feel of a champion, then the one-piece suit is your answer. Not only do the racers use them for their streamlined effect, but recreational skiers find them very functional. Ease of movement is maximized. There are no bulky clothes or extra layers, just sleek, tight-fitting material covering our inner layers.

Racers usually wear one layer of polyprophylene underwear, a turtleneck and the one-piece suit. They ski fast and work their muscles, creating an abundance of body heat, and clothes that dissipate moisture take priority. Suits for telemark racers even have built-in kneepads to protect them from the ski and slalom poles.

Less active skiers require more insulation. A double layer of long underwear and a sweater underneath maintains body heat. The one-piece

suit gives the recreational skier a fashionable look and a tight-fitting outer layer that shields the entire body from the elements. Ease of movement is, again, maximized.

REVIEW

I n summary, when dressing for active winter sports, remember these three important considerations: (1) prevent moisture from building up next to the skin; (2) insulate the body from heat loss; and (3) protect against external weather such as wind, rain, snow, and sleet.

The layer system is one way to meet all these needs. An active skier wearing several layers of clothing can regulate body temperature by taking off or adding clothes. Maintaining a comfortable body temperature helps lessen the energy drain when you are too hot and sweating profusely. The same holds true when the body is cold, because muscles become stiff and energy is used staying warm rather than skiing.

Avoid bulky, heavy layers. Remember, movement is the key to efficient cross-country skiing. Clothing that restricts natural movements, like heavy down parkas, jeans, and tight pants, are not the best clothes for skiing. Parkas are great for inactive spectators, but they provide too much insulation for active cross-country skiers. Blue jeans may look great, but they act like sponges in the snow and turn into hard shells when frozen.

We lose body heat in the following ways:

Radiation: Heat is constantly emitted from the body and from exposed areas of the face, neck and head. Insulating the body from this type of heat loss is important in staying warm.

Conduction: Here you are losing heat from a warm to a cold area. You feel conduction when you pick up a pair of cold skis with your bare hands. The heat is immediately transferred to the ski, causing your hands to become cold.

Evaporation: The dissipation of moisture from the body causes cooling. Preventing excessive perspiration build-up and wicking it away from the skin is a function of our inner layers of clothing.

Respiration: The loss of heat through breathing cools the body, causing dehydration. "Drink before thirsty, eat before hungry" is a good motto to follow when cross-country skiing.

CARRY IT!

"Nothing to excess."

Anonymous

From the guide's pack to the racer's small fanny pack, skiers love to bring along extras. Cross-country skiers are a prepared bunch. They always seem to be carrying something with them. Whether it's a camera or the day's lunch, cross-country skiers tote things. (Racers don't tote much, though, as they want to be light and agile, like a deer bounding through the woods. A small fanny pack with extra wax, a scraper, and cork might be all a racer would carry, and that would only be on the longer course, thirty kilometers or more.)

Tour skiers have reason to carry the most. Skiing out on all-day tours away from civilization demands that the leader have everything needed to handle any problem that might arise. If you ski with a certified guide, even on a day tour, you can be sure he will have a large pack with everything from matches to water to overnight gear. The

education required to become certified with one of the divisions of PSIA is very thorough. Potential guides are tested on the specific items required on commercial tours.

Choose a framed or unframed pack depending on intended use. A frame pack carries plenty of weight in the summer for backpacking, but that same load in the winter is tough to ski with. Keep in mind that your pack must be suited to skiing, leaving your arms free to swing to the side. If not, carrying your pack may feel like carrying someone on your back up the stairs in your gym class. Pretty bulky, to say the least!

A lightweight, internal frame pack might be the best thing. They can be stuffed with waxes and water bottles and they even have room to tie a snow shovel on the side. Anywhere from ten to forty pounds is a comfortable load.

Don't overload packs. Remember, you have to carry them. "The lighter, the better" is a good rule to follow. Your pack should fit your body well and not bounce or shift while skiing. Check to see if the pack has a waist or chest strap to stabilize it; too much bounce and the extra weight shift may throw you to the ground. It helps to pack infrequently used items on the bottom, along with heavy gear. Distributing weight lower on the back and using a waist strap will prevent you from getting nailed in the back of the head after a forward fall. Ski cautiously with heavy packs as subtle mistakes are accentuated. Take the easy way down; traverse, rather than turn. It might mean leaving that untracked slope for the next skier, but it may save you from a hair-raising fall.

For short trips, the small day pack or fanny pack works fine. Fanny packs buckle around the waist like a large belt with a carrying compartment in the back. These are smaller packs, but are convenient to swivel around in front to get things out.

Consult the mountain shops, summer hiking stores, or your certified guide before you buy. Check around and try on different packs and go through the motions of skiing. Make sure your arms move freely.

SLEDS

For extra-large, heavy loads, a small sled is used. Called "pulks," they were named by the Laplanders of northern Scandinavia, who use them for loads they don't want to risk carrying on their backs. Today's pulks are fiberglass sleds about one and one-half to two feet wide and varying from four to nine feet long. The sides curve up like a small boat to give the sled buoyancy in powder. John Dostal writes of famed winter expedition leader Ned Gillette: "During Ned's high arctic expedition to Ellesmere Island, each man hauled his gear in an eight-foot fiberglass sled. It was the only practical means of transporting two hundred and forty pounds apiece. They got the sleds through chaotic ocean pack ice, up steep glacier tongues and down rocky river valleys." Sleds are pulled by a long metal or wood pole harness fastened by a belt buckle around the skier's waist. The long harness allows the skis to clear the sled's bottom and still stride out.

Pulks are becoming popular in the states for pulling small children along on tours. The family that ski tours together, stays together. Pulks are a great way to enjoy the winter scenery as a family and keep the load off your back!

At the Scandinavian Lodge in Steamboat Springs, Colorado, we use pulks to carry our ice fishing supplies onto the lake, looking for that perfect fishing hole. The ice auger, tackles, and smoker fit nicely into the sled and take a load off my back. It's a good way to transport all our fish out, too!

SKI PREP

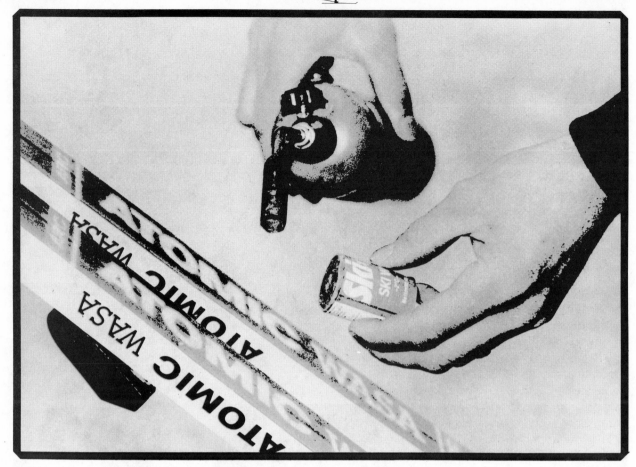

THE ART OF WAXING

"A good lather is half the shave."

William Hone

Wax is that sometimes mysterious substance that is applied to the bottom of skis to prevent slipping, influence momentum, and help maintain glide.

Finding the correct wax for the snow conditions is sometimes an art, other times a science. The principles are simple; the application and techniques take practice. The wax itself is a constant; each wax has its range of ideal snow conditions. The type of snow, the temperature, the skis, the trail—all play a role in what wax you choose and how you apply it. Depending on your goals, waxing can be as simple or as complicated as you want to make it.

Snowshoe Thompson, who delivered mail in the Sierras in the late 1800s, devised a wax for climbing hills and sliding. "Sierra Dope" was a concoction with enough ingredients for a witch's brew. These early waxes were derived from natural components including beeswax, tars, and animal/vegetable by-products. Thompson was more concerned with hold than glide.

What are your goals? Do you plan to ski only two or three times a season? Then waxing needs to be convenient and simple. If you plan to ski every weekend and enter a citizens' race, select wax for its performance qualities. Do you plan to ski and race extensively? Then waxing becomes quite intricate; its correct selection is crucial for overall speed and grip. Where do you stand in this spectrum?

As with anything mysterious, the exploration is exciting. Remember the old caves and houses you used to explore as a kid, if for no other reason than to add a little adventure to the moment? The wax box may awaken the youngster hidden inside. Waxing is an adventure and, fortunately, the consequences are the increased enjoyment and self-fulfillment that come with mastery.

WAXING—ART OR SCIENCE

To be considered an "art," waxing must provide some potential for human creativity and require skill in application. To be considered a science, it must be derived from systematized knowledge obtained through observation or study. It must show an organization of facts, principles or methods related to a skill.

Therefore, waxing is at times an art form while maintaining its status as a science.

WHY WAX?

Skiing without wax is like sailing without wind. Wax is the skier's source of momentum. It provides the firm, momentary platform from which to push off. Without wax, the sport of cross-country skiing is incomplete. It's like playing tennis without a net.

The no-wax ski has been developed by ski manufacturers to promote wax-free skiing. The convenience of no-wax skis definitely has a place in cross-country skiing. They are especially good for beginners. This section in no way intends to belittle the use of no-wax skis, but is written to explain how performance using a properly waxed ski is enhanced. Once a balance is achieved between grip and glide, there is nothing like it. The properly waxed ski is a joy to ski on. It does not slip back when pushing off and it glides effortlessly.

The reason for waxing really hinges on these two words—grip and glide. *Grip* describes the holding characteristic of the ski when the skier pushes off. *Glide* refers to the resulting slide of the skis on the flat and downhills. The goal of waxing is to find the proper wax combination for optimum grip and glide, without sacrificing either. Revealing the intricacies of waxing, discovering its hidden simplicity, is the purpose of this chapter.

SNOW

Snow is one of nature's miracles. It creates our winter playground. Without it, we would be hard aground, and with it, the sky is the limit! There are hundreds of different kinds of snow, each produced by different temperature and weather conditions. Each flake is a unique study in crystallization. Snow's composition is broadly based on air temperature: it is either dry (when temperatures are below freezing) or wet (when temperatures rise above freezing). It may be further described by these three main categories:

(1) **Fresh fine-grain snow**—usually occurring after a snowstorm, when temperatures are cold.
(2) **Coarse-grain snow**—developing one to three days following a storm.
(3) **Granular snow** (sometimes referred to as "corn snow")—frozen and refrozen snow crystals.

Imagine the well-formed snowflakes of a fresh snowfall, with air temperature around 20-25°F. Each flake has very distinctive features, like the fingers of your outstretched hand. This is what is referred to as fine-grain snow—frozen and sharply defined.

The second type of snow develops after it has been on the ground for twenty-four hours or more. It undergoes a transformation in which the crystals begin to lose their shape. Evaporation and compression cause a rounding of the fresh snow's sharp points, like taking your outstretched hand and starting to form a fist. Without any new snow, coarse-grain snow will develop after one day and continue to change until it snows again.

The third major type of snow develops when the temperature rises above freezing. Once the snow melts and refreezes, a granular snow evolves. This form is often referred to as "corn snow" because of its large crystals and loose bonding. It is similar in shape to your closed fist, with no relationship to the original snowflake that floated to the ground.

MATCHING WAX TO SNOW

Cross-country wax is needed for hold and glide. The objective of waxing is to select a wax to match the texture and hardness of the snow. The wax applied to the middle third of the ski must allow the snow crystals to penetrate it and give hold. The crux of waxing is encompassed in that statement.

When wax is spread on the ski's bottom, it provides a cushion for thousands of tiny snowflakes to stick into. For a brief moment, when all the skier's weight is on one ski, a multitude of snow crystals are embedded in the wax, holding the ski firm while the skier pushes (or kicks) off. As the ski begins to slide forward, the pressure release and friction of the sliding ski release this bond. A thin, microscopic layer of water—a result of friction between the ski's bottom and the snow—causes the ski to glide until it stops and downward pressure is again applied.

Wax-snow behavior			
Correct Wax	▼	▲	➤
Wax too hard	▼	▲	➤
Wax too soft	▼	▲	➤
	▼ Ski weighted during kick	▲ Ski unweighted	➤ Ski Gliding

To wax properly, therefore, you must select wax of an appropriate hardness to allow the snow crystals to penetrate and provide a brief moment of hold. The type of wax you choose to accomplish this depends on whether the snow is dry and hard or soft and wet.

Waxing, based on theory, sounds easy, but application and use are where the "art of waxing" comes through.

WAX ZONES AND TYPES

The bottom of a cross-country ski can be divided into two zones. Due to camber (stiffer flex under the foot), the middle third of the ski is waxed for hold (grip) while the tip and tail are waxed for glide. We will refer to these areas as the *grip zone* and *glide zone*.

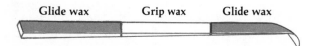
Glide wax   Grip wax   Glide wax

There are two main types of waxes to work with: (1) *grip wax* and (2) *glide wax*. Used in the right combination, the skis do not slip back when pressured and slide easily forward when pressure is released.

Grip waxes provide hold by creating a layer for the snow crystals to stick to. Grip waxes come in various hardnesses, from super hard for dry, frozen snow to very soft for wet, mushy snow:

(1) **Hard wax**—for fresh or coarse-grain snow.

(2) **Klister wax**—for newly fallen wet snow.

(3) **Klister**—for granular or melt/freeze snow.

Hard waxes, usually used on dry snow, come in small metal or plastic cans similar to the little plastic cans for exposed 35mm film. Each can is color coded and marked with an air temperature range, plus brief instructions. All wax manufacturers use cool colors (white, green, and blue) for dry cold snow, and warm colors (purple, red, and yellow) for wet snow.

Klister wax is really the softest hard wax before a klister is used. It is in the middle range of temperatures, around freezing (32°F.) or slightly above. Klister wax varies depending on the manufacturer, but generally is only one consistency—soft. Applied from a small can, the wax is usually pushed up from the bottom and daubed on the ski, then smoothed with the palm of the hand or a scraper.

Klister is a wax for old snow that is very wet or has been melted and refrozen, such as spring snow and that found in icy tracks. Klister is the Swedish word for "glue" and can live up to its name if you are not careful. Because of klister's toothpaste-like consistency, it is packaged in tubes with instructions and a color code like that for hard wax.

Applying a glide zone wax is necessary to properly prepare new synthetic skis. Most new skis come with a somewhat hairy-looking bottom. Apply a glide wax to the tip and tail. Let dry, scrape, then wax again. The end result should be a smooth, glossy base.

There is no need to apply a base wax each time you go skiing. Rewaxing is only necessary if you are a racer and need to switch wax to fit the changing snow conditions or if the glide wax has worn completely off from use. You can always tell if a new wax job is needed by close examination of the base. White spots will be apparent on the bottom where all the wax has been worn away.

Generally the base wax is scraped thin but, depending on snow conditions, a thicker layer can be left for protection. For example, the abrasive nature of coarse granular snow calls for a thicker layer of wax. The same is true for wet, moist snow. Scrape only minimally, leaving the wax rougher than for colder snow. Racers even run a wire brush over the wax, creating small striations to help break the suction between the wax and snow. In extremely wet snow, suction is sometimes so great it will almost stop you on slight downhills.

GLIDE WAXES

The primary purpose of glide wax is to maximize the ski's forward speed. If you are at all concerned about making your skis slide easily and efficiently, then a little attention paid to waxing the tip and tail can really improve the overall operation. The tour skier can get by without it, but a performance skier will seldom be without a fresh layer of glide wax. New synthetic polyethelene ski bases have made glide wax a requirement for proper ski care. Just as pine tar is used on wooden skis to impregnate the bottom to resist moisture absorption and facilitate wax retention, the new fiberglass skis need a glide wax to seal and protect. Polyethelene bases, fresh from the factory, contain thousands of microscopic pores and are very porous when new, much like wooden skis. The application of glide wax to synthetic skis and pine tar to wooden skis fills these pores.

To improve glide, select just the right wax for the specific temperature and snow condition. Alpine waxes can be used, but are sometimes complicated and are designed for higher speeds. Cross-country glide waxes are made specifically for the speeds a cross-country skier attains and are available for three to five broad temperature ranges. The color code is like that for cross-country hard waxes: green and blue for cold snow, red and yellow for warm snow.

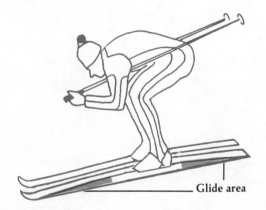
Glide area

GLIDE WAX APPLICATION

With a hot waxing iron, the paraffin-based glide wax is melted and spread over the tip and tail sections of each ski. With the skis placed on benches, wax is dripped on both sides of the groove, leaving the middle third of the ski free for the cross-country wax. Running the waxing iron back over the ski reheats the wax and spreads it evenly on the gliding portions of the ski.

Always keep the iron moving to avoid overheating the bottom and possibly melting the base and sealing the pores. Use a temperature setting at which the wax melts easily but does not smoke. Using too hot an iron will break down the wax characteristics and may damage the ski. An old household iron with an adjustable setting works best. Set it near the "wool" reading. Allow the wax to cool for at least twenty minutes (preferably overnight) to solidify. Then, using a plastic scraper to remove the excess, scrape until only a paper-thin coat of wax remains on the base. Use the rounded corner of the scraper to clean the groove and check the side wall for excess drippings.

On wooden skis, the hardest cross-country grip wax is used for glide. On the tip and tail, rub on one or two coats and use a cork to smooth them. Because the wax is very hard, it will resist most all snowflake penetration, unless it is very cold snow (–20° to –40°F.). If it is this cold, *any* wax will feel slow.

GRIP WAX SELECTION

The following considerations will help you choose the correct wax:

(1) **Temperature**. What is the outside air temperature? Each wax can is marked with an air temperature range, plus simple instructions. Generally, if temperatures are below freezing (32°F.), the snow is dry and a hard wax is used.

(2) **Humidity.** What is the moisture content of the snow? High humidity usually calls for a softer wax, low humidity a harder one. Use the "snowball test" to determine whether the snow is dry or wet. With your gloved hand, grab some snow. If you can make a snowball, it is wet; if the snow crumbles and falls out of your hand, it is dry.

(3) **Weather.** What does the weather forecaster predict? More snow, clearing, warm or cold temperatures?

(4) **Snow condition.** What type of snow will you be skiing on ? Fresh, granular, icy or wet? Will the snow crystals be hard or soft?

(5) **Track preparation.** In what condition are the tracks? Have they just been reset in new snow? Are they old and washed out?

(6) **Technique.** What kind of a skier are you? Can you adapt to the wax on your skis, or does the wax work against you? Is your timing at push-off exact, with weight over your foot, or are you late with the push?

(7) **Skis.** Are you using a stiff, double-cambered ski that allows use of a softer wax, or a soft-cambered ski where the wax is not held off the snow as much? Generally, the racer will use a stiff camber for icy, hard tracks and a soft camber for powdery, soft tracks.

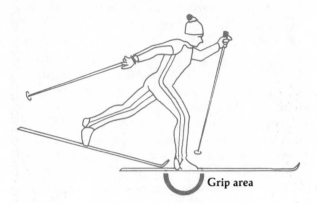

Grip area

GRIP WAX APPLICATION

Say we have two skiers of equal ability using skis with the same camber, but one is slipping while the other is holding and gliding around the trail. Selecting the same wax does not assure you of the same hold as your friend. How you apply that wax makes the difference.

There are three concerns when applying wax:

(1) **Length.** To keep it simple, plan on applying wax to the middle third of the ski, from twelve inches in front of the binding to six inches behind the steel plate. Once you determine the stiffest section of the ski, then you will have determined your "wax pocket." This is the area where the ski bottom does not touch the snow until all the weight is on one ski. The paper test is the best way to mark the waxing pocket. Refer to the Equipment chapter, page 21.

(2) **Thickness.** One thin layer of wax may work well for very cold, hard snow; but soft, wet snow needs more of a cushion. Therefore, wax thickness can increase grip. For instance, if your skis are slipping slightly, instead of going to the next softer wax, apply a thicker coat of the same wax. On the other hand, if the wax is *too* soft, the snow crystals will penetrate the wax but won't glide out once the ski is sliding. This creates an icing or clumping problem.

(3) **Firmness/hardness.** Applying wax to match the snow crystals can pertain to hard waxes, klister wax and klister. A wax that matches the current snow conditions must be hard enough to allow the snow to penetrate it and give hold. Read the instructions to help match wax to snow. If the wax on your skis is slipping, apply a thicker layer. If that doesn't work, use the same wax and go longer in front and behind the heel plates. If you are still slipping, apply the next softer wax. Waxing is a building process. Start from the harder waxes and go softer to arrive at the perfect combination.

HARD WAX APPLICATION

Hard waxes are rubbed on the ski like a crayon on a picture. Ideally, apply the wax to a warm ski bottom. When you are outside on the trail, remove all snow and make sure the bottom is dry. Rubbing a hard wax on a wet ski is like trying to find traction on an icy road. It just doesn't work! Apply wax to both sides of the groove at a thickness, length and hardness necessary for good hold.

It would be nice if we could always wax at home, where it is warm and toasty. More often than not, though, people who select and apply wax at home end up changing it once they start skiing. The best approach is to ski five or ten minutes on whatever wax is already on. Then you will have a better idea of the overall snow condition and can choose the correct wax and method of application.

Building up wax layers adds to durability. Many thin layers of wax, applied one at a time, each smoothed with a synthetic or natural cork, will help assure an adequate supply of grip wax for the length of the tour or race. Applying one thick coat of wax and corking it smooth accomplishes the same thing. It is a matter of preference, but the end result is durability to go the distance.

KLISTER WAX APPLICATION

Klister wax is the in-between wax for wet, newly fallen snow. It is very soft and gooey, like klister itself, but applied from a can like hard wax. Klister wax is dotted onto the ski for the length of the grip zone, then smoothed with a cork or hand. A carefully used torch and rag make quick work of spreading the wax, as long as you keep moving and don't scorch the bottom.

Klister wax also works well in very wet spring snow, the kind that drips with water. Longevity is not one of its traits, though, as it tends to wear off fast. It is not as durable as a klister.

Snow	Typical Grip Wax	Typical Glide Wax
Wet	Red klister	Red Glider
Transition	Violet, Red, Klisterwax; violet, yellow or silver klisters	Violet Glider
Cold	Blue, Blue extra, Blue klister	Blue Glider
Very cold	Green, Special green	Green Glider

Klister, the toothpaste-like wax, is squeezed from a tube. It is often said, "If your car is stuck at the bottom of an icy hill and you have nothing but your summer tires and a wax kit, take out the yellow klister." A little yellow klister spread on the tires just may get you up and over.

The gooey consistency of klister calls for careful application. Careless waxers may find themselves like flies on flypaper—all stuck up. With practice, applying klister is an easy, clean procedure.

Start with a warm tube of klister; room temperature is fine. If outside, use your hands or carry the wax next to your body. A small torch is also helpful. Cold klister is difficult to use. Once the klister is squeezable, run a bead down both sides of the groove for the length of your wax pocket—or longer, if you plan on climbing a lot. Take a plastic scraper or the palm of your hand to smooth the klister evenly on the ski. Remove any excess from the edges or side walls to start with. As you ski, a certain amount may naturally spread itself over the edges and will be evident at the end of the day. Sometimes this indicates too much wax. When waxing with klister, it is usually a problem of too much, rather than too little. Start with a thin coat and build if you are slipping. Try a little less next time out and experiment with grip. If the track is very dirty, apply a shorter length of klister. Klister will pick up every little bit of dirt along the track and, if you have a long klister section, it will be slow. Generally the harder klisters tend to stay on the ski bottom much better than the softer ones. They are sometimes used for binding a softer wax to the ski because of their durability (see section on Binder Waxes, following).

Klister skiing is some of the best and fastest skiing you will ever enjoy. On a properly waxed ski, the glide and hold balance themselves. Mastering klister selection and application definitely has its rewards. Cool spring mornings and evenings are the klister skier's paradise.

WAXING SYSTEMS MADE EASY

In an effort to simplify waxing, the cries of the public and the wax manufacturers finally brought a halt to the constantly expanding array of waxes. The racer, of course, benefitted from the great variety. The fifteen- to twenty-wax system, once understood, is easy to work with, but the recreational skier is sometimes short on experience and would rather be skiing than waxing. It was the recreational skier who became stymied by the myriad array of waxes on the ski shop shelves.

Enter the "one-wax system," the universal wax to cure all woes. It works by applying layers, varying in thickness, to match dry or wet snow. A thin layer is laid down for cold, dry snow, just thick enough to provide grip when snowflakes are well formed and sharp. As the snow becomes wetter, the wax coat is thickened to ensure a cushion for the rounded snowflakes to stick into. But for icy or extremely wet snow, the system is lacking. At these extremes, a klister was needed.

Not to be discouraged, the wax manufacturers have come up with the next best combination—the "two-wax system," in which only two waxes are all you need for a season of kicking and gliding. The system is very easy to understand and work with: one wax is for air temperatures above freezing (32° F.) and one is for air temperatures below freezing. They are, appropriately, named "Wet" and "Dry" for easy reference. First-time waxers now have an easy system for learning how to wax, conveniently and reliably.

The first variable is air temperature. For example, if the temperature outside is 24° F., the choice is the dry two-wax system. Apply a thin coat of cross-country wax to the grip zone, enough wax so a fingernail can scrape some up. Ski a little ways and, if it slips, simply make the wax layer thicker. Then go longer to achieve correct grip. Use a cork to smooth the wax to improve durability and glide.

Layering is the secret in the two-wax system: wax hardness can be varied by wax thickness. If slipping is still a problem, apply a rougher, uncorked layer of wax to aid grip. The opposite is true if you are sticking. Scrape off the wax and start anew, building layers until you hit the right combination.

Temperature	Snow	Apply wax
35°		Rough
	wet	
32°		Smooth
30°		Rough
under	dry	
26°		Smooth

For extremely warm temperatures, wet snow wax will work all right on the flat, but climbing could be difficult. It is better to use a red klister at this point. The same holds true for icy tracks, as dry snow wax just won't last. It will wear off as quickly as you put it on; therefore, try a blue klister.

I've tried to keep it simple, but as you can see, we've added waxes to come up with a four-wax system. For general touring in midwinter conditions, however, the two-wax system is a good bet. From there, your waxing knowledge will grow. Like anything, start slow and easy, working up to the need for other waxes. After a year or two, you might be walking to the ski trails with your own tackle box full of waxes!

BINDER WAXES

For those long ski trips or days when the snow is very coarse and abrasive, wax retention becomes a concern. To keep cross-country waxes on the ski longer, a binder wax is used. Applied in a thin coat, the binder wax acts to bond the grip wax to the ski bottom. Like a double-sided piece of tape, the binder prevents excessive wax wear.

Binder wax comes in two forms: hard and klister. The hard wax binder is primarily used for binding hard waxes. It comes in a can, like hard waxes. Using a torch to warm the top layer, the binder is daubed on the ski and spread to a thin coat. I'm always amazed at how little binder wax is needed. A thin coat does the job; too thick a coat is hard to cover completely. Binder wax alone may hold, but the skiing is not very fast.

Klister binders include the hard green or blue klisters. Using a thin layer on the grip zone, the softer klisters will bind with other waxes and resist wear better. The combination of klister on top of klister creates a much better bond than mixing hard wax and klister binders. Likenesses tend to stick together.

But klister binders can also be used to bind hard waxes. If the klister is applied warm, then frozen, hard waxes can be rubbed on top. This is a good combination for granular tracks with a light dusting of fresh snow. The klister will act as a cushion for the icy snow and the hard wax will keep the ski from sticking.

WAX KIT

Eventually, the tools of the trade will become too numerous for you to carry in your back pocket. The wax kit provides a carrying and storing case for your expanding array of tools. Fishing tackle boxes make ideal wax kits. The small shelves keep waxes separate and the bottom bin collects odds and ends.

Generally a wax kit should contain a variety of tools, not only for waxing needs, but for repairing and cleaning. Use this checklist as a reference in assembling your personal kit:

(1) Thermometer to determine air temperature.
(2) Scrapers, both metal and plastic.
(3) Corks, preferably synthetic (one for hard waxes, one for soft waxes), if you're into racing.
(4) Torch for spreading and smoothing waxes.
(5) Waxing iron for applying glide wax and spreading cross-country waxes.
(6) Cleaning solvent and rags for cleaning off grip waxes.
(7) Extension cord for those long distance plugs.
(8) Newspaper for depositing klister scrapings.
(9) An adequate supply of cross-country waxes, from hard waxes to klisters.
(10) Waxing vises for clamping on any table to hold skis firmly for waxing or repairs.
(11) Hand cleaner, when the job is over or for that drop of klister on your coat.
(12) Drill for mounting bindings and other repairs.
(13) Extra screws. You always lose one.

IRONS AND TORCHES

Heating waxes is a frequent practice when waxing or cleaning skis. The household iron is a great tool for this purpose. From heating and spreading glide waxes to applying grip waxes, it is reliable and efficient. Just be sure you travel with an extension cord.

Square, flat irons made out of a rectangular piece of aluminum are small and fit nicely into any wax kit. However, a torch is needed to heat these waxing irons. Usually a small propane or butane torch is ample. Several torches with different nozzles are available commercially. A broad-tip nozzle is preferable, as it heats a larger area. If you want to travel light, butane torches are lighter, propane torches are heavier. But propane will burn at a much lower outside air temperature than will butane. Propane gas burns well below freezing (–20° F.) while butane will freeze below 32° F.

Torches come in handy for warming cold klister tubes, cleaning stubborn messes, mixing waxes and bringing life to a cold day. However, the torch can be a menace to plastic ski bottoms. Excessive or prolonged heat on the bottom will seal the base or even bubble it, depending on the heat's intensity. I would highly recommend electric irons for waxing needs and solvent for cleaning. Leave torches to the experienced racer who knows how to use them.

CLEANING SKIS

You wouldn't wear the same shirt over and over again until it became encrusted in perspiration and dirt. No, you would wash it periodically to bring back its full luster and the fragrance of the day you bought it. The same holds true for your skis. Cleaning is simply the ongoing process of eliminating excessive wax buildup and dirty ski bottoms.

Using a plastic scraper, remove as much of the grip wax as possible. Plastic scrapers are used because metal scrapers can gouge or nick the ski's bottom or edges. Clean the groove and side walls of any excess wax. With a waxing solvent and a rag, wipe off the remaining wax and totally clean the ski, top and bottom. Cleaning fluids made specifically for this purpose and sold commercially will not damage the polyurethane bases or cause other harmful effects.

It is best to clean skis indoors at room temperature, before rewaxing or storing them. But after a day of klister skiing, you will need to remove the wax before transporting and storing your skis. Storing a klister-waxed ski in the closet all week will result in a small puddle of klister on the closet floor. Once the klister is

warmed up again, it turns liquid and runs whichever way is down. So take time to clean klister off before you throw your skis into the car.

WAXING THE NO-WAX

Even though the name implies otherwise, waxing is required to properly care for and prepare a no-wax ski for glide and grip. The tip and tail need to be prepared with a glide zone wax. This base impregnation is the same used for any new synthetic-based ski. The microscopic pores of the bottom material need wax to smooth the base and provide a good gliding surface. When an older ski begins to show signs of losing its initial glide wax and the base looks rough, reapply a base wax with a hot iron and a universal or specific glide zone wax. This will also help to avoid icing due to moisture absorption.

The main goal of waxing a no-wax ski is to improve glide and prevent icing. The two main waxing agents are paraffin-based glide waxes and silicone-based sprays. Simply rubbing a glide wax on the entire bottom of a patterned no-wax ski may be enough. Carrying a small bar or section of glide wax will be a quick remedy for sticky skies. An aerosol can of silicone spray is another way to increase glide and prevent icing, especially for mohair. Spray the entire bottom of the ski first, and let sit for ten to twenty minutes before skiing. The product wears quickly and may need to be reapplied during longer tours.

There are certain snow conditions when even a no-wax ski won't work—in fresh, deep powder or on icy trails. To alleviate the deep-powder woes, the best cure is to follow in someone else's tracks where the snow is compacted and your no-wax pattern will grab. If that is not possible, use a cross-country hard wax on the tip and tail to hold for climbing, then scrape, once the majority of climbing is done. This is a better method than applying a cross-country wax right on the ski's pattern, which is difficult to clean on the trail and will cause clumping or sticky skis if the wax is too soft.

On hard, icy trails no-wax skis use mohair or a similar rough surface. Mohair has a tendency to ice up when skiing from icy tracks to powdery, dry snow if there is any moisture present. A silicone spray applied liberally to the hair strips will ease this icing problem. Pattern-based skis are the least effective on ice. You may even have to use a cross-country wax such as a klister for grip in this condition, which is a good reason to switch over to a waxable ski.

WAXABLE BASES TURN NO-WAX

Creating a no-wax surface on a regular synthetic base is a possibility. Waxing is never an exact science, especially when temperatures hover around freezing. Skiing in such conditions may require technique adjustments to withstand lessened grip or decreased glide. A compromise is sometimes the only relief.

When these "in-between" conditions come up, particularly in the early fall and spring, try changing your waxable base into a dynamic, gripping no-wax base. Sound far fetched? Listen to this. By roughing up the wax pocket of any synthetic-based ski with #80- to #100-grit sandpaper, you can turn the base into a waxless surface not unlike the no-wax skis on the market today. The plastic based material when raised up and roughed up creates small irregularities to bind with the snow crystals when downward pressure is applied to the ski. There are some commercial "wax abraders" for this specific purpose.

Once the ski is roughed up, use a silicone spray over the area for glide. If you want to reprep the area back to a smooth base for waxing again, scrape it smooth and melt a hard wax, such as a blue grip wax, onto the base with an iron. Using warm heat, spread the wax evenly over the grip zone to impregnate the base. Let it cool overnight and scrape thin. One important caution: the ski bottom will not last long if this method is used constantly. The base will eventually wear down from repeated sanding.

SKINS

The use of skins is reminiscent of the early days of skiing when fur on the skis' bottoms was used for climbing. That way the early ski pioneers could climb hills without the aid of waxes. Nowadays ski mountaineers and alpine tourers who use skins can climb through a two-thousand-foot elevation gain without having to change waxes constantly.

Climbing skins were originally made from sealskin. Cut in long strips, they were attached to the ski so the hairs slanted backward. Today's climbing skins are made from synthetic fur called "mohair." Like the mohair strips on a no-wax ski, these climbing skins will allow you to slide forward, but not back. They extend almost the entire running surface.

The best advantage of climbing skins is the sense of assurance they give you. Carrying a heavy pack in changeable snow conditions is tricky business, even for the experienced waxer. With skins on, ascents can be quicker with fewer traverses, and the back slippery ski is eliminated, easing the work load.

Skins are either strapped or stuck to skis. The stick-on variety are handy: simply unfold the entire strip and apply a little sticky glue. When you have reached the summit, peel the strip off, fold it (stick sides together), and down you go.

WHAT TO DO IF . . .

(1) **Slipping.** Slippery skis are indicative of too hard a wax or not enough wax. To correct this imbalance, first add a thicker coat of the same wax. Then add a longer section of the same wax. If that combination does not work, go to a softer wax.

(2) **Sticking.** Icing or clumping problems are just the opposite of slipping; too soft a wax has been used for the snow conditions. The snow crystals stick into the wax, but won't let go. To correct this problem, either stop, scrape the wax off, and start anew, or rub a correction wax (paraffin) over the too-sticky wax.

(3) **Nothing works.** There may be days when the snow seems to change around every corner. The snow is wet in the meadows and dry in the trees. Waxing to fit both condition will only cause frustration. Instead, if you are waxed for cold dry snow, ski in the trees where the snow is consistent. Remember, we can't talk waxing without talking about technique, too. Wax will work when the skier on top is using correct technique. Next time you are slipping, take a look at your technique before adding a softer wax.

(4) **It all looks too complicated.** Start simple. Waxing "starter kits" are available that give you the essentials—two hard waxes, one klister, a cork, and a scraper. Learning how to wax takes practice and experience. The two-wax system is a good way to begin. From a thorough understanding of waxing basics, it won't be long before you discover how the complete array of waxes can help with improved glide and grip. The best way to learn waxing is to stick with one brand of wax. Learn it well, discovering its peculiarities and small idiosyncrasies before delving into another brand.

CARE & REPAIR

"An ounce of prevention is worth a pound of cure."

T. C. Haliburton

Your equipment will serve you as long as you serve it. This means properly caring for the skis' well-being. Their requirements are not elaborate. They don't eat much and they are very quiet in the off season. A little attention to the things that bring you joy is the aim of this care and repair section.

Ski care involves cleaning, storing, prepping and repairing. Time spent on each area will assure long life to your skis, an investment worth preserving.

CLEANING AND STORING

Skis get dirty. There is no way around it. Even though they glide over some of the purest, whitest snow, they do act like magnets, collecting dirt, leaves and pine needles. The soft grip waxes and klisters are the biggest culprits. Sometimes after skiing with klister on a warm spring day, the bottoms may look like an old dirt road after a summer rain. Scraping and cleaning the skis on such days is a must. (There may be cold, fresh powder days when the wax can be left on for several days before cleaning.)

Always scrape the wax off first. Then use a commercial cleaning solvent and rag to remove what remains. A racer may want to use a lint-free cloth (fiberlene) to wipe the skis dry after cleaning. Usually when the bottoms are dirty, the side walls and tops are too, so wipe the whole ski with mild solvent. Use only cleaning fluids specifically designed for this purpose. Gasoline, lighter fluid or turpentine can be harmful, preventing wax adhesion.

Before storing skis, thoroughly clean the tops,

bottoms and side walls. Wooden skis need a fresh coat of pine tar to protect them from moisture absorption. Synthetic bottoms require a coat of glide wax. Performance skis need this protection in the off season to prevent oxidization, which slows glide. Apply a thick coat of glide wax, leaving it rough until fall. Then it is ready to be scraped thin for the first trip of the season. Store skis in a cool, dry area where the temperature will not rise about 90° F. I've stored many a ski in cool, dark basements horizontally or vertically and have had no problem with warping or loss of camber. Skis are designed to retain camber patterns. There is no need to block and tie skis together to maintain camber. As long as the ski can stand freely, its camber will be retained.

PREPPING

Old or new, wood or fiberglass, the objective of prepping is the same: to prepare the skis' bottoms for waxing. New wood skis are usually factory sealed. Proper preparation of the base requires a metal scraper, a torch, rags and pine tar. Scrape the bottom, removing any seal, even to the point of shaving the wood slightly. This should open up the wood's porous surface to accept the pine tar. Using a small paintbrush or rag, spread an even coat of pine tar on the base while heating it with a torch. Reheat the pine tar and spread it around again. Heat it to a point where a little smoke and small bubbles appear. This will liquefy the tar enough for it to penetrate into the wood, sealing and protecting the ski against moisture absorption, the biggest threat to wooden skis. Warping is not uncommon with wood skis, and it can occur in a poorly sealed ski (or even in a well sealed one during storage in a humid environment).

Once the pine tar is burned in, use a rag and torch to remove the excess, leaving a clean-to-touch bottom surface that looks brown in color. No white wood should show after a thorough job. Pine tarring, like glide waxing, is done during the season when the wood base loses its nice, chocolate-brown color. Pine tar is, itself, a good cross-country wax on cold, dry snow. It was used exclusively during the early years of waxing. Pine tar also binds other cross-country waxes to the ski and prevents wax wear.

Preparing synthetic-based skis follows a similar procedure. A glide wax and waxing iron are used in place of pine tar and a torch. Use a universal glide zone wax or a specialized wax. Hold the wax to a warm iron and melt a bead of wax onto the tip and tail sections only. If you are using a household iron, the "wool" setting should be about right. If the wax begins to smoke, then the iron is too hot and you run the risk of melting or delaminating the base. Too hot an iron can seal the porous plastic, causing it to lose its wax-holding capability. Spread the wax evenly over the tip and tail. Keep the iron moving. The bond between wax and polyethylene bases is improved with heat.

The grip zone is left free of glide zone wax because cross-country waxes do not bind very well to a glide wax. It is better to apply a grip zone wax, such as a blue, to the middle third of the ski and spread it with an iron. Wax retention is improved when grip wax is applied onto a base impregnated with the same type of wax.

Following the heating of the glide and grip zone waxes, let the ski cool overnight. Then, using a plastic scraper to avoid damaging the base, scrape the wax from tip to tail, leaving a thin, smooth layer.

For the racer who is concerned about creating the best possible gliding surface, a sanding procedure may be used for preparing new polyethylene bases. Before any wax is applied, sand the entire base with silicone-carbide sandpaper (wet or dry). Make sure the ski is held firmly, either clamped in a vise or held steady between two benches. This process will eliminate any irregularities on the base and take down high spots, producing a consistent texture. Begin sanding with #100-grit paper wrapped around a sanding block. Work from tip to tail using long strokes. When you feel the entire base has been sanded, scrape off the raised fibers and switch to #150-grit paper, which is finer grained, to do a finish job on the bottom. Some racers take this sanding a step farther and finish up with a #180-grit paper for an even smoother finish—all in an effort to create a faster, more porous base for wax retention.

During the season, the racer may need to reprep his skis to again open up the polyethylene base. From constant heating and waxing, bases may become hardened or they may get oxidized from storage. Clean the ski thoroughly first. Then, using a stiff wire brush, rough up the base, removing any excess wax and hardened P-Tex. Then clean the base again with solvent. Once the ski is reprepped, you are ready to start anew. Proceed to apply glide wax and kick wax as previously explained.

Depending on your specific skiing needs, ski preparation varies slightly. The mountaineering skier who intends to climb uphill for long stretches has different requirements than the strictly downhill telemark skier.

The skier who plans to climb and glide should prepare the glide and grip zones separately. He will apply glide wax to the tip and tail sections and a cross-country wax to the middle of the ski. The telemark skier, who plans only to ride ski lifts and ski downhill, can apply glide wax over the entire bottom.

We keep glide and grip wax separate from each other only to help wax retention on the ski's bottom. If you wax with glide over the whole ski bottom, you have not ruined the ski. Waxing the whole ski with glide wax was once the accepted method. Changes in waxing technology may again change the approach for base preparation. Don't let your own experimentation with different methods be threatened.

Mountaineering ski edges are usually metal, either steel or aluminum, for hold on hard-packed traverses and for turning. Preparation of metal-edged skis should proceed in the following manner:

(1) **Cleaning.** Clean the entire ski, removing any excess wax from the base.

(2) **Base level.** Using a scraper, run its edge down the ski to determine if their edges are excessively railed (higher than the base) or beveled (lower than the base). Sight for any light showing through.

(3) **Flat filing.** Set a flat, eighteen-inch, mill-basted, single-grooved metal file at an angle across both edges and pull down from tip to tail in long strokes. Make sure the hand pressure is distributed evenly over the edges not on the very ends of the file. Flat filing will flatten the ski base, lowering the edges and removing the high spots on the P-Tex.

(4) **Side filing.** Use the file to square the edges. Turn the ski on its side and run the file at an angle along the sides of the edges. Finishing up with a sharpening stone or emery paper will create the perfect edge. In some cases, a very sharp edge may not be desired. Sometimes a sharp edge may feel like it is always catching in soft-packed powder, especially if you are not used to it. But for the telemark racer who skis on a hard-packed course, a sharp edge means less skid and faster turns.

(5) **Dulling.** For ease of ski control, the tip and tail edges should be dulled. Using the file or sharpening stone, dull the tip edges from the very tip of the ski down past the ski's shovel about three to five inches. The same procedure is done on the tails, dulling the edges for a shorter distance from the very tail upward about two to four inches. If the tip edges are left too sharp, the ski will always feel like it is hooking or turning too quickly when placed on edge.

(6) **Cleaning.** Use a rag to dust off the ski and finish with a good cleaning job to remove all metal filings and P-Tex from the bottom.

REPAIRING

Ski equipment, like the family car, must be maintained and repaired for continued dependability, enjoyment, and longevity. Neither will last long if we don't follow routine maintenance schedules.

Breakage. Cross-country skis are vulnerable to load stress, particularly the tips and tails where the stress can be greatest. Taking a good eggbeater of a fall can do more damage to your equipment than to your body. Breaking a ski at the tip is probably the most common accident. Another frequent spot is mid-ski, at the heel plate. If skis are old and have not been cared for, this is a possibility. Always keep the skis covered with a protective glide wax or pine tar to guard against moisture and dirt.

Delamination. Fiberglass construction has greatly reduced the chances of breakage. These skis are stronger and more durable, able to withstand much more abuse than wooden skis. But delamination is a more common occurrence. You may have seen skis whose tails have split apart from being constantly jammed into snowbanks or whose tips have their top layers pulling away. These classic problems are cured with a little epoxy and "C" clamps.

Clean and dry thoroughly the areas to be glued. Mix an appropriate supply of epoxy. Don't skimp—it is better to have extra than to run out before the job is done. Place waxed paper around the area to be clamped, then use wood blocks to distribute the pressure of the "C" clamp and tighten. (Waxed paper will not stick to the glue.) Let sit for twenty-four hours, then remove the clamps and paper. Use a file or metal scraper to smooth the rough spots.

Prevent delamination by checking skis regularly for nicks or small separations between the layers. Fill these little cracks with epoxy or water-repellent glue. How many times have you stood your skis in the garage after a tour and let the snow melt down the skis, leaving their tails in a puddle of water? Either clean the skis of snow before storing, or hang them off the ground. Water absorption should be avoided.

Gouges. There always seems to be a hidden rock somewhere along the trail to scrape your ski's bottom. Gouges hamper glide, making you work just a little bit harder. Take the time to keep on top of gouges. Repair involves filling each scratch or hole with P-Tex, a material similar to that of the base.

(1) Clean the base and remove any hanging or rough-edged P-Tex.

(2) Drip P-Tex candle (or similar product) into the gouge. P-Tex will adhere better to a warm ski, forming a permanent bond. Hold the candle away from the base to prevent the P-Tex from burning on the base itself.

(3) Let cool and scrape off the excess. Use a sure-form or wood working plane to carefully smooth the area. Then use sandpaper to finish the job.

Bindings. Bindings are the mechanical marvels of cross-country equipment. The safety pin and the cross-country binding have a lot in common. Both will function properly for long periods of time unless they get bent out of shape.

Binding screws have a tendency to work loose. Check for tightness periodically. If the screw hole has become enlarged, simply plug the hole with a splinter of wood. Cut and level the wood before reinserting the screw. Toothpicks make good stuffers and will work for quick repair while on tour. Steel wool and epoxy are also used for oversized screw holes.

As with any repair, it is prevention that will save you in the long run. Proper care is not expensive, but it does take time on your part. Next time you look at your skis, use the careful eye of a ski mechanic.

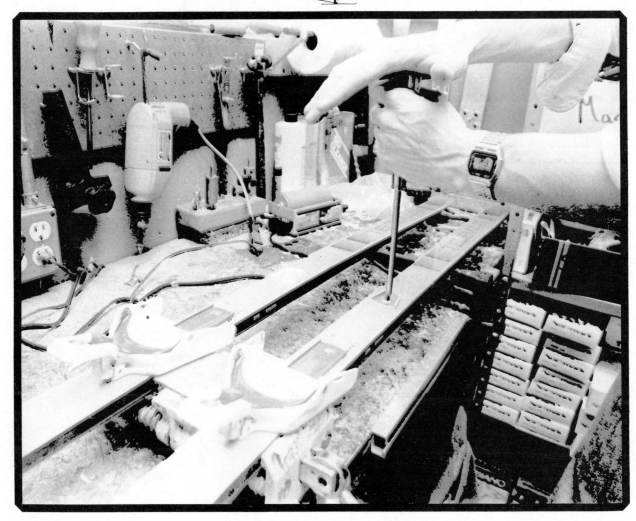

MOUNTING BINDINGS

"You might as well fall flat on your face as lean over too far backward."

James Thurber

Have you ever seen a ski with the hole drilled all the way through it? If you are not careful, it could happen to you. Whether you mount your own skis or have a trained ski mechanic do the job, follow these simple guidelines:

(1) Read all instructions for the specific binding to be mounted. Follow any instruction on the ski for binding location.

(2) Assemble the necessary tools: drill, bits, posi-drive screwdriver, glue (white or epoxy), ruler, mounting jig, and marking awl.

(3) Determine which mounting method to use and mount the exact end of the boot's toe on the ski's balance point. The *mounting jig* is a tool for easy mounting that uses a metal plate with guide holes for spotting exact drilling locations. Holes

are usually compatible with most bindings. Check the hole spacing before drilling.

For *freehand* mounting, locate the binding on the ski in the exact center. Mark and drill the center hole and attach the binding with the front screw. Then place the boot in the binding and center the boot heel on the ski. Remove the boot and mark and drill one of the rear holes, leaving the third hole until last for minor adjustment if the binding is slightly off kilter.

Fill each hole with either a white (Elmer's) or epoxy glue, using an awl or a toothpick to poke the glue into the hole. Then tighten the screw and turn the ski over to let the glue set up around the top of the ski. (If the ski has a foam or honeycomb core, this becomes especially important.)

Heel plate. Mount the heel plate at the center of the boot heel. If using a wedge or similar kind of plate, the proper location is critical to smooth operation. Attach either with small nails or one screw in the center of the plate.

Drilling. Use either a hand or electric drill. Select a drill bit size with a diameter slightly smaller than the screw's shaft. This leaves the threads room to bite into the ski's core. Use a piece of tape to mark the bit at the appropriate depth so you avoid drilling through the ski.

Removing bindings. After the glue has set up, removing tightened screws may be tough. If you have to take a binding off for traveling or to use it on a new ski, first use a firm hand on a posi-drive screwdriver. If this does not loosen the binding, place a wood block under the ski at the binding. Put the screwdriver in the slots and hit the top with a hammer. This should break the bond,

loosening the screw. Still no luck? Use a torch; heat the screwdriver while it's on the screw. The heat will transfer to the metal screw and loosen the bond.

MOUNTING TELEMARK BINDINGS

Measure the entire length of the ski from the tip to the tail (cord length). Use a tape measure from the tip in a direct line to the tail. Mark a line at half cord length. This is where the three binding pins should be located.

Since nordic downhill skis are primarily used on the slopes, placing the bindings so the boot is centered on the ski becomes important for proper utilization of the ski's side cut versus the wax pocket on a track ski.

PRE-SKI CONDITIONING

PHYSICAL TRAINING

"Nothing happens to any man that he is not formed by nature to bear."

Marcus Aurelius Antoninus

Yes, there is a physical side to cross-country skiing; the exercise it affords is one of the drawing features of the sport. The continuing awareness of the benefits of regular exercise to body and mind is becoming overwhelmingly evident. The fact that you are reading this chapter is proof of the increasing recognition of physical exercise as a part of a fulfilling life.

Getting in shape for cross-country skiing differs for each individual. It is an individual sport; the level of fitness you strive to attain depends on the extent to which you want to involve yourself. Cross-country skiing can be a very physically demanding sport, requiring the utmost of a person's strength and endurance. Cross-country skiing can also be as relaxed and invigorating as a walk through the park.

"The racer trains to race and races to train." The recreational skier is training for enjoyment.

With these objectives in mind, the training activities you select can be the ones you enjoy. If your job is physically demanding or you're involved in other sports, then you are probably already doing your part to tone and strengthen your muscles.

The physiological benefits derived from cross-country skiing itself are many: improved muscle tone, oxygen intake, circulation, and stamina. Of course, the mental aspects of engaging in any physically stimulating activity are also a boost to individual well-being. Simply putting on the equipment and skiing a little—even if it is only in the local park—makes your body undergo changes. Cross-country skiing is one of the best physical activities for exercising the whole body. It ranks at the top of the list, with swimming, as the best total body conditioner. And if you are a calorie counter, cross-country skiing is one of the highest fuel-burning activities, requiring about

1,200 calories per hour at racing speeds and about 800 calories per hour when touring. Depending on how much time is spent skiing during the winter, improvements in mind and body follow accordingly. Frequent skiing on a regular basis improves the body's physical capabilities to the degree of effort put forth. If the time available for skiing is limited, then engaging in similar activities when not skiing will continue or prolong the physiological benefits of exercise.

Cross-country skiing is movement, repetitive movement like long distance running or swimming. The body is asked to perform a pattern of motions over and over. The body must endure this type of continued movement if training for the demands of cross-country skiing is to be successful. Muscles are the source of the power for motion. Training specific muscles, along with the heart and lungs, is the goal of a physical conditioning program. The purpose of training is preparation: fine tuning the body to withstand the demands of the sport, dependent on individual goals.

GOALS

Every person is born with certain natural abilities, such as reaction time, fast or slow twitch muscle fiber, coordination, balance, speed or agility. All these elements can be refined through training to help each individual reach his or her potential. Training to reach maximum physical output is very systematic and progressive in nature. For the serious racer, exercises are tailored closely to actual skiing movements. Training is oriented toward speed; being able to move faster over long distances without tiring is the goal of the racer.

Recreational skiers have different goals. They may just want to ski a five-mile loop and not fall over from exhaustion, or enjoy a day of ski touring without being so stiff afterward they can't walk.

Determine your goals. What you want to get out of a training program? Do you plan to ski every weekend or just once a month? Are you planning any long tours or races during the winter? Having the commitment to stay with the training program you have outlined is the next step.

Pace yourself. Don't overestimate what you can do. Allow time for the body to adjust slowly to your increasing demands. Cross-country skiers tend to be an active lot anyway, and it's likely that some of your daily activities are conditioning your

body naturally. Walking to work, climbing stairs, summer hiking, tennis, bicycling, skating, and golfing all involve the legs, the most powerful muscle group used by skiers.

To maintain a training program, it is important to start slowly. Keep the work load reasonable for your own needs and available time. Too many training programs have been started but never realized because of trying to do too much too fast. If you plan on staying with an exercise program, have the mental discipline to progress gradually. Let us look at areas of development, and then how to accomplish our goals through different exercises.

TRAINING EMPHASIS

In training for cross-country skiing, whether the goal is racing or pleasure, the physical conditioning is the same. The difference lies in the degree of effort put forth. To maximize the benefits from a conditioning program, training should be geared toward increasing (1) muscle strength, (2) muscle endurance, (3) flexibility, and (4) cardiovascular capability.

Muscle strength has a direct relationship to power and speed. In a strong, long stride, the explosive power is generated from the leg push-off and subsequent poling motion. Speed will increase as muscles become stronger and more power is exerted, while the possibility of injury will decrease.

Muscle endurance is enhanced to continue repetitious movements without fatigue. Have you ever noticed how easily your arms tire when skiing? Few sports emphasize, or even require, arm strength. Runners, for one, can get by without even using their arms. That is one reason a good runner may tire quickly when skiing, because the arms, as well as the legs, supply power for the sport.

Strength training for skiing does not mean we end up looking like Mr. Universe; quite the contrary. The cross-country skier would rather have the slim, sleek muscles of a gazelle—powerful muscles that can supply a quick burst of speed and will continue to do so without tiring. The big, bulky muscles of a weightlifter have no place in the rhythmic, flowing stride of cross-country skiing. The goal is muscles that provide endurance, not large, showy pectorals and deltoids. The nature of cross-country skiing lends itself well to adaptation of existing exercise routines that simulate the diagonal stride or double poling movements. These are two of the major techniques to concentrate on during off-season training.

The third component of a well-rounded training program is flexibility. Ask a runner or skier if he maintains a regular stretching routine and the response may be varied. Stretching is often the most neglected aspect of an athlete's training, but it is by no means any less important. Listen to what Marty Hall (past U.S. Cross-Country Ski Team coach and author) has to say about stretching: "Stretching improves flexibility so that you can perform the movements of your sport through a full range of motion without muscle tension. Stretching keeps you relaxed while training and racing. It also develops your kinesthetic sense, an awareness of where each part of your body is and what it is doing. Stretching encourages buildup in fatigued muscles."

Stretching the different muscle groups is best done after a brief five- to ten-minute warmup, when the blood is flowing and the peripheral blood vessels have warmed the outer skin slightly. Muscles that are loose and warm before stretching are less prone to injury by over stretching. Think of a frozen rubber band. If you grab it and give a quick pull, it might just break in half. But warm that same rubber band in your hand and then pull it gently; it will extend to its fullest. This is a pretty simplistic analogy, but muscles react in a similar fashion. That is why stretching after exercise is also important, especially after a fast, hard run or interval workout. Stretching the muscles slowly will help them recover and may alleviate soreness and stiffness.

The final concern of your physical training program is the cardiovascular system. The heart, lungs, and blood vessel network are the key to overall fitness. Improving the heart's ability to pump greater volumes of blood through the entire body will increase the oxygen supply to the tissue and, therefore, improve performance.

We speak of cross-country skiing as an aerobic activity, which, as defined by Kenneth Cooper in his book, *The New Aerobics*, is "any activity that stimulates heart and lung activity for a time period sufficiently long to produce beneficial changes in the body. Running, swimming, cycling, jogging and cross-country skiing are typical aerobic exercises. The main objective of an aerobic exercise program is to increase the maximum amount of oxygen that the body can process within a given time. It is dependent upon an ability to (1) rapidly breath large amounts of air, (2) forcefully deliver large volumes of blood and (3) effectively deliver oxygen to all parts of the body. In short, it depends upon efficient lungs, a powerful heart and a good vascular system (blood transport).

Any exercise, to be beneficial, must be performed for a long enough time to effect a change in the body. For training to transpire, an exercise must be done at least three times per week for a minimum of twenty minutes with a minimum heart rate of 120 beats per minute. Heart rate is a good indicator of intensity and effort. It depends on age, weight, and physical condition. Consult the chart on page 77 for information regarding heart rate levels and exercise.

Improvements in the cardiovascular system are dramatic for the previously sedentary person. Simply getting out and doing some aerobic activity will build strength. The more intense and frequent the exercise, the more improvement in oxygen intake. If we can increase the oxygen intake to the lungs, the blood transport system carries more hemoglobin and fuel to the muscle tissue, enhancing overall endurance. The stroke volume (the amount of blood pushed through the arteries and capillaries) is increased, allowing the heart to beat at a slower rate and rest more between beats. This reduces the heart's total work, a definite benefit to overall fitness and well-being. Less work for the heart means living efficiency is improved.

Skiing is usually done in an aerobic state, meaning there is enough oxygen supplied to the muscles to meet the requirements of the workload. During aerobic activity, the muscles can efficiently burn glycogen, which fuels them.

There may be times, in an emergency, when you have to reach a phone or injured skier in a hurry. You may reach a state, referred to as "non-aerobic" or "anaerobic," in which your muscles work in an oxygen debt. What happens is this: lactic acid builds up in the muscles from insufficiently burned glycogen. This build up of unused fuel results in muscle fatigue and, eventually, a stiff, sore muscle. Because recreational skiers and racers may sometimes need to ski fast or climb a steep hill quickly, it is good practice to ski into an oxygen debt now and then when training. By doing so, the body adapts and can push back the "anaerobic threshold" learning to accept heavier workloads.

Both aerobic and anaerobic training should be done, but aerobic exercise is far more efficient, easing heart rate and muscle fatigue; moving into the anaerobic realm will increase the muscles' ability to store fuels and enhance stamina for short bursts of speed.

PROGRAM PLANNING

Once goals have been determined and you have a good idea of what you want to accomplish, the next step in your training program is planning. The amount of time you will be able to devote will direct your decisions on appropriate activities. Use each section of this chapter for suggestions in program content and appropriate exercises for planning your own training.

Prior planning allows individual programs, tailored to specific needs. Each activity is designed as a stepping stone, progressing ever so slightly each week or month to achieve the desired result.

Before engaging in any physical fitness program, have a physical checkup. Let a doctor evaluate your present conditon and point out your weak or strong points. If you are over forty, a checkup is a must, if for no other reason than knowing where you stand when it comes to putting out a little effort.

How much training is enough? This is, again, individually decided. If you have been involved in other sports or if you are a regualar jogger, then simply add onto your current workload. If you have never been involved in an exercise program before, then you are starting with a clean slate and the sky is the limit. Use the following pages to acquaint yourself with different types of appropriate exercises.

Allow enough lead time before you intend to actually begin each season. About four to five weeks should be ample time to condition the body for the beginning skier (exercising three times per week). Take it slowly at first and build up your aerobic base.

TRAINING LOG

Keeping track of your training and program outlines is a fun way to watch for improvements. The training record will guide you from the day you start. Knowing exactly how long, how many, and how much helps you evaluate progress and direct future decisions. If you ever have a chance to train with a group, the training log is a good indicator of your competitive edge.

Training logs can be kept daily, monthly or yearly. The daily log is more like a diary, recorded in a spiral notebook or an elaborate chart. A sample chart is printed on page 87. Usually, you will write down how many miles or kilometers you ran, how much time you spent in hard exercise, and how you felt during the workout, and correlate it with daily diet and sleep time. Write down resting and working heart rates. Keep track of weight gain or loss.

With a little time and persistence, you will be able to decipher the correlations of good days and poor days. The results are revealing and interesting, and they guide future decisions.

SPECIFICITY

Program planning will set the stage for your performance. Planning each workout with skiing in mind puts quality into your training, not just quantity. The quality program is goal specific, meaning the exercises you do closely simulate the movements of on-snow skiing.

Plan each workout to specifically focus on important physical characteristics, such as strength, endurance, flexibility, or cardiovascular capability. Involving the body in activities closely aligned to skiing is a great psychological, as well as physical, boost to your self-esteem. Knowing you are working toward something, not just running around taking up time, gives more value to your workout.

Roller Skis. Roller skis are essentially sawed-off skis with wheels. A ratchet wheel that only rolls one way—forward—acts as the wax, so when the ski is pushed from, there is no slippage. If you do a lot of roller skiing, be careful to employ proper technique and don't come to rely on the sure-holding roller ski that never slips back.

Roller skiing is the closest you can come to actual skiing and is an ideal activity for training in the snowless seasons. If you can't be on snow, do the next best thing—roller ski!

Ski Pole Exercises. Another way to practice the ski stride is to take ski poles along whenever you go walking, hiking, or running. Think of the double impact of hiking mountain trails with your poles. Not only do you work leg muscles, but your arms contribute to moving you forward.

Besides, with a pair of poles, you strengthen specific arm muscles and work on technique. By winter, the ski poles will feel like a part of you.

Ski-striding up gradual hills with poles is like doing the diagonal stride. Take long strides and land on the heel first, then roll off the ball of the foot and extend the leg behind.

A combination of ski-striding and running will add speed to the exercise. The natural running movements coordinated with poles emphasizes forward lean. Used on hills, the workload increases and it provides a good simulation of uphill snow skiing.

Rowing. For the water enthusiast, rowing has gained acceptance as a good skiing-specific exercise. The rowing itself, combined with a leg push using a moveable seat, works the arms, back, shoulders, and legs. Rowing adds variety to a training program and provides a lift on those hot summer days.

Overall specific exercises such as these will add quality to your training program, developing you physically, technically and in spirit. The psychological benefits of goal-specific exercise are their own rewards. You know the exercise is right when the entire body is moving as if on skis.

Relaxation. Training also has its quiet side. A racer in training needs ample sleep—maybe not nine or ten hours, but no fewer than five or six. Rest is an important part in the overall training effect of exercise. The muscles need time to recover and rebuild. A racer who always is training with his eyes on the gold may end up with an unwilling body on race day. Schedule time for rest; it should not be neglected.

Along with relaxation, racers benefit from visualization. During a relaxed state of consciousness, induced by rhythmic breathing and soft music (preferably 60 beats/minute), athletes mentally rehearse, visualizing themselves performing their skill. With practice, actual performance is improved through involving the senses in intricate detail, enhancing the awareness of feelings associated with proper movements.

Research into the powers of the mind and finding ways to specifically focus this source of energy could become the new frontier of psychobiology/neuropsychology and its relation to the science of behavior. Discovering how we learn and ways to improve the process for our own and future generations is an exciting adventure. A good book to get you started on a program of relaxation is *Superlearning* by Ostrander (see bibliography).

PROGRESSIVE TRAINING

Training schedules should be progressive in nature. Especially for the long run, the serious racer plans on increasing workloads ten to twenty percent every year. The training log will help you in looking back on past years and determining future needs. If you have been fairly inactive prior to training, don't rush it. Coaches look at their young recruits and plan their training schedules to see substantial improvement in three to four years. A fit body doesn't happen overnight. Granted, you will see and feel significant improvement within two to six weeks after starting your fitness program, but reaching your potential will take much longer. Be patient.

DIET

Advanced nutritional studies have confirmed the benefit of eating a diet high in carbohydrates if you are exercising regularly for at least thirty to sixty minutes per session. Carbohydrates are the most readily burned calories. Stored in the muscle tissue as glycogen, they provide quick, readily available energy for muscle contractions. Cross-country skiers, who are working under the pressures of cold temperatures and extensive physical demands, burn calories quickly—about 1200 per hour at racing speeds. Because carbohydrates are burned so quickly, a stockpile is needed or the furnace will go out and the racer will, in layman's terms, "hit the wall" when carbohydrates are totally depleted. At this point, the body begins to burn fats, which are not so readily processed and are slower sources of fuel. This makes the racer feel sluggish.

Studies have shown that diets high in fats and low in carbohydrates reduce energy levels significantly, but a high-carbohydrate, low-fat diet increases energy. The reason is that to metabolize a unit of carbohydrate takes about ten percent less oxygen than to metabolize the same unit of fat.

In favor of increased energy levels, some athletes have adopted a diet of eighty percent carbohydrates, ten percent fat, and ten percent protein. (Although protein plays an important part in body tissue regeneration and other life-giving functions, protein does not easily convert to useable energy for muscle work.)

The term "carbohydrate loading" has gained popularity among distance athletes, even though the medical community hasn't fully endorsed the idea. They deprive the body of carbohydrates for two to three days prior to competition, then take in large amounts of carbohydrates, and as a result the muscle tissue will accept much higher amounts of stored glycogen. The muscle can then function for longer periods and—the athlete hopes—help him avoid "hitting the wall."

Breads, cereals, grains, spaghetti, and pasta are carbohydrate-rich foods. Eating a normal diet is still best, but try staying away from fatty foods—oils, creams, organ meats, nuts—and feel the difference!

Vitamin and mineral supplements should not be necessary. Athletes may go heavy on the carbohydrates, but they still get enough variety in their diets, a prerequisite to acquiring an adequate supply of nutrients. Athletes need to emphasize vegetables and fruits for their vitamin content, required to metabolize carbohydrates and fats.

L iquids are needed in the process of turning food into useable energy. Losing more than a quart of fluid hampers performance and may lead to damaging effects if it is not replenished. The cross-country skier must definitely be concerned with maintaining a balanced liquid state. Race times can be significantly reduced by dehydration. Usually races of more than ten kilometers have at least two on-course feeding stations for liquid replacement. Always be sure to stop, even if you are not thirsty at the time. The marathon course may have as many as five feeding stations along the trail, depending on the distance. Plan on a feeding every seven to ten kilometers to maintain energy supplies.

D iets are an individual aspect of training. An athlete's lifestyle is a vital part of his success—and a little attention to what passes through your lips may give you that psychological edge on race day. I have always used the "caffeine theory" before a ski marathon to give myself that little extra boost. Caffeine has been credited with facilitating the breakdown of carbohydrates and fats in races longer than one hour. Dr. David Costill of the Human Performance Laboratory at Ball State University has shown that "coffee drinking before an event enhances endurance performance." Improved times in endurance events have been attributed to drinking two cups of coffee before a race, which causes elevated levels of free fatty acids in the blood. Fats are stored in the muscle tissue. But unless they are released into the bloodstream, they are not as easily used for energy. The caffeine releases more useable fats into the bloodstream which, when combined with existing glycogen stores, will prolong high energy levels. But caffeine *is* a drug, a stimulant, as any college student knows, producing excitement, sleeplessness, nervousness, and gastrointestinal unpleasantness.

D ecide what works for you and record diet changes in your training log. See if a correlation develops between diet and performance. Then you will discover the optimum nutritional requirements for living a healthy life, full of energy and enthusiasm to meet the challenges of training.

HEART RATE

K nowing your heart rate is your training guide. The number of beats per minute your heart pumps at rest and after an intense effort is the body's way of communicating its internal state of affairs. The heart itself is the strongest muscle in the body. Its efforts are never ending; from birth until death it circulates life-giving blood throughout the body.

The idea of aerobic/anaerobic exercise is to strengthen the heart muscle so it can pump more blood per beat. Physiologists speak of increasing oxygen uptake as a measure of physical fitness. To increase oxygen uptake, there has to be more blood per unit pumped by the heart. Volume per heartbeat is the true measure of our engine, an engine that is strengthened by exercise and that is the key to a healthy body. The following chart gives you an indication of maximum heart rate per minute, depending on your present level of fitness.

AEROBIC FITNESS

Fitness Category: High		Fitness Category: Medium		Fitness Category: Low	
Age	Intensity (in beats/min)	Age	Intensity (in beats/min)	Age	Intensity (in beats/min)
20	164-178	20	153-164	20	140-154
25	162-176	25	151-162	25	137-151
30	160-174	30	148-159	30	134-148
35	157-171	35	145-157	35	130-144
40	154-168	40	142-154	40	126-140
45	151-164	45	139-151	45	122-136
50	148-161	50	136-149	50	118-132
55	145-158	55	133-146	55	114-128
60	143-155	60	130-143	60	110-124

Monitoring your heart rate will tell you whether your heart is being overworked or underworked. A sedentary person may have a resting heart rate of fifty-four to sixty beats per minute, while the trained cross-country skier's rate may be as low as thirty-five to forty beats per minute. Record your resting heart rate at the beginning of your training program to help guide future decisions. A lowered resting heart rate indicates a training effect is occurring. If your resting heart rate has remained the same for some time and suddenly goes up five to eight beats one morning, you might be overdoing it. Overtraining or pushing your body too hard too quickly in your quest for physical prowess will manifest itself in sleepless nights, lack of appetite, and overuse injuries, resulting in an increased resting heart rate.

To determine your maximum heart rate, take your pulse immediately after an intense effort, either in the large carotid artery on either side of the neck or by placing your hand directly over your heart. Using a watch that reads seconds, count the pulse for six seconds, then multiply by ten. This reading should be somewhere between 170 and 220 beats per minute. Your heart will slow down quickly afterward, so it is important to take a reading right after the exercise.

TRAINING FOR RACING

We know that cross-country ski racing is the most demanding of winter sports, requiring total body/mind preparation. The physical training necessary to perform up to your potential takes commitment and dedication. If you are serious about improving your physical fitness, then adopt a mental toughness to correspond with your training.

The full-time racer has the whole day in which to schedule training. He will usually plan two workouts a day, with time for rest and relaxation in between. The tendency to skip a workout is a constant test of a person's motivation. With the whole day to train, it is easy to say to yourself, "I'll make it up tomorrow." The part-time athlete can't afford such luxury. His training time is limited to either before or after a full day's work. If training time is limited, then program planning must be goal specific. Know your weak areas and organize every hour of training to accomplish definite objectives. Time is of the essence and grabbing every opportunity to sneak in a little training is important.

Analyze your work week. Decide if there are any holes to fit some training in. How about stair-climbing instead of riding the elevator? Parking the car farther from your place of business and walking? Cross-country is an endurance sport. The commitment to endurance activities must be emphasized. Juggling a training schedule along with job and family takes commitment. Nobody said training for skiing would be easy. But the extra work will more than pay for itself in a healthy, fit body that is ready to meet the demands of life and skiing. The pride and self-fulfillment of sticking to and completing a workout is a great feeling. To experience it is to enjoy it, again and again.

YEAR-ROUND TRAINING

To be successful at ski racing requires a year-round training schedule. A preseason conditioning program may be all right for the recreational skier, but the serious racer must develop a year-round program. Here is a sample of the yearly schedule used by the United States Ski Team.

YEARLY PLAN

Goals	April–July	August–October	November–December	January–March	Total Overall
Total Distance					
Running					
Roller Ski					
Hiking					
Biking					
Skiing					
% Endurance Hrs.					
% Interval Hrs.					
% Strength Hrs.					
% Race Hrs.					
Total Hrs.					

TRAINING WITH A PURPOSE

Cross-country skiers may take part in several different activities during off-season training. No matter what the exercise, the way it is performed determines the result. The exercise is tailored depending on the physical characteristic to be developed (strength, muscle endurance, flexibility, or cardiovascular endurance). Any exercise has an overlap effect;

when you do an uphill ski stride with poles, you are building strength *and* working the cardiovascular system. If the hill stride is repeated several times, muscle endurance is also increased.

Intensity is the amount of force exerted to perform a skill. This varies with the exercise. For example, if you are working on muscle endurance, you would not run hundred-yard sprints all week. Rather, you would run long, slow distances interspersed with short bursts of high-intensity sprints.

Load is the resistance used to develop strength, muscle endurance, or cardiovascular conditioning. An "on-deck batter" who swings three bats at once demonstrates the principle of "overloading," working the body at greater resistance than is required for normal operation. Overloading increases the body's ability to handle the demands of sports.

PRACTICAL EXERCISES

Many kinds of exercises meet the demands of many different sports. The common goal of all sports training is to develop and refine the participants' physical, technical, and mental abilities. With basketball, football, baseball, and soccer players, the overall goal is the same: to be physically fit, to endure, and to improve in the technical aspects of the sport. All athletes concentrate on the same four aspects of physical training: (1) strength, (2) muscle endurance, (3) flexibility, and (4) cardiovascular efficiency. This section will briefly define each area and suggest possible exercises to fit each type of training.

Strength training. Muscle strength is what enables long strides. The skiers who can combine a powerful kick with an equally efficient poling motion will have the best formula for increasing stride length and, therefore, velocity. Developing muscle strength is an important part of the well-rounded training program.

It is developed in two ways: (1) overload and (2) progressive resistance. Overload means, simply, working the muscle with more weight than usual, resulting in increased strength. Progressive resistance is the continual addition of weight, as the muscle becomes stronger, to maintain an overload situation. The formal approach involves the use of free weights, Nautilus machines, universal gyms, etc. The informal strength program is based on the most readily available source of weight—the body.

The exercises and tools described on this page are practical and easily applied to develop muscle strength and endurance.

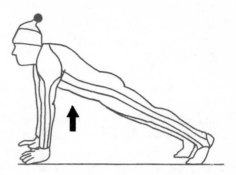

PUSH-UPS Do three sets of eight, three sets of four and three sets of two—three times a week while maintaining a rigid body position.

SIT-UPS Do three sets of eight, three sets of four and three sets of two—three times a week with knees bent.

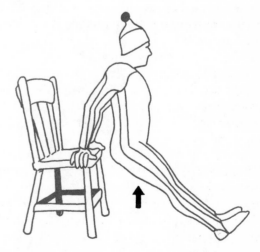

CHAIR DIPS Do three sets of eight, three sets of four and three sets of two three times a week with legs straight, heels on the floor and lowering body by bending arms.

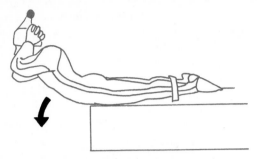

BACK EXTENSIONS Lie face down on table, extend upper body over edge, hands behind head, feet firmly held. Bend at waist, down and up three sets of eight—three times a week.

INNER TUBE PULL Cut two bicycle inner tubes in half and tie together. Hang on wall or door to simulate cross-country poling motion. Fifteen to forty minutes—two times a week.

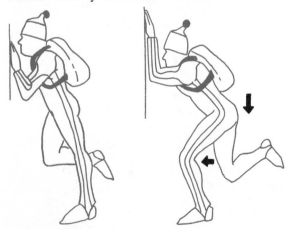

SAND BAG Loop a weighted inner tube or bag over shoulders and practice single leg extensions while leaning against a wall. Three sets of eight (each leg)—three times a week.

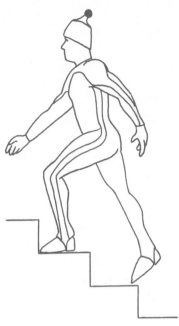

STEP-UPS One step at a time, walking or jogging pace, twenty to thirty minutes—two times a week.

Muscle endurance. The cross-country skier is concerned with reaching a certain level of muscle strength, but then developing muscle endurance becomes important. Muscle endurance is best achieved by exercising repeatedly with light resistance. This type of exercise will help eliminate muscle fatigue at the end of a race. Here is the difference between the body builder and the skier. The same analogy is drawn between the elephant and the cheetah. The elephant is strong and powerful, but the cheetah is fast and powerful. Which would you rather be?

Flexibility. The person who stretches regularly is less injury prone and more able to utilize his full range of motion. Bob Anderson (longtime promoter and author of several books on stretching) says, "With a regular, relaxed and proper stretch program, it is relatively easy to keep your body tension free and flexible throughout the season. Combined with other activities (such as development of the cardiovascular system and fine-tuning your ski technique) stretching can prevent injury and produce a high degree of physical fitness.

"As we grow older, we gradually lose our flexibility. We can no longer bend or twist as far as we once could. Muscles become stiff and unresponsive; sports like cross-country skiing become more difficult and more likely to cause injury. But this loss of elasticity and joint flexibility can be prevented by including stretching in a program of total fitness training."

STRETCHING FOR CROSS-COUNTRY

The following stretches are designed for cross-country skiers. Shaded areas of the illustrations indicate the muscles stretched in each exercise. Remember to stretch on a mat, carpet, or other firm, but not hard, surface.

ARMS AND SHOULDERS

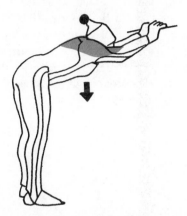

Hold onto something that is about shoulder height. With your hands shoulder-width apart on this support, relax, keeping your arms straight and your chest moving downward. Bend your knees slightly, and make sure your feet remain directly below your hips. Hold for 30 seconds.

With arms overhead, hold the elbow of one arm with the hand of the other arm. Keeping your knees slightly bent, gently pull your elbow behind your head as you bend from your hips to the side. Hold an easy stretch for 10 seconds, then repeat on the other side.

In a standing or sitting position, interlace your fingers above your head. With your palms facing upward, push your arms slightly back and up. Feel the stretch in your arms, shoulders, and upper back. Hold for 15 seconds. Breathe slowly and deeply as you stretch (this stretch is excellent for slumping shoulders).

Hold a towel near both ends so that you can move it with arms straight up, over your head and down behind your back. Do not strain or force the motion. Your hands should be far enough apart to allow for relatively free movement up, over and down. Hold this stretch at any point in the arc for 10 to 20 seconds.

Kneel down and place your palms on the floor, with your fingers pointed back toward your knees. *Slowly* lean backwards to stretch the forearms and wrists. Be sure to keep your palms flat. Hold for 20 to 25 seconds, being careful not to overstretch.

With legs bent under you, reach forward with one arm and grab the end of the mat, carpet, or anything you can hold. If you can't grab onto something, just pull back with your arm straight while pressing down slightly with your hand. Hold for 20 seconds.

NECK AND BACK

Lie on your back, with knees bent and feet flat on the floor. Interlace your fingers behind your head and rest your arms on the mat or floor. Using the power of your arms, slowly bring your head, neck, and shoulders forward until you feel a slight stretch. Hold for five seconds. Repeat three times.

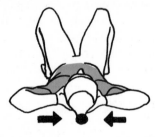

From the bent-knee position, push your shoulder blades together to create tension in the upper-back area. As you do this, your chest should move upward. Hold for five seconds, then relax.

Lie flat on your back, with legs outstretched. Lift one knee, grasp with both hands, and pull toward your chest. Keep the back of your head on the floor if possible, but don't strain. Hold for 30 seconds, then repeat with the other leg.

LEGS AND HIPS

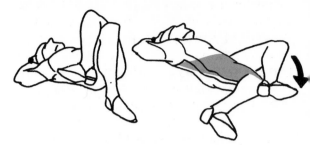

From the bent-knee position, interlace your fingers behind your head and lift the left leg over the right leg. From here, use your left leg to pull your right leg toward the floor until you feel a stretch along the side of your hip and lower back. Stretch and relax—don't overstretch on this one. Remember to keep the upper back, shoulders, and elbows flat on the floor. Hold for 30 seconds, then repeat on the other side.

Sit with your right leg bent, with your right heel just to the outside of your right hip. The left leg is bent and the sole of your left foot is next to the inside of your upper right leg (try not to let your right foot flare out to the side). Now, slowly lean straight back until you feel an easy stretch in your right quadriceps. Use your hands for balance and support, and be sensitive to any pain you may feel in your knees. Hold for 30 seconds.

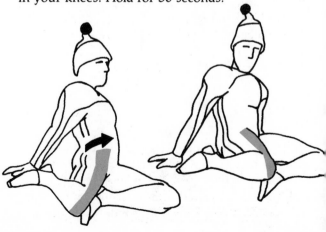

After stretching your quadriceps, practice tightening the buttocks on the side of the bent leg as you turn the hip over. This will help stretch the front of your hip and give a better overall stretch to the upper thigh. After contracting the butt muscles for five to eight seconds, let the buttocks relax. Then continue to stretch the quadriceps for another 15 seconds.

Sit on the mat, with your right leg straightened out. The sole of your left foot will be resting next to the inside of your straightened leg. Lean slightly forward from the hips and stretch the hamstrings of your right leg. Find an easy stretch and relax. If you can't touch your toes comfortably, use a towel to help you stretch. Hold for 50 seconds, then repeat on the other side.

Put the soles of your feet together with your heels a comfortable distance from your groin. Now, put your hands around your feet and slowly pull yourself forward until you feel an easy stretch in the groin. Make your movement forward by bending from the hips and not from the shoulders. If possible, keep your elbows on the outside of your lower legs for greater stability. Hold for 30 to 40 seconds.

Sit with your right leg straight. Bend your left leg, cross your left foot over and rest it to the outside of your right knee. Then bend your right elbow and rest it on the outside of your upper left thigh, just above the knee. During the stretch, use the elbow to keep the leg stationary with controlled pressure to the outside. Now, with your left hand resting behind you, slowly turn your head to look over your left shoulder, and at the same time rotate your upper body toward your left hand and arm. Hold for 15 seconds, then repeat on the other side.

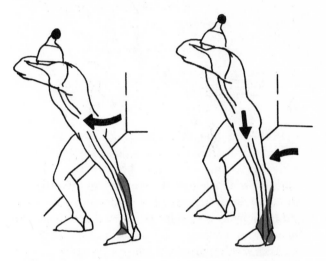

Stand a little ways from a solid support and lean on it with your forearms, your head resting on your hands. Bend one leg and place your foot on the ground in front of you, leaving the other leg straight and behind you. Slowly move your hips forward until you feel a stretch in the calf of your straight leg. Be sure to keep the heel of the foot of the straight leg on the ground and your toes pointed straight ahead. Hold for 30 seconds. To stretch the Achilles tendon, keep the same posture, but bend the back knee slightly, keeping the back foot flat. Hold for 15 seconds.

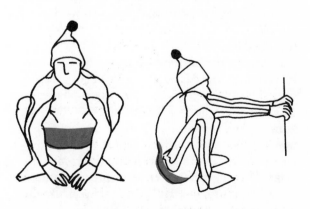

With your feet shoulder-width apart and pointed out at about a 15-degree angle, heels on the ground, bend your knees and squat down. If you have trouble staying in this position hold onto something for support. Hold for 30 seconds. If you feel any pain in your knees, discontinue this stretch.

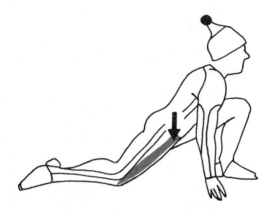

As in the drawing, move your leg forward until the knee of the forward leg is directly over the ankle. Your other knee should be resting on the floor. Lower the front of your hip downward until an easy stretch is felt in the front of the hip and possibly in your hamstrings and groin. Do this without changing the position of the knee on the floor or the forward foot.

Cardiovascular endurance. From simple walking to sprinting uphill, increased workload benefits the heart, lungs, and circulatory system. Besides the specific exercises previously mentioned (roller skiing, ski poling, hiking, striding, running, and shell rowing), other beneficial exercises are also readily accessible to use in training. Try walking, jogging, cycling, swimming, kayaking, and canoeing.

Walking is a much underrated exercise with all of the emphasis today on jogging and running. Walking briskly, or even at a leisurely pace, is a good way to slip a little exercise in during lunch hour or after work. A brisk walk will work the leg muscles, elevate your heart rate and make you feel good overall.

Jogging is the next step in intensity, followed by running. The difference is speed. Joggers are seen throughout cities and towns, usually before dawn, at lunch hour, and after the 5:00 P.M. whistle. The runner is also out there, but is moving faster. The difference is like that between a recreational diagonal stride and the racer's diagonal stride. The movements are the same, but the amount of effort and power supplied by the muscles determines the speed.

Hiking, either for the day or longer, is an enjoyable way to tone up the leg muscles for skiing. Hiking fast will condition the cardiovascular system. To make this exercise goal specific, use ski poles to hike with and double the value of time spent on the trail.

Cycling, although not specific to skiing movements, does provide a beneficial workout. It is good for leg muscle strength, particularly the quadriceps (thigh muscles), but a poor upper body exercise. If you do ride, try standing up as you pedal and notice how the upper body muscles are involved. Cycling builds aerobic capacity and long, extended trips keep the heart rate in a comfortable aerobic range. Bike for variety, but don't rely on it totally for cross-country conditioning.

For the water enthusiast, swimming provides a total body workout. Swimming laps in a pool or distance swimming will build arm strength and also develops muscle endurance on extended swims.

Kayaking and canoeing are fun alternatives to supplement more specific exercises. The arm work required by both sports is similar—repetitive movements where workload depends on how fast and hard the paddles move. Rowing is a good general conditioner for the shoulders, arms, and back muscles.

STRENGTH TRAINING

Strength training encompasses the entire body musculature, from the smallest muscles in the wrist to the large leg muscles. The idea is to build strength in the primary muscles. Once the technique of cross-country skiing is mastered, it is the powerful push-off, or kick, that contributes to increased speeds. Remember: the formula to increased speed is speed = stride length × stride rate. Studies have shown that increases in stride length result from a powerful kick, not lengthened glide (Charles Dillman, 1979, *United States Coaches Journal*). Stride rate between faster and slower skiers is similar; the power supplied by each kick makes the difference.

Strength training for cross-country skiing should focus on exercises that are goal specific. Free weights or Nautilus equipment are good for building up weak areas, but bulky strength by itself won't make the best cross-country muscles. Training should focus on building the strength necessary for the repetitive performance of the diagonal stride. The ability to perform a movement over and over again is something to keep in mind when you are training.

DISTANCE TRAINING

Distance training, whether you choose to run, hike, walk, or ride, is oriented toward increasing your body's ability to endure a full day of touring or complete that fifty-kilometer ski marathon. The idea is simple: continuous exercise for a distance compatible with your abilities. Racers and coaches endorse training for a distance of half to one and one-half times the intended course length. For tour skiers, this may mean running or jogging for one-half to one hour continuously, or hiking a full day with a lunch stop. Hiking trails is a good way to simulate actual skiing because of the uphill climbs and downhill recoveries. Distance training should be performed at an intensity that provides a constant supply of oxygen to the muscles. We have previously referred to this as "aerobic" (with oxygen). When our aerobic pace intensifies and the increased demand for oxygen is not met, the body begins to function in an anaerobic state (without oxygen). In a purely anaerobic state, the muscles will function for no more than a few minutes. The moment of shift from aerobic to anaerobic work is sometimes called the anaerobic threshold. One reason for training is to push this threshold back. In other words, training builds up the heart, lungs, and circulatory system to withstand heavier, more intense workloads without going anaerobic.

The best measure of fitness is how much oxygen we can take into our lungs, how readily that oxygen reaches the blood, and how fast (and how much) blood is delivered to the muscles where the oxygen is extracted for use. It is aerobic exercise that enables the body to take in more oxygen and transport it more efficiently. Cardiac output, the stroke volume of blood delivered from the heart, increases as the muscle tissue extracts more oxygen for fuel. Therefore, distance training can develop both aerobic and anaerobic functions, depending on its intensity. In distance training, it is better to work just below your own anaerobic threshold and leave the intense sessions for an "interval" workout.

Continual efforts to push your anaerobic threshold will raise this barrier to higher limits. One purpose of interval workouts is to force the body into the anaerobic realm, building its ability to endure aerobic work longer and at higher intensity levels. This strength is a prerequisite for short-term, high-load efforts, such as a mass start when you want to get out in front or during the final push to the finish. Anaerobic efforts are short term and intense; aerobic efforts are long term and constant. And cross-country skiing is primarily a long-term effort. Races or tours are usually planned to last from thirty to sixty minutes (in ten-kilometer races) to between two and one-half and six hours for marathons and eight to nine hours for the all-day tour. The cross-country skiers, therefore, is not involved in a short-term effort very often. The ideal is to be working aerobically, just below your anaerobic threshold.

INTERVAL TRAINING

Interval training, the alternating of fast, hard activity with rest periods, performed on a predetermined schedule, is a vital part of a fitness program. Any aerobic activity will fit into an interval workout. Intervals improve the body's ability to take in and utilize oxygen. During rests between periods of exertion the heart rate is monitored for signs of recovery or overuse. The activity itself should cause the heart rate to shoot up to 160-170 beats per minute. During the ensuing recovery period (an interval of anywhere from one and one-half to three minutes), the heart should return to 120-130 beats per minute. If it takes longer, the effort demanded may have been too severe or too long.

Interval training can follow any type of fast/slow pattern that resembles cross-country skiing. Cross-country trails are usually set in rolling hills where there are a series of increased workloads (uphills) and rest periods (downhills). The cross-country racer is well aware of the pattern of fast movements and slow recoveries. The natural intervals of a cross-country ski trail may be simulated during off-season training by working out in the same type of hilly terrain. The Swedes have a word, "Fartlek" (which, translated, means "speed play"), a technique developed by Gosta Holmer, coach of the 1948 Swedish Olympic Team. It consists of fast, untimed runs on varied terrain over a set distance. It is a great way to avoid the rigid, formal timed runs on a track. "Fartlek" opens up the woods, streets, and parks for fun alternatives. Because of the natural occurrence (or nonoccurrence) of terrain suited to fast bursts of speed, "Fartlek" should not be relied upon totally for your interval training. However, this type of natural interval is closely aligned to the cross-country skiing environment and adds spice to a training program.

A similar idea has gained popularity around the U.S. The "par course," a jogging loop with a series of exercise stations spaced over a distance of one to three miles, is a European concept that was introduced in the United States around 1973. Each station provides an apparatus and sign describing the exercise to be performed, along with a suggestion on how many repetitions to do. All the while, the participant is walking, jogging, or running between these stations. Sounds like fun! It is! Par courses are popping up everywhere. Local parks, schools, and college campuses are good places to look for your nearest par course—the total conditioner.

When designing an interval workout, the number of high-intensity runs will vary, as will the rest intervals between those runs. A good interval workout usually will take about forty-five minutes to an hour, including warmup and warm-down time. If you are monitoring your heart rate or timing the runs, you should stop when your heart rate does not drop to 120 beats per minute during the rest interval, or when the time it takes to complete the run increases. Be careful to ease up when signs of fatigue set in. Know your body; recognize when you have had enough and stop before you injure something.

T he interval workout is not set off by itself. Preparing the body for such an intense session requires a definite warmup period. Warm up for ten to fifteen minutes by doing some light jogging and stretching exercises. This way the muscle tissue will respond to the workload more efficiently. Do it, if not for any other reason than that a warmed, stretched muscle is less injury prone.

The same is true after the workout. Take time to wind down and cool off before stopping all activity. Don't sit or lie down immediately after a hard workout. Keep moving, even if you are only walking. Your muscles have worked hard, and they need time to cool down while blood circulation removes any waste products and lactic acid buildup. If you stop and sit down right after a fast run, getting up again may not be so easy!

SAMPLE INTERVAL WORKOUTS

Warmup: 10-15 minutes—*easy jogging* to prepare the body for increased demands. *Stretching*—especially the muscles involved in the activity.

Interval length: Short—30-60 seconds; long—3-7 minutes.

Terrain: Flat or gradual uphill, with or without poles.

Short sprint workout: *5 x 30 seconds;* rest interval of 45-60 seconds. *4 x 60 seconds;* rest interval of 1½-2 minutes. *3 x 45 seconds;* rest interval of 1-1½ minutes. *2 x 30 seconds;* rest interval of 30 seconds.

This should only be used as a sample. Adjustments can be made according to individual needs.

- Start out easy, with an intent to finish each set strong.
- Take about 3 or 4 minutes' rest in between each set.
- Heart rate should be near or at your maximum level at the end of the last set.
- A good indicator of fatigue or overly long sets is an inability to maintain speed throughout the workout.
- Be careful to monitor your body; be aware of unusual discomfort or pain. But, if there is ever going to be a time to push yourself into an uncomfortable state, this is it. The result of this type of cardiovascular training is an increase in the body's oxygen uptake. This reward could offset any temporary discomfort!

Long sprint workout: 2 x 5 minutes; 3 x 7 minutes, 2 x 3 minutes.

Terrain: Flat or gently rolling terrain. Jogging or ski trails are good ideas.

Rest interval. Equal to or less than the sprint time. The entire workout should take from 30 to 60 minutes.

The long sprint should take slightly less effort to maintain speed. If speed drops, it is time to stop. The muscles (or mental state) have tired.

Tempo workout: For the serious racer, tempo training simulates the actual race pace. It is used to prepare for a competition. Preferably an on-snow exercise, it is also adaptable to roller skiing or other endurance activities. Tempo training is skiing at race pace or above for ten to twenty percent of the intended race length. If you are training for a ten-kilometer citizens race that will take you approximately forty minutes, plan a ten- to fourteen-minute fast ski with a total recovery following. Use tempo workouts to tone up for competition and progressively build quickness and speed.

ON-SNOW TRAINING

O nce the snow falls, training begins to shift gears from a purely dryland experience to on-snow workouts. As much as we try to make our dryland training like actual skiing, there is still an adjustment period. I know from experience that the transition from purely dryland training to on-snow skiing awakens all the small, seemingly untrainable muscles, especially in the groin area. No matter how hard or specific my summer training, there are nearly always stiff muscles after my first real skiing of the season.

Make the transition from dryland training to on-snow training with caution. Don't let your enthusiasm take hold and make you forget about gradually easing into actual skiing. This

adjustment period may be quick for some racers (five to eight days), but it can be longer for others, especially the recreational skier.

Now that the snow is on the ground, the chance to ski yourself into shape is also a possibility. Use those first ski trips to further condition and tone your body muscles. Many skiers favor this approach over preseason training.

On-snow training follows a program similar to that for off-snow training. The same approach taken to summer training is adapted for winter. Emphasis is placed on starting slow, building a base of many hours of on-snow skiing before increasing intensity. The best part of on-snow training is the fact it is really skiing and not a simulation.

WEEKLY TRAINING SUMMARY

NAME: DATE: WEEK NUMBER:

WEIGHT:

DAY	ENDURANCE							INTERVAL			STRENGTH		SLEEP	RACE/TEMPO	GENERAL	STRETCH	TIME	DISTANCE	RESTING PULSE
	SNOW SKIING	ROLLER SKIING	VERTICAL	SKI RUN-NING	SKI HIKING	ROW-ING	VERTICAL	HILL RUN-NING	ROLLER SKIING	SNOW SKI	GEN-ERAL	SPE-CIFIC			LIST				
MON																			
TUES																			
WED																			
THUR																			
FRI																			
SAT																			
SUN																			
SUB TOTAL																			
TOTAL																			

THE SKI SCHOOL & YOU

"For the things we have to learn before we can do them, we learn by doing them."

Aristotle

Whether you are just starting or a seasoned pro, lessons by a PSIA-certified instructor will enhance your skiing experience. The first-time student will benefit immensely from an instructor's talents to guide and direct his ski experiences. The skills of cross-country skiing are not highly mechanical, intricate movements, but natural outgrowths of fundamental motion. The will to move is born in all of us. Our bodies naturally move, from the first steps of childhood to our high school 100-yard dash. People must move to survive, and healthy persons move to thrive.

For further insight into why you should take a lesson from a PSIA-certified instructor, consider the following: When a person becomes seriously ill, who is the first person they look to? They see a doctor, an individual knowledgeable about the inner workings of the body, who they hope will find a cure and relieve whatever discomfort they are experiencing. To maintain our teeth in a pearly white, cavity-free state, what do we have to do? Seek out a trained professional in dental care. Where does a skier go when he has a problem with his skiing or just needs a checkup to keep his technique development on track? A PSIA-certified instructor, who is specifically trained to provide preventive maintenance, and who can bring the natural feeling back to a person's skiing technique. The rhythmic, flowing movements of cross-country skiing can, at times, be lost, and the person to see for a maintenance checkup is a trained professional. So, next time you feel something is just not right with your skiing, take your body to the expert in movement analysis, the PSIA-certified instructor, for a simple tuneup or a complete overhaul. You will be glad you did. It could be the extra little lift to put the zing back in your skiing.

Here is a listing of PSIA Certified Ski Schools around the United States where skiers can go for instruction.

● = Services, Facilities Offered ○ = Contact for Further Information

		Prepared Tracks	Touring Trails	Telemark Inst.	Track Inst.	Rentals	Lodging
WESTERN							
Alaska Nordic Ski School, 2300 Homestead Ct. #3A, Anchorage, AK 99507	907-563-8614	●	●	○	●	●	●
Asplund's Nordic Ski School, 1544 N. Wenatchee Ave., Wenatchee, WA 98801	509-662-6539	●	●	○	●	●	●
Bear Valley Nordic, Bear Valley, CA 95223	209-753-2834	●	●	●	●	●	●
Eagle Mountain Nordic, Box 89, Emigrant Gap, CA 95715	916-389-2254	●	●	●	●	●	●
Echo Summit Nordic, Box 8955, S. Tahoe, CA 95731	916-659-7154	●	●	●	●	●	●
Grant Cove Ski Touring, Kings Canyon Nat'l Park, CA 93633	209-335-2314	●	●	●	●	●	●
Hatcher Pass Ski Touring Center, Box 2655, Palmer, AK 99645	907-745-5897	●	●	●	●	●	●
Leavenworth Nordic Ski Programs, Leavenworth, WA 98826	509-548-5165	●	●	●	●	●	●
Mt. Bachelor/Rossignol Nordic Sports Center, Mt. Bachelor, Bend, OR 97709	503-382-2607	●	●	●	●	●	●
Northstar Nordic Center, Box 129, Truckee, CA 95734	916-562-1010	●	●	●	●	●	●
Outing Club, 5601 N.E. 77th St., Seattle, WA 98115	206-525-8171	○	○	●	●	●	○
Quiet Mountain Nordic, 419 Spring St., Nevada City, CA 95959	916-265-9186	●	●	●	●	●	●
REI Ski School, Ski Acres Nordic Center, Seattle, WA 98102	206-323-8333	●	●	●	●	●	●
Ruby Mountain Heli-Ski, Lamoille, NV 89828	702-753-6867	●	●	●	●	●	●
Sahale Adventures, Mount Vernon, WA 98273	206-424-1831	○	○	●	●	●	●
Sequoia Ski Touring, Sequoia Nat'l Park, CA 93262	209-565-3463	●	●	●	●	●	●
Sierra Summit, P.O. Box 236, Lakeshore, CA 93634	209-893-3316	●	●	●	●	●	●
Snow Summit Nordic Center, Big Bear Lake, CA 92315	714-866-6117	●	●	●	●	●	●
Ski Acres Nordic Center, Snoqualmie Pass, WA 98068	206-434-6646	●	●	●	●	●	●
Strawberry Ski Touring, Kyburz, CA 95720	916-659-7200	●	●	○	●	●	●
Sun Mountain Lodge, P.O. Box 1000, Winthrop, WA 98862	509-996-2211	●	●	●	●	○	●
Tahoe Nordic Ski Center, Box 1632, Tahoe City, CA 95730	916-583-0484	●	●	●	●	●	●
Telemark Cross-Country Sports, Box 11975, Tahoe Paradise, CA 95708	916-577-6811	●	●	●	●	●	●
Timberline Nordic, Inc., 4312 S.E. Morrison, Portland, OR 97215	503-236-4005	●	●	○	●	●	●
Uni. of Nevada, Reno Nordic Ski Programs, Rec./P.E. Dept. Reno, NV 89557	702-784-4041	●	●	●	●	●	●
White Pass Ski School, Box 354, Yakima, WA 98907	509-453-8731	●	●	●	●	●	●
ROCKY MOUNTAIN							
Ambush Ranch Nordic Touring, Box 1230, Crested Butte, CO 81224	303-349-5408	●	●	●	○	●	●
Aspen Touring Center, Galena Street Trolley, Aspen, CO 81612	303-925-7625	●	●	●	●	●	●
Beaver Creek Cross Country Ski Center, Beaver Creek, CO 81657	303-949-5750	●	●	●	●	●	●
Big Sky Nordic Ski School, Big Sky Area, Big Sky, MT 59716	406-995-4211	●	●	○	●	●	●
Bigwood Nordic, Box 3637, Ketchum, ID 83340	208-726-3266	●	●	●	○	●	●
Breckenridge Nordic Center, Box 1058, Breckenridge, CO 80424	303-453-2368	●	●	●	●	●	●
Brighton Ski Touring, Box 21096, Salt Lake City, UT 84121	801-359-3283	●	●	●	●	●	●
Bruce Batting Nordic Ski School, LaVeta, CO 81055	303-742-3351	●	●	●	●	●	●
Busterback Nordic Touring Center, Star Route, Ketchum, ID 83340	208-774-2217	●	●	●	●	●	●
Copper Mountain/Trak Cross-Country Center, Box 3001, Copper Mtn., CO 80443	303-968-2882	●	●	●	●	●	●
Crooked Creek Ski Touring, Box 3142, Vail, CO 81658	303-949-5682	●	●	●	●	○	●
Crosscut Creek Ski Touring, Bozeman, MT 59715	406-587-3122	●	●	●	●	●	●
Eldora Touring Center, Eldora Ski Area, Box 430, Nederland, CO 80466	303-447-8013	●	●	●	●	●	●
Grand Tour Backcountry Guides, Box 1683, Jackson Hole, WY 83001	307-733-4821	●	●	●	○	●	●
Jackson Hole Karhu Cross-Country Ski Center, Teton Village, WY	303-733-3560	●	●	●	●	●	●
Keystone Cross Country Center, Box 38, Keystone, CO 80435	303-468-2316	●	●	●	●	●	●
Medley's The Other Place, McCall, ID 86338	208-634-2171	●	●	○	●	●	●
New Park Cyclery, Inc. Rossignol Touring Center, Park Emporium #4, Park City, UT 84068	801-649-2320	●	○	●	●	●	●
Nordic Adventure/Trak Touring Center, Crested Butte, CO 81224	303-349-5435	●	●	●	●	●	●
Nordic Ski School of Idaho, 1811 Leadville, Boise, ID 83706	208-343-3313	○	●	○	●	●	○
Pagosa Pines Touring Center, Pagosa Springs, CO 81147	303-731-2403	●	●	●	●	●	●
Payette Lakes Ski Touring, Little Ski Hill, McCall, ID 83638	208-634-5307	●	●	●	●	●	●
Purgatory/Rossignol Touring Center, Purgatory Ski Resort, Durango, CO 81301	303-247-9000	●	●	●	●	●	●
Red Lodge Mountain, Drawer R, Red Lodge, MT 59068	406-446-2663	●	●	●	●	●	●
Rocky Mountain Ski Tours, 156 E. Elkhorn Ave., Estes Park, CO 80517	303-586-2114	●	●	○	●	●	●
Snowmass Club/Ski Touring Center, Snowmass Village, CO 81615	303-923-5600	●	●	●	●	●	●
Steamboat Powder Cats, Box 2468, Steamboat Springs, CO 80477	303-879-5188	●	●	●	●	●	●
Steamboat Ski Touring Center, Steamboat Springs, CO 80499	303-879-8180	●	●	●	●	●	●
Sun Valley Nordic, Box 272, Sun Valley, ID 83353	208-622-4111	●	●	●	●	●	●
Telluride Nordic Center, Box 307, Telluride, CO 81435	303-728-3856	●	●	○	●	●	●
Togwotee Mountain Lodge Rossignol Touring Center, Moran, WY 83013	307-543-2847	●	●	○	●	●	●
Vail Cross Country Ski Center, 458 Vail Valley Dr., Vail, CO 81657	303-476-3239	●	●	○	●	●	●
Wood River Nordic At Bigwood, Ketchum, ID 83340	208-726-3266	●	●	○	●	●	●
CENTRAL							
Bendix Woods County Park, St. Rd. 2, New Carlisle, IN 46552	219-654-3155	●	●	●	●	●	○
Camp Sagawau Nordic Ski School, RR 2, Lemont, IL 60439	312-257-2045	●	●	●	●	●	○
Love Creek County Park, Berrien Springs, MI 49103	616-471-2617	●	●	●	●	●	○
Minocqua Winter Park, Minocqua, WI 54548	715-356-3309	●	●	○	○	○	●
Nordic Sports Cross Country Ski Center, Holden Arboretum, Mentor, OH 44060	216-238-2181	●	●	●	●	●	●
Nordic Sports Cross Country Ski Center, Wallace Lake Metropark, Berea, OH 44017	216-826-1173	●	●	●	●	●	●
Spirit Mountain, 9500 Spirit Mt. Place, Duluth, MN 55810	218-628-2891	○	●	○	●	●	●
Sugar Loaf, Route 1, Cedar, MI 49621	616-228-5461	●	●	○	●	●	●
Telemark Lodge Nordic, Telemark Lodge, Cable, WI 54821	715-798-3811	●	●	○	●	●	●
EASTERN							
Birches Ski Touring Center, Box 81, Rockwood, ME 87440	207-534-7305	●	●	○	●	●	●
Blueberry Hills Ski Touring Center, Goshen, VT 05733	802-247-6735	●	●	○	●	●	●
Bretton Woods Ski Touring Center, Bretton Woods, NH 03575	603-278-5181	●	●	○	●	●	●
Bromley Mountain Ski School, Manchester Center, VT 05255	802-824-5522	○	●	○	●	●	●
Burke Mountain Touring Center, Box 101, East Burke, VT 05832	802-626-8338	●	●	○	●	●	●
Butternut Ski Touring Center, Rt. 23, Gt. Barrington, MA 01230	413-528-0610	●	●	●	●	●	●
Carrabassett Valley Touring Center, Kingfield, ME 04947	207-237-2205	●	●	●	●	●	●
Cataloochee Touring, Rt. 1 Box 500, Maggie Valley, NC	704-926-0285	○	●	●	●	●	●
Catamount Nordic, Governor Chittenden Rd., Williston, VT 05495	802-879-6001	●	●	●	●	●	●
Cummington Farm Nordic, South Rd., Cummington, MA 01026	413-634-2111	●	●	●	●	●	●
Four Seasons Ski Center, 8012 E. Genesee St., Fayetteville, NY 13066	315-637-9023	●	●	○	●	●	○
Gunstock Cross Country Center, Route 11A, Gilford, NY 03247	603-293-4341	●	●	●	●	●	○
Hickory Hill Ski Touring Center, Worthington, MA 01098	413-238-7765	●	●	●	●	●	●
High South Nordic Guides, 835 Faculty St., Boone, NC 28607	704-264-6565	○	●	○	●	●	○
Inside Edge Ski Trails in Crandall Park, Glen Falls, NY 12801	518-793-5676	●	●	●	●	●	●
Intervale Nordic, Route 16A, Intervale, NH 03845	603-356-5541	●	●	●	●	●	●
Jackson Ski Touring Foundation, P.O. Box 90, Jackson, NH 03846	603-383-9355	●	●	●	●	●	●
Ligonier Mountain Outfitters, Route 30, Laughlintown, PA 15655	412-238-5246	●	●	●	●	●	●
Mad River Glen Nordic & Touring Center, Waitsfield, VT 05673	802-496-3551	●	●	●	●	●	●
Mountain Meadows Ski Touring Center, Route 4, Killington, VT 05751	802-775-7077	●	●	●	●	●	●
Mountain Top Ski Touring Center, Chittenden, VT 05737	802-483-6089	●	●	●	●	●	●
Northfield Nordic Ski Touring Center, Rt. 63, Northfield, MA 01360	413-659-3714	●	●	○	●	●	○
Pinnacle Mountain Ski Touring Center, Roxbury, NH 03431	603-352-5712	●	●	●	●	●	●
Ski Tours of Vermont, RFD 1, Chester, VT 05143	802-824-6012	●	●	●	●	●	●
Ski Touring Nordic Center at Saddleback, Saddleback Ski Area, Rangeley, ME	207-864-3380	●	●	●	●	●	○
Stratton Cross Country, Stratton Mountain Touring Center, Stratton Mountain, VT 05155	802-297-1880	●	●	●	●	●	●
The Nordic Ski Touring Center, N. Main St., Wolfeboro, NH 03894	603-569-3151	●	●	●	●	●	○
Twin Pines Nordic, Route 16, Delevan, NY 14042	716-496-5510	○	●	○	●	○	○
Tussey Mountain Resort, Boalsburg, PA 16801	814-466-6810	●	●	●	●	●	○
Viking Touring Center, 70 Little Pond Rd., Londonderry, VT 05148	802-824-3933	●	●	●	●	●	●
Waterville Valley Ski Touring, Waterville Valley, NH 03223	603-236-8311	●	●	●	●	●	●
White Grass, Canaan Valley, WV 26260	304-866-4114	●	●	●	●	●	○
Wild Wings Nordic, Box 132, Peru, VT 05152	802-824-6793	●	●	●	●	●	●
Woodstock Ski Touring Center, Woodstock, VT 05091	802-457-2114	●	●	●	●	●	●

CROSS-COUNTRY ETIQUETTE

"The very pink of courtesy . . ."

Williams Shakespeare

In society, we speak of morals. In sports, we speak of etiquette, the specialized "dos and don'ts" known by the frequent participant, but many times misunderstood by others.

Have you ever played golf and noticed how much etiquette contributes to the total experience? From the moment you step onto the first tee box until you reach the last green, there are a multitude of unspoken rules of the game. Unless you spend time studying, these rules go unnoticed until that game with Mr. Etiquette himself.

Cross-country skiers are just as concerned with playing by the rules, but skiers, like golfers, may be unaware of them. Many of the rules are for safety. For instance, what would you do if you were on the eighth fairway and someone behind you yelled, "Fore"? Part of being courteous is playing safely. The same courteous behavior carries over to the automobile. There are certain rules of the road we all follow when driving, such as obeying traffic signs, signaling when passing, following at a safe distance for the speed we are traveling, entering freeway traffic, etc. The rules and etiquette of golf, driving, or skiing help to make for a safe and enjoyable day.

Acceptable behavior on touring trails and race courses creates a safe environment. The high speeds reached on downhill trails and sharp curves decreases reaction time, so knowing which way to move ahead of time when someone is barreling down on you may save a collision. The following rules of etiquette apply to both the touring trail and the race course.

(3) When overtaking another skier on a touring trail, the faster skier steps out of the track and passes. Give a verbal signal indicating which side you will pass on, i.e. "track right." If it is double-tracked, as a matter of courtesy, the faster skier passes in the open track.

(4) When overtaking another skier on a race course, the tracking rule states: the overtaking skier verbally signals "track," then the slower skier must yield by stepping to the side into the free track.

(5) On downhills, yield the track to the faster skier. The downhill skier has the right of way. Step to the side, but do not block the track.

(6) Avoid stopping on blind corners. When stopping on the trail, move to the side to let others pass. Do not block the trail.

(7) Most touring center trails are one way. Ski the indicated direction to avoid two-way traffic on narrow downhills.

(8) If the touring center is having a race, stay off the race tracks and avoid crossing them when racers are near.

(1) Be considerate of other skiers. Courtesy should guide your actions.

(2) Ski within your ability. Know the trail difficulty before you venture out.

(9) Dogs and prepared tracks do not mix. The dog will be happier walking on firm ground rather than punching holes in a ski track, and so will the skiers.

LEARNING RIGHT

AMERICAN TEACHING METHOD

"In seed time learn, in harvest teach, in winter enjoy."

William Blake

The American Teaching Method (ATM)—developed by Horst Abraham, technical director of Vail's Ski School, with the support of many colleagues and PSIA Demo-Team members—has been changing the way people learn. With the burning desire to discover how people learn, Horst has compiled his thoughts, experience, and knowledge into an unconventional methodological approach to teaching. The ATM favors an easier, more natural way to learn that makes use of thought processes we used as kids. As adults, we have almost lost this natural ability to learn. We tend to think too much before we move. Our schoolteachers have always evaluated our progress, telling us where we need work and exactly how to do it. So much critique results in less free expression. We have been raised with the idea that teachers are right and students are wrong, and have lost some of our own ability to judge what is correct. This is

especially true in sports, in which evaluation of right and wrong is largely subjective. The pleasure derived in sports is for the student's benefit, not the teacher's. Each skier dictates his or her own skiing style more than the instructor does.

If this line of thinking interests you and you want to delve into the philosophy encompassing the American Teaching Method, I highly recommend that you read Horst Abraham's book, *Skiing Right*. An easy-to-read review of Horst's life as a student, teacher, skier, and learner, *Skiing Right* is a book for learning how we learn and applying it to skiing. It's an excellent source for teachers and students alike.

Cross-Country Skiing Right should be used as a companion to *Skiing Right*, to further your knowledge and experience of both alpine and cross-country skiing. Although they have their differences, the two sports share many similarities. All skiing has developed from one seed and, with time, has grown into a large tree with many branches and plenty of foliage.

The following excerpt from *Skiing Right* compares traditional teaching to how we learned during early childhood.

In earliest childhood, we learn by experience, intuition and inference. No one teaches us to crawl, though we later learn to walk using already-walking people as models. Experts tell us that during the first five years of our life, we learn at a rate never again equalled. During these years, our spatial and sensory abilities are our guides for development. At this time, brain hemispheres are capable of functioning interchangeably. As we grow older, the brain halves become more specialized.

Once we enter school, the educational goals of a sequential and logical world concentrate on the development of left brain functions. Our ability to succeed (to do well in school) is based upon rote memorization, mathematical skills and verbal proficiency. Spatial and holistic skills are neglected in favor of analytical and linear thinking.

The acquisition of skills is viewed by ATM as holistic, meaning that skills are learned in totality, not fragmented into sub-parts. In *Skiing Right*, Abraham writes: "Regarding a movement as a whole, rather than as many parts, can make learning considerably easier. The ability to move is a sensation, not an explanation." The American Teaching Method serves the student by allowing a controlled environment for self discovery and individual improvement above and beyond traditional methods. The learner should feel a certain flow as previously learned skills mesh together as one. A learner who knows what the target or goal is may naturally combine steps and even progress to steps not yet demonstrated by the instructor. All the better. This freeing of the learner from the bonds of conventional teaching is helpful. It eliminates situations where students are reprimanded for exceeding the limits of the task and told to pay attention to the lesson—an attitude that is a hindrance to the natural abilities hidden in all of us.

A feeling of excitement should be communicated to learners being introduced to flat and slope skiing. The excitement should be maintained and encouraged as the new skill is learned, *not* squelched by the directorial, limiting methods of a helpful friend or instructor. ATM

encourages self-exploration and discovery, which frees the judgmental mind, releasing inner potential. At this point, I would suggest the person who is intent on learning how to ski read the exercises again and start skiing.

With ATM, students have been freed from dogmatic, traditional approaches to learning. Once discouraged from daydreaming or fantasizing, you are now encouraged to use these right brain functions. ATM departs from the analytical, verbal mode of learning and places more emphasis on the feeling, nonverbal aspects that assist in the acquisition of physical skills.

There were no books written about how to walk. When you were a year old, you didn't pick up the latest copy of Jean Piaget's *The First Steps* and proceed to study its contents before you moved up from all fours. The move came naturally. You'd been watching big people stand on two feet since birth. When the time was right, and with a little coaxing, you were on two feet, only to fall over. But while you were up, the praise was enough of a reward to encourage you to try it again. And try you did, adjusting and readjusting, trying to feel the sensation once more. And one day, when you least expected it, everything came together! Not only did you walk to the kitchen, but you didn't feel like sitting down at all for awhile.

From then on, you were walking, just like the big people. All that watching had paid off. Although you were totally unaware of what you were doing, you were learning how to walk. If only we could tap the natural learning processes we used as kids and begin anew, without any preconceived or judgmental notions of right or wrong! Learning could become a continual process whereby experiences shape awareness.

Horst Abraham, Educational Director of the PSIA, writes, "Traditional education is based upon the behaviorist learning theory. It contends that acquisition of a new skill is the result of repeated trials with differential reinforcement of responses (reward or punishment). The frequency of the desired response is gradually increased as the organism associates its performance with positive reinforcement. Behavioristic theory separates tasks into parts; each segment of the ultimately desired outcome is stressed by itself.

"The humanistic alternative to behaviorism, developed in the 1920s, states that understanding is neither random nor accidental, but is based upon clearly perceived experiences. The individual approaches the task or situation as a whole."

My walking example is indeed a simplistic observation of learning. But if we could only start anew and begin learning with a clean slate (mind), dealing with sensations and feelings rather than engaging our philosophical, inquiring, thinking mind . . . doesn't the idea seem exciting? Making such a switch is what ATM is about.

Ask any ski instructor how he or she became such a good skier. What do you think the answer will be? Ski instructors became good by doing. They are fortunate to be making their living by skiing—skiing every day, practicing and reinforcing their skills. Instructors also develop the technical knowledge necessary to analyze their students' skiing and make appropriate corrections. The combination of practice and continual feedback from fellow instructors is how those individuals became good.

People learn more if they discover new revelations on their own rather than being told what to expect in intricate detail. As Dr. Jim Tunney, National Football League referee and motivational speaker, states, "Practice does not make perfect. Perfect practice makes perfect." It's only after repeated attempts at moving correctly that the body's "muscle memory" becomes fixed on the correct moves.

ATM approaches learning through experience. Its methods provide students with the unhindered opportunity to experience skiing first, to develop the sensations associated with gliding on skis. Horst Abraham writes:

Tapping into methods like rhythm in skiing, exploring rather than being directed, appealing to feeling, awareness and intuition, we build a strong basis from which we can develop confidently, rapidly and autonomously. While we know that optimal results in learning are achieved by using both hemispheres, the real key to learning is to teach skillfully to the "right side of the brain." Spontaneity and intuitiveness make learning a joy and, when people enjoy what they are doing, they progress much more quickly.

Too often have we been told how to do something. We have had the movements described to us in the smallest detail, yet we find ourselves unable to do what it is that has been explained so thoroughly. Though we are physically capable, our nervous systems function, and we have a perfect run-down on the task we wish to accomplish, we cannot perform it! ATM, the American Teaching Method, addresses these

very issues; the approach combines our physical energies with our intellectual capabilities, making it easier for us to learn and perform. It blends the powers of each brain hemisphere and its respective function to facilitate learning through experience. Utilizing joint capabilities in this fashion, we can develop skills along with the necessary perceptions that are shaped by our attitudes about what we are doing.

I have just given you a taste of the American Teaching Method, as presented in Abraham's book, *Skiing Right*. The concepts are universal and have been known for years. They are presented in an understandable, provocative manner by someone who has actually tested the techniques. The joy of moving on skis is something everyone should experience. The physical and mental exhilaration of moving effortlessly over the snow, uphill and down, is a feeling difficult to describe in words. Those who have been there know what I mean.

From personal experience, I remember those perfect days when the wax was just right, the weather sunny and cool, the effort needed to glide along so minimal that I felt as though I could ski forever. I didn't want the track to end. Foot runners, I'm sure, experience this same feeling—the mind and body are one, each drawing energy from the other to continue the life-giving movements.

Cross-country skiing is movement. Movement on skis. Differing from walking or running, cross-country skiing is a free-flowing expression of energy, created not only by muscles, but by gravity. The skis' innate ability to glide forward gives cross-country skiing its special appeal. Learning to cross-country ski takes your natural ability to propel yourself on dry ground and transfers that same movement to the medium of skis. However, the sensations and feelings change. The skis' glide alters the perception you have.

Cross-country skiing is unique among winter sports. No other sport, except swimming, exercises the whole body so perfectly. It is often referred to as the total aerobic exercise. Dr. Kenneth Cooper, exercise physiologist, promotes cross-country skiing for snowbound exercisers.

Once the fundamentals are learned, cross-country skis can take you anywhere there is snow, from your back yard to the highest mountains. Maybe you only want to ski in local parks after a new snow. Perhaps you want to maintain your physical condition throughout the winter or take on the challenge of telemark skiing. The variety of ways to enjoy winter on skis makes cross-country a great stepping stone to the wide world of skiing.

Learning to cross-country ski is like learning to walk, best done slowly over a period of time as balance, confidence, and strength increase. Deciding one day that you are going to learn how to ski, buying equipment and setting aside the whole day might be a good way to turn you off on skiing forever. More ill-advised cross-country skiers have tried the sport and quit after one day than have continued. That is why I suggest taking short ski trips at first. Give your body a chance to adjust to the demands you are placing on it. If you are not very active in your daily life, move into skiing gently. Take half an hour or an hour just to put the skis on and slide around on the flat. No-wax skis give you hold without wax. (You can learn about waxing later.) Select easy terrain. In swimming, you don't climb up to the high dive before you've tested the water. Start on the low board first and build confidence.

A PSIA-certified instructor creates an ideal learning situation, taking care to introduce you to cross-country skiing the easy way. As Sven Wiik says, "There's not much to cross-country skiing, but what there is, is important." A lesson will emphasize the areas of your stride that need attention. The careful eye of an instructor can catch major errors before they develop into habits. The immediate feedback of an instructor facilitates learning. To know what you are doing wrong, and immediately practice the correction, speeds the learning process.

Group lessons are nice, but a private lesson, where you are one on one with an instructor, is the best way to learn. Lessons individually tailored to your own skiing personality give you optimum opportunities for improvement.

Cross-country skiing using good technique is an exhilarating feeling. You know when you are there! Moving on skis involves muscles; you can work hard or easy, depending on what you want. Racers ski fast and work their muscles hard, but not much harder than a novice skier who is inappropriately straining every muscle in his or her body. Inefficient movement is tiring; efficient movement is effortless. Keep this in mind as you work at becoming a good skier. Skiing becomes easier with practice when you begin to learn

which muscles to use to contribute to forward motion and which nonspecific muscles to relax. By moving slowly at first, you will be assured of not working your muscles needlessly. Think of moving in such a way that effort is minimized. Even if you go more slowly than your friend, take long deliberate glides. Push off from one ski onto the other. Prepared tracks are by far the best terrain to learn on. They're flat, so it's easy to control your speed, and you ski in previously made tracks, so fear is kept at a minimum.

Off-track skiing can be tiring. Because of the resistance of deeper snow or powder, the glide after each push-off is diminished. There is therefore more friction and consequently more work. Try prepared tracks first.

The diagonal stride is the most common technique used to move on the flat. It is characteristic of your walking stride, but with extension and slowed timing. Because you pause slightly on the gliding ski after each push-off, there is a time delay in moving the leg and arm forward.

Watching better skiers whenever you have a chance will ingrain the proper moves and look of the technique you want to learn. It gives you the right image to copy and to think about. According to Mike Gallager, coach of the 1984 U.S. Cross-Country Olympic Team, "The improvements in the next ten years in cross-country skiing will not be in technique or physical training methods or equipment. The major advances will focus on mental imagery."

It is worth spending time to develop the mind's ability to imagine how the body will perform a physical skill. If we would use the powers of the mind, we could tune our skiing skills even while at work. Creating the perfect image of how we want to ski and feeling the accompanying sensations in your mind can do more for your weekend skiing than you might think. Please refer to the bibliography for books on the subject. There has been a lot of research on imagery and, now, its application to learning skilled sports.

Developing your technique is exciting. I look forward to your efforts as you begin and perfect your skiing. Use the following instructions as a starting point. Read through the suggested exercises, then practice. Use the mechanical section to reinforce your on-snow movements. Practice like a child, in short bursts, until you feel a certain ease in skiing. Keep up the good work and have fun!

The following sections are useful both to students and teachers, and may be adapted to either. Teachers will benefit from the lesson plan development and students will learn through practicing the different suggested exercises.

For the inquiring enthusiast, the mechanical section will focus on the functional analysis of the different techniques, delving into the detailed mechanics associated with efficient movement. However, my concern is that you spend more time skiing by *feel* rather than by analytically picking apart the intricacies of the technique. Mike Gallager comments about biomechanical tests and sports medicine: "There's an expression which has reflected the problems of the United States team for years: 'Paralysis by analysis.' We tend to over-analyze wax, equipment and technique. We've put too much black magic into international racing. I like a simplistic approach. Technique should be good to a certain level, but after that, I'm interested in an athlete's natural flow on his or her skis. If I have to destroy that natural flow to develop a technical point so that it goes 'by the biomechanics,' then I've ruined that skier. If I can work with that flow, and make some suggestions with his or her style, then I've accomplished something."

Keep the details in the back of your consciousness to help you understand the sport and to analyze other people's skiing. But learn by doing and feeling what's right for *you*, developing your individual style within the spectrum of efficient technique. Once the mechanics are learned, you will progress with simple directives from the teacher that will lead to more self discovery.

Skiing requires a mixture of many skills. Viewing cross-country skiing as composed of three main skills—pressure control, turning, and edging—can simplify our teaching methods. Skill is relative and varies among individuals, and the instructor needs to be aware of each student's abilities. Pressure control includes elements of poling, timing, and power—all integral parts of the whole. Whether it's a pole plant or push-off, the resulting force provides propulsion. Although the "skills of skiing" may be viewed as similar for both track and downhill, cross-country skills deal with ways to impart speed, while downhill skills deal with ways to control speed.

BEGINNING FLAT TRACK

GOALS

- Developing a familiarity with equipment
- Developing balance while walking and sliding on skis
- Turning, using stationary step turns
- Changing direction while moving on the flat
- Speed control while in the track

CHOICE OF TERRAIN AND SNOW

- Flat terrain with prepared tracks, either set up in a loop or straight

MECHANICAL DEVELOPMENT

- Balancing on slippery skis
- Coordination and timing of arms and legs
- Edging the skis

EXERCISE EMPHASIS

- Exploring the nature of equipment: length, weight, maneuverability, and the loose heel
- Discovering ways of moving forward, backward, sideways, turning in place. With a good model to imitate, learning through imitation may transpire without detailed instruction.
- Provide students with success-oriented tasks. Create a sense of accomplishment at appropriate levels. Recognize student successes and build on their strong points.
- Pace practice carefully while attending to individual energy levels. Select a defined area or section of trail for practice. The overall winter environment, the extra concentration and muscle demand is tiring for the first-time skier. Allow for frequent breaks.
- Focus attention on *feeling* body movements while skiing. Feel how much leg muscle is used to move; how much arm muscle. Develop a sense of how the ski feels on the snow. Experience the amount of leg force possible before the ski slips back. This type of kinesthetic awareness at early stages develops student sensitivity to the overall skiing experience.
- Stationary balance, combined with moving balance, allows individual exploration. Relating the sensation to other physical activities such as ice or roller skating, tennis, jogging, dancing, or horseback riding may trigger corresponding feelings.
- Balancing games, developing one-foot support. The rhythmical nature of moving on skis is similar to the walking stride. Balance should be introduced as a push from one foot forward to a support foot. The resulting glide is dependent on the push-off power. Balancing on a gliding ski is introduced early, through demonstration or observation of better skiers, to point out that balancing on one ski after the push-off is inherent to good skiing. Visual imagery is an ideal reference source on and off the track. Watching other skiers or looking at still or moving pictures emphasizes balance in motion.
- Create a feeling of complete movement. Standing tall, squatting low, long stretch, wide stretch all change perspective and equilibrium.
- Discover equipment problems or any physical impairment restricting movement. Equipment malfunctions or wax problems directly affect the student's ability to imitate proper technique. Ski length and camber stiffness affect progress. Make sure skis are not too long or short and the camber is not too stiff for the student.
- Move on skis, as in walking, alternating arm and leg, and then using only the poles. Utilizing such movements may happen spontaneously following a demonstration. Let this kind of immediate natural movement be a trademark of learning.
- Discover how to change direction, while stationary and while moving, to maintain either speed or control.
- Explore how the skis' edges can prevent side-slipping on a stationary turn. Use the ankle and knee joints, emphasizing a self-discovering approach, following demonstration.
- Use exercises as a means in themselves, not to critique skiing. The errors made visible through practice, unless grossly out of place, may disappear on their own if no attention is called to them.

EXERCISES FOR WALKING AND SLIDING ON THE FLAT

. . . Move along the track on level terrain, as in walking . . .

. . . Turn 180° and walk back without poles . . .

. . . Alternately raise one ski high off the snow, then the other. Then "hop" both skis off the snow . . .

. . . Raise the ski up and balance, using the poles for support . . .

. . . Balance on one ski without pole support . . .

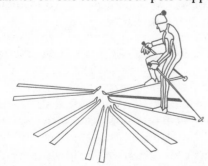

. . . Make a 360° turn while standing in place . . .

. . . Turn 360°, keeping the tails together; the tips together . . .

. . . Push along the track using only your poles—both poles together, then one at a time . . .

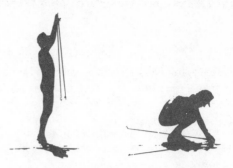

. . . Stand and raise up on your toes—reach for the sky—then get small and touch the snow. Ski under a ski pole held to side . . .

. . . Slide one ski way behind and touch the knee to the ski; alternate . . .

. . . Move in the track fast, then slow . . .

. . . While sliding, raise one ski off the snow. How long can you hold it up? Then switch . . .

. . . With speed, use the poles to apply pressure, slowing you gradually in the track. Think of the brakes on your bicycle . . .

. . . Take off one ski and move down the track; then switch. What does that feel like? Slipping? . . .

. . . Standing still, notice where your weight is centered. Focus attention on your feet. Feel where the pressure is on your foot as you walk forward. Now walk fast; push off the ski powerfully . . .

. . . Push off one ski, then push with both poles. Keep time by repeating the words, "push–double pole; push–double pole."

"I LOSE MY BALANCE WHEN THE SKIS SLIDE!"

. . . If balance is difficult, emphasize stationary balance exercises. Raise one ski off the snow, then the other. Start slowly and take small steps . . .

. . . Ski without poles, then take a series of short quick steps as in jogging. Feel that the body stays forward over the gliding ski. With practice, combine a series of quick steps and pause longer on the gliding ski . . .

. . . Practice gliding while standing on one leg; hold the other out behind. Where are the arms? . . .

. . . With poles planted to the side, balance on one leg and swing the free leg back and forth easily. Stand tall and swing; bend low and swing . . .

. . . Imagine yourself as your instructor and visually feel how you would move. What does it feel like to be in balance over your gliding ski? . . .

. . . Play "scooter." Bend low, put both hands on one knee and scoot along the track, pushing with one foot. . .

"MY SKIS KEEP SLIPPING BACK WHEN I PUSH OFF."

. . . Start slowly and try to push off when all your weight is on one foot . . .

. . . Without poles, imitate the jogger on skis . . .

. . . Is the camber too stiff, not allowing the whole bottom to contact the snow for grip? . . .

. . . If all else fails, check the wax. Put on the next softer kind. . . .

"MY ARMS REALLY GET TIRED WHEN I'M SKIING"

. . . Think of your arms when you walk. Are they bent at right angles? No, they are comfortably at your side . . .

. . . Start skiing slowly. Keep the hands low, plant the pole at an angle behind you . . .

. . . When skiing, move your hands no higher than your belly button and push on the pole all the way behind you . . .

. . . Check whether your poles are too long. Use the standard measuring method to select the proper length. . .

TURNING ON THE FLAT

. . . Remember how we turned 360° with the tails together? Let's try that same turn while moving. Get some speed by using both poles; bend low and step the skis in the direction you want to turn . . .

. . . Now let's get small and turn to the left, and then right, without using poles; using poles . . .

. . . Have you ice-skated before? Let's try skating on skis . . .

. . . Now, let's skate in a circle, first one way and then the other. As you push from one ski onto the other, is the ski flat or edged? . . .

"I DON'T FEEL ANY POWER IN MY TURNS."

. . . Try bending low, like a cat that's ready to jump; then push off one ski and turn . . .

. . . Edge the ski you are pushing off more, so it doesn't slip sideways . . .

. . . Turn to the beat of "skate–double pole, skate–double pole . . .

THE MECHANICS

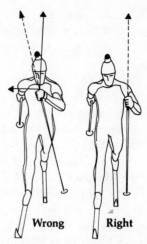

Wrong   **Right**

The diagonal stride is the fundamental cross-country technique, used predominantly on the flat and for skiing up slight hills. The term "diagonal" refers to the diagonally opposite arm and leg movements as in walking. Movements are similar to walking or running, but employ the additional components of gliding on skis and using poles to push with. Because cross-country equipment allows a free heel, the diagonal stride gives skiers that special ability to propel themselves through varying terrain: uphill, downhill, and across the flat.

Learning efficient technique follows a gradual acquisition of skills. For example, driving a car requires certain skills. You need to develop a feeling for how much to push the accelerator to speed up and pass, or how hard to hit the brake to miss another car. Parallel parking takes practice to perfect. (With all the driving you've done, how's your parallel parking?) Driving on icy roads is no easy matter. A definite skill is required for each of these tasks. The ability to deal successfully with each situation makes you a good driver. In other words, you have developed the mechanics of successful, efficient driving. Progressing from this basic skill level to more refined levels involves repetitious practice.

Let's look further into the mechanics of cross-country skiing on the flat. These are the component skills of the diagonal stride:
(1) Arm-pole movement
(2) Leg-body movement
(3) Timing
Separate skills combine to form the whole movement of diagonal stride. It's only for purposes of analysis that the diagonal stride is broken down into separate skills so, as teachers and students, we can gain knowledge and foresight.

ARM-POLE

In cross-country skiing, the entire body moves. The legs and arms function as a unit. The poles contribute to the overall momentum by providing propulsion.

By slipping the hand up through the strap, the strap and handle are gripped together. When poling, the pressure is exerted on the strap rather than the pole. Arm movement is related to the

pole angle when planted in the snow. If the hand is ahead of the basket, the angle is correct. As speed increases, the pole plant can approach vertical—hence less speed, more angle between the pole and snow. Why angled? So you can apply force to the pole immediately for forward propulsion. By keeping the arm swing parallel to the skis and tracks, force is directly transmitted to the pole and into forward momentum.

When planting the pole, the arm is comfortably flexed at the elbow and wrist. Once the pole is planted, the arm begins to pull down on the pole strap. As the hand passes the hip, the arm is totally extended, creating a straight line from the shoulder down the arm to the pole basket. At first, slight pressure on the pole is adequate, but as skills improve, begin to apply more power to this motion.

With properly adjusted pole straps, when the pole is planted, there's an initial pull-down, then a push-back on the pole. The push is down toward the knee, rather than pulling back horizontally. From a fully extended arm position with a properly adjusted strap, the grip on the pole is released as the arm and hand extend to the rear. An adjustable strap allows the pole to fit so that only a light grip between the thumb and forefinger is needed to maintain pole control. This eliminates needless muscle tension, which does not contribute to forward motion. It's the same fruitless tension you experience driving your car on icy roads with a death grip on the wheel. Knuckles are white as you tense muscles needlessly. It is not the muscles that will help you in this situation, it's your reaction time—and a tense muscle is slower.

But, driving or skiing, you can learn to relax more with practice. Think how practice has eased your muscle tension when driving a car. Some drivers feel so comfortable and carefree, you wish they would pay more attention to the road!

The recovery phase of poling forward takes advantage of the pendulum-like motion of the arm. Here's the area of the diagonal stride that can be the most relaxing. The upper arm, when loose, swings easily forward from the shoulder, relaxed and fairly straight by the side. The proficient skier uses this forward swing to relax and prepare for the next pole plant. The recovery forward is a chance for the arm muscles to relax and release the tension. It's a short amount of time, but it adds up to energy saved. Tense muscles are always burning fuel; relaxed muscles ease the demand.

I've found in teaching poling that the best advice is to start slowly. Keep the hands low with pole baskets dragging on the snow. Raise the hands only high enough to stick the pole in and push. The key is relaxing the hands to eliminate extra work for the shoulders.

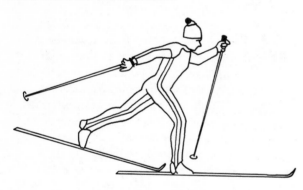

LEG-BODY MOVEMENT

While cross-country skills are inherent in your walking stride, transferring them to skis is a new experience. Think of how you walk. You push off from one foot onto the other; the body moves forward to balance momentarily over the new front foot and another step is taken. When the pace is quickened, as in running, the push from one foot onto the other becomes more forceful and, as a result, the body leans forward more to keep up. The body must keep up with the new front foot or else forward motion is thwarted. Now think of a runner in a 100-yard sprint. A stop-action photo would show a marked forward body lean, needed to maintain momentum. It's such a marked lean that if the runner's feet were to stop, he would fall flat on his face.

Performed on skis, the same movements apply. The new sensation is the slide—or, as it's referred to in skiing, the glide. When the new foot swings through, to take advantage of the ski's ability to glide, the body must be leaning forward to stay balanced over the front or gliding foot.

At first, a slow, shuffling motion will facilitate balance. Speed will increase as you develop balance over the gliding foot. Trying to go fast without technique is like trying to tie a square knot without knowing the procedure. It's very tiring and frustrating. Start slowly and develop the technique first—the speed will come. By applying more power during the push-off, speed increases in proportion to the energy exerted. With a more powerful push-off and forward body lean, the ski will tend to lift off the snow behind you as a result.

Pictures and advertisements in magazines usually depict the cross-country racer with one ski way up behind, arms stretched—the epitome of speed. If you imitate that technique, you'll tire and stop. The racer's speed is a result of proper technique, not an acrobatic maneuver.

The legs work in an alternating push-glide mode. Push from the ski as if you were walking briskly. The push down flattens the ski's camber, allowing the wax or pattern to grip the snow. The amount of downward pressure needed for grip varies with different cambers and wax, but generally a brisk walking step should do it. The push should come from the whole foot. Then the wax is set, creating a stationary platform from which to project forward.

The leg, like the arm, becomes fully extended behind the skier. The knee and ankle straighten. The recovery forward is again a pendulum motion from the hip joint. The knee and ankle are flexed while the body is supported on the gliding ski.

PUSH-OFF VS. KICK

For all practical purposes, the recreational skier pushes from a stationary ski onto a gliding ski. The movement is not very dramatic, not an exhibit of explosive power; there's just enough push to move the body forward. Therefore the term "push-off" is used for the recreational and first-time skier, and the term "kick" is used to denote the same movement performed quickly and powerfully by racers. The terms are synonymous.

TIMING

The timing of the diagonal stride involves the coordination of movements between the arms and legs. As in walking, the opposite arm and leg work together in diagonally opposite directions. Efficient skiing depends on the timing of the push-offs as the feet come together. It is during this momentary position that the legs, hips, and upper torso apply direct pressure to the ski.

Having spent considerable class time with the analytical skier who thinks through his every move, I know that timing can develop backward—meaning that the skier moves the same arm and leg forward. Instructors have come to call this parallel poling. If you've never watched a camel walk, take a second look. The camel is the perfect example of parallel walking—it moves both right legs at the same time, then both left legs. An easy remedy to correct this counterproductive motion is to try jogging on skis. Keep your hands low; take short, quick steps, and notice how the arms move naturally in diagonally opposite directions. This will solve parallel poling problems without focusing any conscious thought on the problem. Exercises that direct students toward the desired behavior without calling their attention to problems keep them in the feeling, experiencing mode rather than awakening the thinking and analyzing side of the mind.

The diagonal stride typifies cross-country skiing. The smooth rhythmic nature of the movement suggests the phrase "poetry in motion." Movements are eloquent in their simplicity. The racer is the prime example of efficiency in motion. By eliminating wasted movements, energy output is directed to specific muscles, contributing to forward momentum. Skiing with a good diagonal stride is like learning to ride a bike for the first time. Balance comes. You feel the ease of moving.

PACE

As an instructor, ski with empathy. Realize the physical nature of skiing and work accordingly. Take time for breaks, both physical and mental. Try to pace the lesson by introducing the more vigorous exercises early, and plan breaks near the lesson's end.

Keep a mental note of each student's progress and adjust the pace to maintain interest and attention. A fatigued skier does not learn much about cross-country skiing, except that it's hard

arms and upper body do all the work
remain slightly flexed, however. A
knee bend works the thigh musc
should be avoided. Maintain a
for efficiency. This is not a
soldier; it is only intended
awareness of your low

DOUBLE POLE
DOUBLE POLING WITH A PUSH

I once knew a skier who constantly used both poles to move. I couldn't get him to use his legs to push and glide! Then I found out he was a weight lifter who found double poling the easiest way to move. If you are not a strong weight lifter, then I'd reserve double poling for gradual downhills or double poling with one push for flat terrain.

Double poling is the fastest technique available to the cross-country skier. Used primarily on gradual downhills when the diagonal stride becomes ineffective, the technique includes the simultaneous use of the arms and poles in a forceful push, employing the upper body for added energy.

As the arms swing forward, poles are planted at an angle and initial pressure is applied on the pole strap, pulling down first, then pushing back. The arms initially remain in a flexed position to better transmit power and maintain momentum. As the hands pass the hips, the push continues until the arm, hand, and pole are in a straight line to the rear. At the front extension, the grip is released and the fingers pointed toward the basket. The recovery forward, like in the diagonal stride, is a relaxed pendulum swing. Allow a brief rest before the poles are planted at an angle and another sequence begins.

The upper body and hips extend forward with the arms. As the poles are planted, the upper body flexes forward at the waist. This additional compression adds to the eventual power of the movement. The upper body moves to a nearly horizontal position before recovering.

Legs can rest when double poling while the

The legs
excessive
les needlessly and
constant knee angle
cense to ski like a tin
to spark your
r legs when double poling.

1

2

3

4

5

6

ONE-PUSH-DOUBLE-POLE

Terrain determines when the one-push-double-pole becomes an effective technique. When the terrain becomes too fast for the diagonal and too slow for the double pole, adding a push-off before double poling will fit the bill. On flatter trails, the one-push-double-pole will add the power of a push-off, combined with a double pole push. This technique is ideal for flats or gradual downhills. Racers have been known to use this technique on gradual uphills. It is a restful break from double poling and long sections of diagonal.

The timing of the one-push-double-pole is "push–double pole, push–double pole." The arms and upper body move as in the double pole. The legs supply the additional force of a push-off onto a gliding ski. The push is with either foot in an alternating pattern; however, some skiers prefer to use the same foot. As the rear foot swings forward, the body weight moves toward the heels and then either recovers to a resting position or stays angled slightly forward for another sequence.

At the moment of push-off with the leg, the arms and upper body extend forward. As the poles are planted, the rear leg simultaneously

swings forward as power is applied to the poles. This movement of the rear leg swinging forward at the exact moment the double pole begins is a good source of potential energy. Try to feel the power of a fast leg recovery versus a slower recovery.

The addition of two or more push-offs before the double pole is a rhythmic move for certain snow conditions or terrain. Timing is the new addition to this double pole variation, using two alternating push-offs before double poling: "push, push, double pole; push, push, double pole." As the push-offs take place, the arms move rhythmically forward. As the last push-off occurs, the arms are forward again, ready to plant the poles. The arms can come forward simultaneously or sequentially in preparation for the double pole.

I remember the sixty-kilometer World Loppett race course in Austria that race organizers said was eighty-five percent flat. With icy, granular snow conditions, double poling with either one push, two pushes or more was the technique for the day. If you have ever double poled for long distances, your arms and back get a real workout. You are thankful for small uphills so you can break out in a diagonal stride.

It may not be the fastest technique available because of the arm rest, but it gives your arms and upper body a rest from the rigors of constantly double poling.

SKATE TURN

The skate turn takes its name from ice- or roller-skating. It can be either a slow, speed-maintaining turn or an aggressive, powerful, speed-increasing turn. The movements

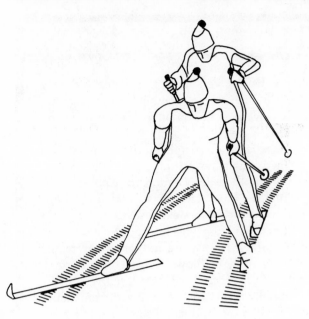

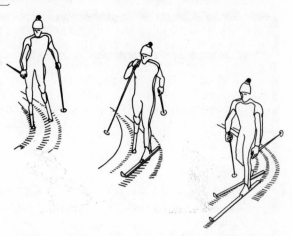

are similar to the stationary step turn around the tails. With skis parallel, sink low and pick up the tip of the inside ski while pushing off an edged outside ski. Transfer weight and bring the outside ski in parallel, and repeat.

Turning on the flat is best accomplished on a firmly packed, level section of trail. The skills involved in this maneuver include edging, leg and body movement, and timing. Pushing off a flat ski is useless. In order to utilize the power of the leg, the outside ski must be on its inside edge to resist the force of the leg push. The edge is achieved by turning the ankle and knee toward the inside of the turn. The inside ski remains flat to the snow during the brief period of glide. The legs are flexed, lowering the body. A powerful extension off an edged ski transfers body weight forward onto the gliding leg and ski. It is this push that will determine speed.

Arms contribute to momentum by swinging forward when the leg pushes off. The poles may be used for a double pole–push as the skis move together. Following the double pole, the skier should be low, ready to repeat the sequence. I suggest that you start students learning the skate without using their poles. This way their attention will be focused on the ski-leg movements first, eliminating any confusion about what to do with the arms.

Setting up a loop or figure-eight track is great for turning practice. That way the student learns to turn in both directions.

STRIDE TURN FOR TRACKED CORNERS

When the turn is a gradual, long, rounded corner, the skate turn is inappropriate. Using the diagonal stride to ski around tracked corners adds a little variety to skiing the flat. Speed is maintained without breaking stride.

The turn is initiated simply by kicking the tail of the rear ski outward beyond the track. The tip pivots on the snow. As the leg and ski swing forward, steer them into the track and glide. The glide on the inside ski may be shortened to help coordinate the timing of the turning radius. Use well-packed, tracked corners for practice. Stride turns are easily made if you ski in the opposite direction on a section of trail where skate turn tracks exist. The outside ski slides easily into the skate tracks. Maintaining the diagonal stride around corners adds to the fluid, continuous motion of cross-country techniques, and characterizes the more proficient skier. No break in rhythm or stride interrupts when turning; momentum is constant and flowing.

SKI POLE CHECK

For gradual speed control in tracks, the poles are used to the side to slow momentum. With hands on the pole straps, turn the palms up. Plant the poles forward toward the ski tips. Apply pressure to the straps, absorbing resistance with the wrist, arm, and shoulder. Once the body moves past the pole baskets, stick the poles in again. Continue in this manner to reduce speed. This is not a technique for high-speed stops, but is ideal for gradual stops on the flat or speed control on easy downhills.

UPHILL

GOALS

- Developing efficient movements for ascending hills, both in the track and in off-track skiing
- Establishing a knowledge of the different techniques
- Adapting the different techniques to the terrain, snow conditions, and wax; terrain utilization

CHOICE OF TERRAIN AND SNOW

- For uphill skiing in tracks, use a gradually increasing hill with well-defined prepared tracks.
- Off-track skiing should be done in powder or hard-packed snow on gentle to moderate slopes.

MECHANICAL DEVELOPMENT

- Transferring the diagonal stride movements to incorporate an uphill climb
- Learning pole use to maintain support and provide propulsion
- Edging creates a stable base from which to step uphill.

EXERCISE EMPHASIS

- Introduce skiing uphill in a modified diagonal stride, starting across the hill or straight up a gradual slope.
- Explore how edging the ski prevents side slip, providing a firm base of support. Use stationary maneuvers to feel how much ankle and knee are necessary.
- Use speed as a guideline for which technique to use. Practice skiing fast, using the uphill diagonal, then slowly using the more secure herringbone.
- Pace the time spent on uphills with skiing on the flat or downhills. Skiing uphill is a demanding task; keep the students within their comfort range. They can let loose after the lesson, if the energetic ones want to.
- Terrain dictates technique variations. Experiment on steeper slopes using a different technique, such as the traverse or forward side step.
- Discover the differences in pushing off a ski on the flat versus on the slope. Use body position examples: leaning forward, leaning backward, and standing directly over the foot.
- Ski pole use on all uphill techniques is shortened, but plays an important role in supporting the skier. Demonstrate pole use behind the hips, arm fully extended.
- Review the balance exercises of the diagonal if balance is a problem.
- Acknowledge waxing and camber problems when student shows poor technique.
- Practice direction changes used when traversing across the slope. Try an uphill tacking turn on gradual hills or a kick turn on steeper slopes.

DIRECTIVES FOR SKIING UPHILL

. . . Let's move up the hill toward my poles . . .

. . . What's different from our diagonal stride? . . .

. . . Try it again, but take shorter steps . . .

. . . Stand taller and take quicker, jogging steps. Does the ski grip the snow better? or worse? . . .

. . . Where do the poles work best? Try to move them only as far forward as you intend to push back . . .

. . . If you feel energetic, let's try a jogging motion up the hill. Where's your body weight now? . . .

. . . Climb the hill in a slow rhythm: 1—— 2—— 3—— 4——. Then faster 1— 2— 3— 4—. How about 1—2—3—4? A ski touches the snow each time you say a number . . .

. . . Continue up the hill until it becomes too steep to climb straight up. Then move one ski to the side in a "half-V" position. Continue climbing . . .

. . . Now continue, but with both skis out of the track in a "V" position . . ..

. . . Look back at your tracks in the snow. What do they look like? . . .

. . . Try turning the edges into the hill. Do you slip back? If so, make a wider "V." . . .

"MY TAILS KEEP CROSSING."

. . . Start slowly and raise the knee high, stepping the whole ski farther forward . . .

. . . How fast are you moving now? Walking speed or jogging? Are you climbing? OK . . .

. . . Plant the poles behind your feet for support. Do you extend your arm completely on each step? . . .

. . . Watch my poles. See how they go in behind my feet? Notice my upright body . . .

. . . Let's ski across the hill toward the trees . . .

. . . Watch my tracks, and try to make yours like mine. Can you see two edge lines in the snow behind you? If not, try turning your ankles into the hill more. What does that do? . . .

. . . Watch me and follow along. Now try the kick turn to face the other direction . . .

. . . Now let's ski at an angle up the hill and see if we can turn and ski in the other direction, like tacking upwind in a sailboat . . .

"MY SKIS KEEP SLIPPING BACK."

. . . Take less of an angle up the hill . . .

. . . Try sliding the foot farther ahead before you move your weight over it . . .

. . . Use the pole to help maintain momentum. Push behind with it . . .

. . . Continue to zig-zag up the hill. Now take one step up the hill as you move across to the trees . . .

"I KEEP SLIPPING SIDEWAYS."

. . . Use the edges to prevent side slip. Turn the ankles and knees into the hill . . .

THE MECHANICS

HALF AND FULL HERRINGBONE

Uphill skiing is one of the joys of cross-country skiing. The versatility of cross-country equipment and wax allows not only flat skiing, but uphill *and* downhill skiing. You've heard the phrase "all-terrain vehicle"; well, cross-country skiers are "all-terrain skiers." No mountain is too steep for the energetic cross-country skier. Descents from such peaks as Mt. McKinley on cross-country gear attest to this fact.

UPHILL DIAGONAL

After you learn the diagonal stride on the flat, skiing hills will come naturally. When you encounter a hill with tracks, continue up as you would in the diagonal stride. When the skis start to slip, adjust by taking shorter steps. Try to stand tall over the feet so pressure is exerted directly down on the ski. Too much forward lean with hands in front renders the ski's grip useless. The skier must be in a position similar to the balanced stride on the flat. At slower speeds the body straightens, and steps and poling become shorter—all in an effort to reduce back slip and to move uphill with the least effort. This is a very stable technique to use when carrying heavy packs.

A faster skier shortens his stride and increases his tempo (the frequency with which the legs and arms move). The push-offs become quick and explosive. The arm swing is shortened in front as the pole is planted at a working angle behind the feet. The arm follow-through may be shortened, adapting to the quicker pace.

When the hill becomes too steep to climb effectively, or skis start to slip back, place one ski out to the side forming a "half-V" position. Keep tails together, with one ski in the track. The ski to the side is turned on its inside edge, and the knee and ankle aid in edging by varying the amount of inward angulation. The poles are used as in the diagonal stride.

On steep, narrow sections of trail, use both skis to the side, forming a full "V" position. Both skis provide an edged, firm platform from which to push off. Body position is like that for the uphill diagonal—fairly upright, weight over the pushing foot, knees and ankles well-flexed to supply power for the push-off, head up, eyes looking ahead.

I've seen skiers with their heads down, concentrating so much on what they are doing that they are oblivious to where they are going—even to the point of running into small trees or bushes. "Look up" has long been a coaching phrase in many sports. Focusing on the horizon or on a permanent feature in the environment helps balance. If you try skiing with your eyes closed, you'll see what I mean.

To practice in a prepared track, pick one with a gradually increasing pitch. Ski in a diagonal stride as far up as you can effectively; then switch to a half herringbone until *it* becomes ineffective; finally place both skis in a wide "V" position, continuing to widen it as the hill becomes steeper. In deep snow, raise the knees high and step the whole ski up and out of the snow. (Some skiers seem to forget, when they are on skis, that their knees can bend.) For deep powder, emphasize bending the knees to make climbing easier.

UPHILL TRAVERSE

Skiing an up angle across the hill can be a relaxing way to climb. Used primarily for off-track skiing, traversing a slope is similar to tacking a boat upwind. Both the boat and the skier are working against natural external forces. The amount of force varies in each case. The sailor adjusts sails for light and heavy winds. The skier adjusts pace according to snow conditions and pitch.

Edging the ski to prevent side slip is the main key to the traverse. In soft snow, edging is easy because the ski is supported by the snow. On hard-packed slopes, keeping the skis on their uphill edge becomes more difficult.

On the flat, practice turning the ankles left and right. Move to a hill and feel how much ankle movement it takes to step sideways uphill. Notice the track, or edge mark, left in the snow. Does the edge make a 90° angle, or is there a smoother edge mark?

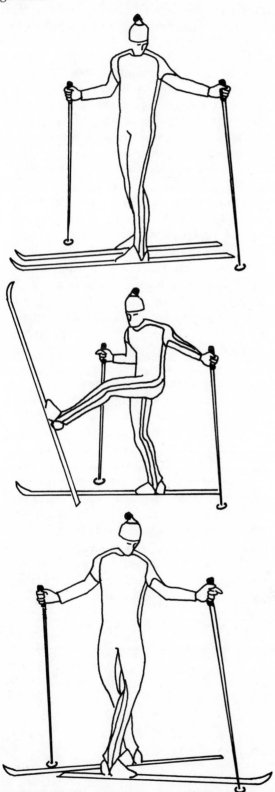

The angle of ascent varies depending on wax and the skier's strength. A well-waxed ski climbs easier. A slippery ski tires the arms, because when the skis slip, the arms have to provide support. When traversing steeper slopes, do not raise the uphill hand unnecessarily to plant the pole. Hands remain low and swing forward only high enough to plant the pole and apply pressure.

Link the traverses with a kick turn to continue up the hill. The kick turn is a 180° turn used to change direction on a hill or on narrow trails. Because the skis are across the hill and edged, poles are planted uphill and a three-point contact is made, forming a firm platform to kick the downhill ski up and around to face the other direction. The uphill ski is brought around parallel and the turn is complete.

On gradual slopes, the kick turn is a step up the hill rather than down. The uphill ski is turned into the opposite direction. The downhill ski and poles provide the three-point balance, while the uphill ski is kicked up and turned. This is called a "tacking turn."

FORWARD SIDE STEP

The cousin of the uphill traverse, the forward side step combines components of the traverse with the side step. Like the traverse, the forward side step is used primarily for off-track skiing. Angles are taken up the hill, tacking back and forth to gain elevation. The difference is that while traversing, the uphill ski is stepped forward and up the hill, making the technique faster, but one requiring more muscle energy.

The forward side step requires the same leg movements as the uphill traverse, but with more flex in the ankles and knees. Ankles are turned into the hill to edge the ski. Lift the ski high enough to perform the step sideways. The terrain and snow affect the size of each step uphill. Usually the forward side step is used on steeper hills, when climbing straight up would be difficult. Flatter hills are easily climbed with other techniques. When wax is slick, use the technique with more side stepping to prevent the ski from slipping back.

The poles are planted either diagonally, as in the uphill traverse, or simultaneously on each side of the skis. The arms help the skier step up onto an edged ski, but may not have a complete follow-through.

BEGINNING DOWNHILL

GOALS

- Development of balance and maneuverability on skis while moving down gradual hills.
- Direction changes while skiing in prepared tracks and in off-track skiing.
- Speed control through stepping and wedging.

CHOICE OF TERRAIN AND SNOW

- Best learned on smooth, gentle slopes ending in a flat bottom.
- Pack or soft-packed snow conditions are best.

MECHANICAL DEVELOPMENT

- Speed control on tracks results from ski resistance, wedging.
- Turning on the hill controls speed and changes direction.
- Edging is refined through step turning and wedging.
- Turning results from stepping in the new direction or from pivoting the outside foot, or both feet, in desired direction.
- Skidding results from increasing speed and from turning with a narrow wedge.

EXERCISE EMPHASIS

- Exploration of the sensations associated when gravity takes hold.
- Provide a smooth acquisition of skills by building on past experiences. This progression should start simply and work toward more specific goals. Individual goals and performance determine, to some extent, the emphasis of the lesson.
- Work on foot-ski control. On the flat, turn the ski tips together; push tails out to form a wedge. Give numbers related to the size of the wedge (small: 1; large: 5).
- Use games that focus attention on a task rather than analyzing the exact movements. Directing the learning to specific goal-oriented tasks keeps wordy explanations to a minimum while allowing skiers to *feel*.
- Learning in a confined area is an excellent opportunity to practice both uphill and downhill techniques. For example, combine an uphill climb with a straight downhill run which is a great way to pack down powdery slopes for turning practice.
- Pacing becomes a concern when alternating uphill and downhill skiing. Fatigue reduces the effective learning time. Monitor each student's progress, checking for excessive perspiration, rapid breathing, or frequent falling. Intersperse informative rest breaks to combat total exhaustion.
- Give demonstrations, effectively showing proper movements, even exaggerating certain moves. A good demonstration is worth a thousand words. Mental pictures provide a good focal point to effect change.
- The ability to equalize weight between both feet and to distribute this evenness is developed. Experiment with equal weight in a wedge; uneven weight is a characteristic of turning symmetry. Most people tend to have a better side. For instance, right-handed people tend to turn better to the left, and vice versa. Eliminate this propensity through exercises and practice.
- Allow individual interpretation of desired responses. The demonstration shows the results of proper technique. Now let students work, unrestricted by the thinking mind, toward unhindered movement. Although some students may need more explanations, keep instruction simple and brief. Direct them toward more skiing rather than having them listen to explanations.
- Fear is common at this stage and is dealt with individually. Select descents that students can manage and feel comfortable with. Success is important to building confidence.

EXERCISES FOR BEGINNING TO
SKI DOWNHILL

. . . While we are on the flat, let's hop on both skis. Now on one . . .

. . . While standing still, let's hop and turn both skis to the right, then left . . .

. . . Stand still, push out the tails and keep the tips together. Again. What do we call this position? ("A.") . . .

. . . Now jump the skis into a big "A." . . .

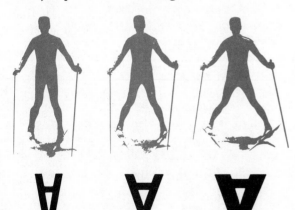

. . . Let's call a narrow "A" a number 1, a medium "A" a number 2, and the largest one you can make a number 3 . . .

. . . Move into a number 2, now 1, now 3, repeat . . .

. . . Stand tall and stretch to the sky. Get small and touch the snow . . .

. . . Follow me—let's ski around in a circle. Now try a figure eight. Now switch directions . . .

. . . Remember our skating? Let's skate around in a figure eight on the snow . . .

. . . Let's climb a little ways up the hill. Sidestep. Herringbone. Traverse . . .

. . . Let's learn the "bull fighter turn." Watch this . . .

. . . Now let's slide down to a stop . . .

. . . Look back at your tracks. Are they close together or wide apart? Shoulder width? . . .

. . . Raise up one ski and balance while moving. Then try the other. How long can you keep it up? . . .

. . . This time when you get to the bottom, make a turn by stepping first to the right then back left . . .

. . . Now let's get real small and step turn around my poles.

. . . Let's try that again, but this time come down in a number 3 "A" position . . .

. . . Now a number 2 . . .

. . . Let's move down in a number 3 to 0 and back to 3 . . .

. . . What does your track look like now? An hourglass? . . .

. . . Can you ski under the pole? With hands on your knees? . . .

"I KEEP FALLING BACKWARDS!"

. . . Try bending your knees more, like you would when receiving a serve in tennis, or like a cat getting ready to pounce on a mouse . . .

. . . Check your ski bottoms to see if there is any ice or snow stuck on them . . .

"MY BOOT HEELS KEEP SLIDING OFF THE SKI!"

. . . Check for heel plates . . .

. . . Retie your boots to tighten ankle support . . .

EXERCISES TO BEGIN TURNING

. . . Let's start straight down the hill in our wedge and come to a stop by my pole . . .

. . . Now start in a wedge and point your "A" slowly to the left and then slowly back to the right . . .

. . . For a different thought, try maintaining your number 2 "A" position and think of pointing your outside foot in the direction you want to go. Notice that if your "A" is pointing straight downhill, the foot is already pointing in the new direction. Stand on it and push the tail to the side while turning it . . .

. . . Make a run without poles and brush the turning ski's tail to the side . . .

. . . Turn with hands on your knees . . .

. . . Weave through the ski poles like a slalom course . . .

"I SEEM TO STIFFEN UP WHEN I START GOING FAST."

. . . Try starting lower until you feel comfortable . . .

. . . Think of bouncing and bobbing up and down as you turn . . .

. . . Ski down, turning to the count of "1, 2, 3, turn" or "1, 2, turn." . . .

. . . Look at your tracks. Now, are they smooth and "turny" or sharp and quick? . . .

. . . Let's make smooth, rounded turns . . .

THE MECHANICS

The progression from flat skiing to small downhills is natural, facilitated by the terrain. Most touring centers or trail systems have easy loops with smaller rolling hills and advanced trails containing steep, curvy downhills. Back-country tours are prime areas for off-track skiing. Downhills are often the main event on such tours. The secluded powder slopes accessible on cross-country equipment allow skiers to experience a variety of skiable terrain.

And cross-country skiing is an "all-terrain" sport. Unlike their alpine counterparts, cross-country skiers climb uphill under their own power, but ski down using some of the same techniques as their slope-skiing friends. There is a trend at alpine ski areas toward skiing on cross-country equipment. The term "nor-pine" has been used to describe this blend of nordic and alpine skiing. Using cross-country equipment, these nor-piners are difficult to distinguish unless they drop into the telemark position, disclosing their free heel.

With a feeling of balance already developed from flat skiing, initial attempts at sliding downhill are experiences in speed control and refinement of balance. The ability to balance while moving is an important developmental stage. Refine this sensation on gradual, packed slopes so the learner develops confidence. Reduce tension or excessive fear by carefully choosing the slope for their first descents. I've known many students who truly appreciated the efforts to ease them into downhill skiing gradually. These students develop a certain trust in the instructor, another step in freeing their inner potential.

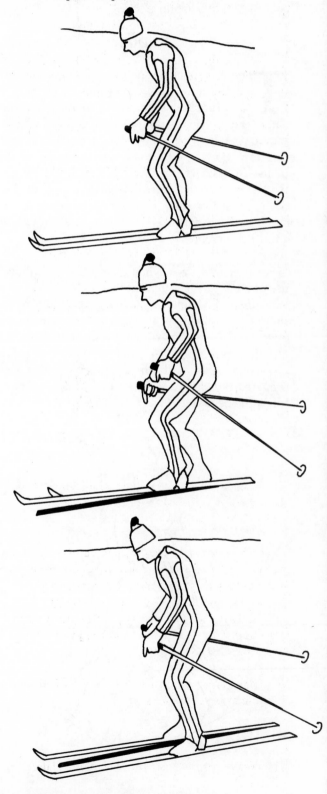

Balance on downhill descents, whether or not in tracks, is strengthened by a comfortable stance. A relaxed posture, referred to in sports as the "basic body stance," enhances stability. By standing straight, knees flexed, hands down and forward, the "center of balance" is over the whole foot. Heels are flat on the ski and arms are forward to the side. The center of balance on any skier is around the belly button.

To realize how the positioning of this center affects balance, think of a heavy bowling ball in your stomach. If the bowling ball is moved forward too much, you will fall on your face. If you keep the ball right over the feet, balancing—even while moving—is easy. To maintain this position, keep skis shoulder-width apart and try sliding one foot forward slightly in a type of scissored stance. As speed increases, flex knees more, lowering the bowling ball.

Using bamboo poles to ski under or trying distracting directives like "look at me; how many fingers am I holding up?" will help put the learner in the feeling rather than the thinking mode.

STEP TURN

Besides being a very functional turn, the sense of balance inherent in the step turn is a key ingredient for success. The ability to pick up one ski and step in the new direction is the basis of the turn. The tail remains on the snow because of down pressure on the heel and upward pressure on the toe. This allows the tail to pivot. The steps are continuous from one ski to the other until the desired direction is reached. Always step the inside ski first. Body weight is naturally transferred to the stepped ski, or else performing the splits is a real possibility!

Step turns are to skiing what pedals are to bicycles. Both supply power, but in different ways. An inverse relationship exists between the two. Pedals move up and down because of leg power; the same up-and-down motion is part of step turning, but gravity provides the movement. The legs are flexed and the body is in a low crouch over the skis, increasing stability and balance. Step turns are possible in a variety of adverse snow conditions, such as crusty powder, windblown powder, or crud. The step turn, when linked with a downhill traverse, is a secure way to descend a slope. On packed trails, stepping around corners is a preliminary move to the more powerful skate turn.

Building on the discovery of edges in the flat

lesson, skiers will improve ski control through their use. The edge engagement necessary to complete a turn varies with snow conditions and terrain. Firm, hard-packed snow on prepared trails, for example, requires greater edging to prevent the ski from side slipping. The opposite is true in soft pack or powder.

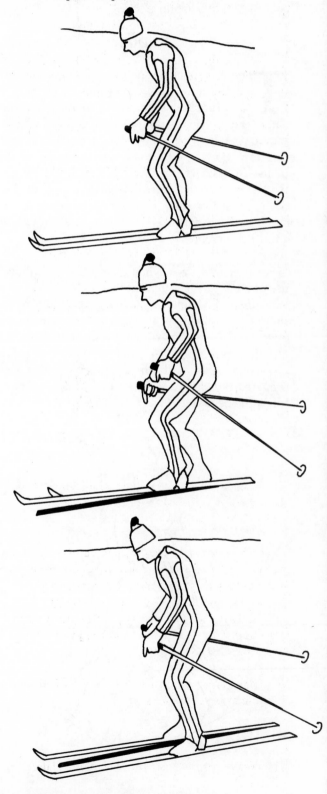

When practicing, begin with small steps to the side from a low crouch. Weight the heels slightly and keep pressure up with the toes, to maintain the ski tails on the snow. The ski's tip is lifted and moved to the side as body weight transfers. Short, quick steps are preferable to slow, wide ones. The arms are held forward and to the side, poles pointing behind.

WEDGE

The ever-popular snowplow has given way to the term "wedge." Terms are terms and function is undisputable. By whatever name, the position is still the cross-country skier's foundation, the sure method of speed control and turn initiation. It is the basis of all other downhill turns. Tour skiers and racers both use the wedge to control speed and turn. The wide stance of the wedge is very stable. The narrow stance makes it easier to initiate turns. Resistance provided by the angled skis creates enough friction to slow the skier.

For prepared track skiing on gradual downhills, use of a half wedge furnishes enough friction to slow down. Pick up one ski and place it outside the track in a half wedge. Body weight remains over the flat, straight-running ski, applying pressure to the edged ski only for speed control. On steeper hills, use both skis in a full wedge. On prepared trails, use both the full and half wedge for both speed control and turning.

Mechanically, the wedge is used two ways. As with track skiing, wedging is a speed-controlling device, or what is called a "braking wedge." A braking wedge is a wide "A" position that reduces speed through width and edging. A combination of both will eventually stop the skier. Wider means slower, when it comes to wedging.

The wedge is also used as a "gliding wedge." With skis closer together in a narrower "A" it becomes easier to initiate turns. Practice both types of wedging to experience how the width of wedge and edging effect speed.

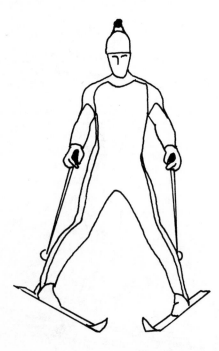

Turning is introduced without much fanfare from a gliding wedge. Once a skier has a good feel for gliding straight down the hill, he or she can begin to learn by steering or guiding the outside foot and ski in the direction of the turn. Very slight changes in direction are encouraged at first.

To add a challenge, use slalom poles or twigs stuck in the snow for skiers to negotiate in order to feel the gliding nature of turning practice on packed slopes. Smooth, soft-packed snow allows for minimal edging, so that attention may be focused on a gliding wedge. Turning is easier from a flatter ski, characteristic of the narrower gliding wedge.

Crossing tips continually is usually a result of too much edge, meaning the ankles or knees are turned excessively inward. This high degree of edge prevents the ski from being slid sideways. By maintaining a stiffer ankle and staying centered over the ski, edging decreases and more foot rotation can occur. The outer foot rotates inward, forming the turning arc (the heel is pushed out, the toe is turned inward).

The use of physically manipulative exercises helps the problem student feel the desired movements. For example, a nice safety net for the fearful student is provided if the instructor skis backward, holding a pole for the student to grasp as he skis. This technique also allows a close one-on-one wedge review. Poles held behind by the instructor and in front by the student, also help the student. The instructor can control speed and suggest improvements while the student leads the way.

Horst Abraham has a comment about skiers at this level. The relation to cross-country skiing, I think, is self-explanatory. "The beginning skier may not be very sensitive to kinesthetic experiencing; gradually though, feeling associations will become better and more sensitive. As part of the instructional or learning process, it is highly beneficial to spend time learning to sense, feeling one's extremities, sensing the pressure increases and decreases of the skis on the snow. Life today often deprives us of such practice; and it may take repeated focusing and practice to come into contact with one's physique and feelings. Take the time!"

The muscles can tire quickly in untrained skiers. Fatigue muscles lose their responsiveness and concentration wanes when working past the enjoyment stage. Be careful to maintain interest and excitement. It is better to end the lesson early rather than dragging it out in order to cover the prescribed lesson plan. There is more to skiing than hard-core learning. The instructor who can intersperse learning and fun will get far better response and student appreciation. The students should leave their lesson with a definite direction and specific goals to work toward. The lesson content, and the instructor, will have then served the students' needs, helping them toward their continuation in the sport.

ADVANCED DOWNHILL

GOALS

- Refinement of turning skills
- Rhythmically linking turns on open slopes
- Development of more skidding at end of turn with increased speed
- Employing a variety of techniques where snow conditions and terrain dictate (versatility characterizes the skier's repertoire as the skis function on all kinds of terrain)

CHOICE OF TERRAIN AND SNOW

- Gradual slopes or trails until confidence develops, then areas of increasing pitch and difficulty
- Packed smoother slopes with some trips into variable snow conditions: powder, wind pack, crust, crud, bumps, etc.

MECHANICAL DEVELOPMENTS

- Using ski displacement through stemming or stepping to initiate turning, gradually decreasing the amount of steering (wedging) in turn initiation; skidding increases
- Increasing independent leg action, intensifying the pressure on the turning ski, building to a rotary push-off from the downhill ski onto the new turning ski
- Edging sensitivity is honed to control speed and vary the radius of the turn
- As turns become smoother, body position is refined, emphasizing upper/lower body separation.
- Poles become a timing aid in turning and for body positioning.

EXERCISE EMPHASIS

- Past skills are magnified in proportion to increased speed and terrain.
- Turn initiation with a feeling of stepping from ski to ski relates to familiar movements: i.e., walking, bicycle pedaling.
- Variations in wedge size, narrow to wide, help in identifying the relationship between speed and terrain.
- Involve the student's perception in discovering the variety of turns available to accommodate the changing situations.
- As confidence grows from repeated suc-

cesses, speed will increase; turning becomes easier with more momentum.

- Visualization of proper movements comes through watching better skiers. The mental process of imagining correct body movements may facilitate learning without detailed instruction. It's helpful to imitate while practicing. The real benefits of mental visualization or imagery come with time. Start now to mentally prepare for future success.
- Employing self-talk enables rhythm and free-flowing movements to become solidified. Involve the learner with verbal cues to guide performance. Once the initial self-consciousness is overcome, talking loudly can trigger appropriate responses.
- Movement games—"standing tall," "sinking low," jumping, hopping, balancing on one ski—emphasize the dynamic nature of turns rather than static positions. Departures back to previous skill practice are valuable.
- Continue to practice pressure and edging. Experimenting with more edge engagement at turn finish combined with a pressure buildup, creating a rebound effect into the next turn.
- Experiment with different body positions while turning as a function of terrain changes and pole use.
- Pole plants become a functional means for turning and fully employing the skis as tools. Incorporation of the pole plant helps time turn imitation and develops forces in the turning arch, such as pressure and edging.
- Skiing steeper terrain or different types of snow allows discovery of related changes in turning technique. Exchange information following runs, asking questions such as, "What's happening in the turn? Where's the weight, fore, aft, etc.?" or "Are you moving during the turn or staying fairly static?" Questions like these keep the lines of communication open.
- Fear can be dealt with through communication. Talking out what causes tension is the first step toward dealing with the fear. Awareness of what causes the fear is more valuable than dealing with the symptom.

EXERCISES TO IMPROVE TURNING

. . . Begin to point your skis straighter down the hill and feel the speed build as turning is executed from a narrow "A" position (wedge) . . .

. . . Ski a run without poles. Let the arms move as they will . . .

. . . Now vary the size of your turns: long and smooth, short and quick . . .

. . . Move across the hill with skis parallel. Is the uphill ski light? Can you pick it up? . . .

. . . Push out into a wedge position. Turn and bring the skis parallel again . . .

. . . Standing on the hill, let's flatten the skis and see if they will slide sideways . . .

. . . Try a little hop and then slide down and forward to a stop. Switch sides . . .

. . . Make turns by stepping with greater commitment to the outside ski. Feel that you step from the outside ski to outside ski with all your weight . . .

. . . Let's make turns to your favorite song. Bounce to the beat—1, 2, and 3, 4—1, 2, and 3, 4 . . .

. . . Try to feel the skis slip sideways at the end of each turn . . .

SPEED CONTROL

. . . Ski a steeper slope; use the side step to control speed . . .

. . . Finish each turn by digging in the edges more . . .

. . . Ski down like a big, tough gorilla—then like a fleet-footed gazelle . . .

. . . Come to an abrupt stop, like a hockey player does to check his opponent . . .

. . . .See if you can stop fast and throw some snow in the air . . .

DEVELOPING REBOUND

. . . Ski down making quick, sharp turns in the snow. Feel pressure build by the turn's end . . .

. . . Let this feeling develop a bounce into the next turn—a kind of rebound effect to initiate turns . . .

. . . Now smooth out the movement, but feel a certain lightness at the start of the turn . . .

. . . Try a series of short, quick turns moving into longer radius turns by the bottom .. . .

EXERCISES TO IMPROVE EDGING AND BALANCE

. . . Step turn uphill while moving across the slope . . .

. . . Using small, quick steps, turn all the way around, then again the other way . . .

. . . Let's skate into the turns: skate, skate, skate, turn; skate, skate, skate, turn. Does speed increase? Decrease? . . .

. . . On a gradual slope, maintain a wedge straight downhill and walk from ski to ski, like a sand crab walking sideways . . .

. . . In powder, try a series of step turns. Try tails together, tips together, and combined. Which type of step works best? . . .

EXERCISES FOR BODY POSITION

. . . Make turns with your body square to the skis, following your direction of travel . . .

. . . Now turn quickly and face the upper body downhill . . .

. . . Try to point your hands downhill as you turn, as if they are six-shooters and you are fending off a barrage of man-eating tigers . . .

. . . Begin turns by touching the pole basket to the snow and turning around it . . .

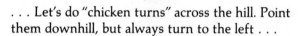
. . . Now tap the pole briefly and turn . . .

. . . Now use the pole plant in coordination with your bounce or "up" movement to initiate turns . . .

EXERCISES FOR LEARNING THE TELEMARK TURN

. . . On the flat, let's sink into this position. One ski moves forward, one back. Then switch . . .

. . . As you move into the telemark position, does the rear heel come off the ski? If not, let's bend lower like this . . .

. . . Try to feel your body weight equally between both feet . . .

. . . Now let's switch skis in the position as you stand up. Now stay low and switch . . .

. . . Jump and land in the position, like a ski jumper . . .

. . . Let's ski using our diagonal stride, but move slowly, dropping into the telemark position on each stride . . .

. . . Where do you feel your weight in the position? Front foot? Back foot? Equal? . . .

. . . Let's go to a gradual hill and try moving into the position on the run . . .

. . . Let's try a run, changing ski positions straight down the hill . . .

. . . Try holding the position while moving across the hill . . .

EXERCISES FOR BEGINNING TURNS

. . . From a straight run on a gradual slope, move one ski out into a half wedge; then let it run in parallel. Try the other side. Weight is mainly on the straight running ski . . .

. . . Let's try the same thing, except now apply slightly more weight to the wedged ski. Let's call this "pressuring the ski." What happens? Did you turn? . . .

. . . Make a series of linked half-wedge turns . . .

. . . Try turning with your weight on the inside ski throughout . . .

. . . Let's do "chicken turns" across the hill. Point them downhill, but always turn to the left . . .

. . . Now let's start the turn with a half wedge, but finish in the telemark position . . .

. . . Make some large, rounded turns like a big "S" in the snow . . .

. . . Add more speed, steeper slopes . . .

. . . Step into the turn with the forward ski . . .

. . . If you feel aggressive, fly into the turn with a skating step . . .

EXERCISES FOR IMPROVING TURNS

. . . From a straight run, sink into the telemark position, turning slightly by pushing the front heel out; then switch lead skis and repeat . . .

. . . Ski to a count of 3, then turn. Keep the rhythm going. 1, 2, 3, schuss; 1, 2, 3, schuss . . .

. . . Turn by pressuring the front ski throughout. Now pressure the back ski in the turn. Then put equal pressure on both skis. Which feels best? . . .

. . . Follow the leader, making the same kinds of turns. Try some synchronized turns. Some figure eights . . .

. . . Watch a better skier. What is he doing differently? Try to ski like that . . .

. . . Try an excursion through the powder; over bumps. What's the difference? . . .

IMPROVING SPEED CONTROL
AND EDGING

. . . Come to an abrupt stop and spray some snow with both skis . . .

. . . As you turn more aggressively, think of your big toe and little toe in relation to the edge. Feel the downhill ski with your big toe, your uphill ski with your little toe. Now feel the pressure build on the turn equally on your big toe and little toe . . .

. . . At the finish of the turn, point the outside knee toward the hill . . .

. . . Do some "tele-two-steps," complete steps over from downhill ski to downhill ski . . .

. . . Try some turns with early lead changes. Before the skis move across the hill, change to the new lead ski. Make it a continuous movement, never holding a static position . . .

. . . Try a "monomark." Is it animal, vegetable, or mineral? . . .

. . . Face the upper body downhill and let the feet swing to each side . . .

. . . Plant the pole forward and downhill of the feet. Turn around it.

THE MECHANICS

Once skiers have reached this level, the whole spectrum of cross-country skills is available. When and where the different techniques can assist depends on the individual's preferences. The type of equipment used is a big factor in realizing the full usefulness of pressure, turning, and edging. Cross-country skiers who want to advance through the entire realm of available techniques can become immersed in the functioning side cut of metal-edge skis, allowing the opportunity for constant expansion of skills. I have found that it is the variety of choices in cross-country skiing that makes the sport so intriguing. You can teach someone how to wedge and control speed on small downhills and the world opens up for them. Now they can enjoy the more elaborate trails at touring centers and feel very comfortable.

The relation of individual goals to skiing advancement becomes evident. Many skiers have learned to move and turn on the flat and feel at home on most all terrain. Their development has progressed far enough to enjoy the touring trails at the local center or city park. If you feel this way, I encourage you to continue skiing before reading further. Come back and read this section when you discover a need for new ways of turning. Then you'll be able to assimilate the knowledge.

On the other hand, if track skiing has broadened your horizons and you are looking for a new challenge, these advanced downhill skills allow you to explore the full potential of cross-country equipment. No slope is too steep, no snow too deep for the adventurous cross-country skier. People on polar expeditions and Himalayan mountain climbs use cross-country skis because of their versatility and mobility. They are ideal for all-terrain use.

Side-slipping is a skill that controls the amount of edging used to stop lateral movement. In order to stand on a hill without slipping, a skier turns his edges into the hill. Flatten the ski, and bingo—you'll move sideways. Dig the edges in and come to a stop. The edge angle and amount of pressure (weight) applied to the downhill ski determine how fast the skis stop sliding.

You can flatten the skis in two ways: (1) turn the knees and ankles downhill, or (2) suddenly stand tall. To feel balanced while slipping sideways, your upper body moves downhill as if you were walking down a snow-packed sidewalk or steep rock face and trying to stay upright. You don't lean uphill, as that takes pressure off your feet and whoops, down you go. But to maintain pressure on the feet, the upper body needs to move downhill, contrary to our survival instinct of moving toward the closest piece of ground.

The concept is called angulation. The position is relative only to a moving turn. Its changing nature helps maintain speed and fulfill the necessary edging to follow the arc of the turn. Just like our friend walking down a slippery hill, to create more pressure and to prevent slipping, the upper body needs to project farther downhill.

What is happening from the waist down to control slipping? The hips, knees, and ankles act independently or in concert to control the turning arc. The ankles are closest to the ski and at slow speeds are easily employed to give a flat or an edged ski. Stand on a hill and feel the effects of moving just the ankles, left, and right. The knees, if moved laterally toward the hill or away, make a similar adjustment. On a grander scale, the hips, when moved toward the hill, will increase angulation in proportion to speed. The joints farthest from the feet contribute to side-slipping as speed and pitch increase. The larger joints provide a greater range of movement to pressure the edge. On a fairly steep, packed slope, begin a side-slip and feel how the ankles act to initiate slipping. Then the knees get involved for more edging and, with more speed and steeper terrain, the hips round out the lower body angulation. This results in a stance that will best use the pressures developed through turning, while maintaining balance—a kind of moving state of momentum in which the body moves to maintain equilibrium created by the centrifugal forces of a turn. A position of balance is found between the inherent tendencies to lean into the hill and the pull of gravity. Turning at this level uses side-slipping skills and body angulation. The turning forces that develop contribute to such a body position, controlling turn radius and its resulting pressure.

STEM TURN

Once speed control and turning are mastered, a logical step to improve turning is to match the skis at the end of the turn. Stemming is the movement of the skis from a parallel position into a wedge. The most frequently used type of stem is to slide the uphill ski out, forming a wedge. The downhill ski provides a firm platform upon which to balance as the other ski is moved. A "down stem"—pushing out the downhill ski into a wedge—will create pressure on the stemmed ski, facilitating a rebound into the next turn. The stem can take the form of a step up and out or a smooth, sliding motion, although snow conditions may preclude the sliding stem.

I've seen many a student use this turn as a helpful means to reach the bottom, especially on slopes or tours where there is no other way down and snow conditions make other turns difficult. A long, gradual traverse across the hill, linked with a wedge turn, is a safe way down for tour skiers carrying heavy packs.

The skills involved in the stem turn relate to edging, body position, and foot steering. When traversing across the slope, the downhill edge holds the ski firm. The edged ski runs straight and leaves a clean edge line behind. Depending on side cut, the ski will run straight when placed on edge or will turn ever so slightly uphill. The more

side cut, the more turning capability inherent in the ski. Maintaining a set edge on the downhill ski is obtained by the three joints referred to in the side-slip exercises: ankles, knees, and hips.

An uphill stem from a set downhill edged ski allows movement from one ski to the other and can develop into a stronger push-off to begin the turn. A push-off may develop without much fanfare. As turning forces increase, the pressure is released by a rotary push-off into the new turn. When snow conditions are smooth and packed, a more dynamic push-off and step into the new turn may result.

To initiate the turn, the body is lowered by a knee bend, balancing on the downhill ski. The upper body stays fairly straight, shoulders rounded, arms held forward and to the side.

When forming a wedge position, the feet steer the skis. This type of steering helps determine the turn radius and controls speed. Once the wedge or "A" position is pointing downhill, the outside foot controls the arc of turn. A strong pivoting of the foot, turning the ski across the hill, causes slowing. With less foot steering, the turning arc is longer. The radius of turn is regulated by pivoting the foot, turning the toes in, and pushing the heels out.

STEM CHRISTIE

Increased speeds and turn initiation from a narrow wedge may spontaneously end in a skidded turn. The sensation has been felt while side-slipping and, when combined with speed and stronger foot steering, momentum releases the skis into a skid.

The rhythmic linking of turns to a count or a song adds the bounce (knee flex and extension) necessary to push off a set downhill edge and steer the new ski into the turn—a more dynamic turn than the stem turn. Vertical motions, to be effective, need a balanced base of support. At this stage, the wedge is used to begin turning, establishing a balanced stance prior to turning and bringing skis together. Initiating the turn early by twisting the torso results in frustration and falling inside of the turn. Practice what is known as "patient turns"—a conscious pause before turning until the skis are pointing straight downhill in the wedge. Then the new turning ski (downhill) is pressured and steered in the new direction.

The stem christie is the student's first introduction to a skidded turn. Terrain and snow conditions contribute to success. Learning on smooth, packed slopes where skidding is encouraged allows the edge release (flattening) to move the skier into skidding. Turning starts to take on new meaning and elation. Efficiency is enhanced, releasing the skier from constant wedging. The ease at which a turn develops is less taxing on the muscles and the skis function as the tools they are made to be.

The term "christie" denotes the skid or sideways movement of the skis at the completion of the turn. The name christie is a reference to Christiana, Norway, where the early ski pioneers developed the first such turns.

The stem christie is initiated with a step, or stem, into a wedge. As the skis reach the fall line, however, the greater amount of steering coupled with increased speed creates skidding or a lateral movement of both skis as they match and come together. The use of a forceful "up-unweighting," or what has already been labeled a rotary push-off, will help to release the edges and allow skidding to begin. Lowering the body in the wedge and the sudden upward extension lighten the skis for an instant. At the height of the up motion, the feet are pivoted into the new turn. With stiffer-cambered skis, this up-unweighting is crucial to edge release and the resulting skid. A softer-cambered mountain ski may require a less pronounced unweighting, but it is still necessary for turning the skis. The more subtle knee and ankle movements used to change edges and to flatten the skis are felt more easily on soft-cambered skis.

As skill develops, body weight is transferred to the downhill (outside) ski more confidently. The commitment to standing on the new turning ski will develop into an ability to increase edge angle and pressure to control the turning arc and speed. Body angulation (as referred to in the side-slip) will facilitate balance and affect the amount of edge and pressure required for control.

Practice in a stationary position. Stem into a wedge while flexing the knees, then extend by pushing off, transferring weight to the stemmed ski and allowing the matching to occur. The idea of bouncing through the turns will combine rhythmic movements to help solidify turning forces. Once a series of linked turns is completed, try turning less and following a straighter line down the hill. At the bottom, see if you can turn both skis together.

PARALLEL CHRISTIE

Parallel christies develop naturally in skiers assuming a basically fall-line run, initiating their turns with less of a stem and a simultaneous ski rotation. The need for a strong, quick leg extension creates the split-second position when the skis are lightly touching the snow and foot steering takes over, turning the skis into a parallel skid.

Beginning with short radius turns is the easiest approach, assuming skills have developed sufficiently. If the skier doesn't feel comfortable at higher speeds, rather than initiating turns with feet locked together, an open stance allows greater mobility. The muscles are freed to act independently, and both edges are involved sooner in the turn. Balance and stability are facilitated from a wider stance. Reaction time is quickened, permitting adaptation to sudden changes in snow conditions or terrain with greater lateral mobility.

Parallel christies are great turns for packed slopes or deep powder. No matter what the snow condition, the well-balanced parallel turn is a stable, functional turn. However, when terrain or snow conditions abruptly change, the feet-together stance does not provide much fore and aft support and the parallel is quick to give way to the more stable scissored or telemark stance.

POLE IMPORTANCE

"I get by with a little help from my friends."

The Beatles

Poles are very functional tools for the cross-country skier on the flat and uphills. They provide less propulsion, but help in other respects when skiing downhill. Poles may, at times, seem to be a detriment to learning downhill skills. I've seen many skiers practicing their turns only to be disrupted by planting a pole and tripping over it. Learning entirely without poles would make the uphill climbs tough, though. To avoid this potential problem, try grabbing the pole shaft in the middle. This will help you avoid unnecessarily jabbing your poles in the snow for balance and will keep them out of the way. And they will still be available for the climb back uphill.

When skiing downhill on prepared tracks, the poles take on a different meaning. Their use is a matter of security; like stabilizers on a plane, they help to sustain balance. They are held to the side, pointing behind at high speeds, or used for a ski pole check at slower speeds. For back country tourers, the poles add even more to skiing technique. Depending upon snow conditions, poles are used for braking and balance. In deep powder or on icy slopes, they are used like a symphony conductor's baton, swinging and directing movements, supporting the brief moments of imbalance. They can also be used as outriggers, dragged on the snow for added support (pole drag)—not the prettiest of techniques, but if adverse conditions exist, I've seen some of the best skiers rely on their dragging pole baskets for stability.

For packed-slope skiing, the longer cross-country poles may be exchanged for poles of a shorter, more manageable length. This is particularly crucial for lift-riding skiers at alpine areas. The shorter poles allow more favorable body positions; hands and arms stay lower. But climbing and flat skiing are definitely limited using short poles.

Pole drag

For those skiers who are interested in the coordination of pole plants in relation to linked downhill turns, read on. The pole plant is used as a turning device to signal an edge change and the initiation of a new turn. The pole is planted forward and downhill of the feet. At slow speeds, the pole plant goes in at the finish of one turn,

signaling the start of another, sometimes triggering the up-unweighting motions of the stem christie. At higher speeds during long-radius turns, the pole is used less vigorously. It is merely touched to the snow prior to the turn, in an effort to orient the body.

Develop the correct timing by saying aloud "plant-turn" in coordination with your movements. At the completion of one turn, say "plant" as the pole goes in, say "turn" as the skis start turning around the pole. The relationship between the pole plant and body position is important. Using short-radius turns as an example, when the pole is planted forward and downhill of the feet, the body assumes an "anticipatory" position, like a twisted rubber band, which, when released, will quickly unwind. The skier is creating this wind-up and release. The muscles are stretched and then contracted. The pole plant comes in as a signal to release the wound-up forces. Planting the pole acts as a momentary stabilizer from which to project into the new turn.

TELEMARK TURNS

". . . As those move easiest who have learned to dance . . ."

Alexander Pope

The essence of cross-country skiing is captured in the graceful beauty of the telemark turn. With the advent of alpine skiing and the tied-down heel the telemark was lost to the media, but not to a few diehards who have always used this very functional turn. The oldest turn, the telemark was named for one of the eighteen provinces in Norway and was developed by the innovative Norwegian ski enthusiast, Sondre Norheim. He invented a binding that added more control over the long skis. He was then able to actually determine the arc of the turn by trailing one leg behind and steering with the leading foot. The telemark was originally used for stability on uneven terrain and in powder. The separation of the feet and a lowered body position enable greater fore and aft support while turning, providing a much broader base of support.

Not only has the telemark been useful in deep powder, but it has seen a revival on the packed slopes of alpine areas. Equipment improvements have contributed to this. Its popularity is growing as skis and boots made specifically for telemarking afford greater regulation of pressure and edging. The turning radius can vary from short, quick turns to long, round "cruisers." The turn has even sparked its own contests. Telemark racing through slalom courses on packed slopes tests individual skills against the competition and the clock.

The turn is at home in deep powder, where ski separation adds stability and when parallel or stem christie becomes ineffective. Dropping into the telemark is sometimes a comforting feeling. For example, I was skiing with a friend down a narrow trail when, unexpectedly, we skied into a rather large dip. My first reaction was to sink into the telemark position to absorb the abrupt jolt. My friend, without thinking, froze up, brought his feet together, and skied into the dip. Once he reached the bottom, his forward momentum landed him on his face. After he picked himself up, we went back and tried the dip again. This time, instead of allowing his momemtum to throw him forward, he simply moved one foot forward and one back. The solid stance was a new form of security for him.

With practice, the position will become second nature for abrupt changes from packed snow to powder or even from snow to mud. Sven Wiik of Steamboat tells the story of skiing at his lodge in the springtime. Unknowingly, he rounded a downhill corner from a north-facing slop to a south-facing one, only to find that the spring sun had melted enough snow to expose the grass and dirt. Reacting quickly, he moved into the telemark position and stayed upright. I wouldn't suggest you try this, unless someday, somewhere, when you least expect it, you ski around a blind corner into the mud.

If skiers have progressed through the suggested lesson plan to this point, then skills necessary to do telemarks have developed sufficiently. The groundwork is complete. The new element involved in the telemark turn is learning to feel comfortable in the telemark position. Experiment on the flat, moving into the position. The knees are bent, weight is flat on the front foot and on the ball of the back foot. The front knee should be positioned directly above the arch of that foot. The back knee should be bent to form a right angle with the back heel raised off the ski. For reference, the thigh of the rear leg should form a straight line from the knee up through the upper body. Experiment with moving all body weight forward to the front foot, then to the back foot.

Now reach a comfortable compromise between both feet, where you feel in balance with the body fairly upright between both feet. Try switching the lead ski while standing up, while staying low, then while jumping up in the air. Feel that the rear foot is initiating the lead change as it moves forward.

The PSIA Nordic Demo Team has developed a progression for learning the telemark turn that incorporates a blending together of previously learned skills. This particular progression highlighted the Nordic Team's presentation at the XII Interski in Sesto, Italy, in 1983. The skill development is easily adapted from prior downhill techniques.

The turn is best learned on packed slopes of moderate pitch. The turning skills are similar to other downhill turns. Again, the new component is body positioning—new, in that the feet are separated, unlike the previous downhill skiing we've covered. The telemark turn takes advantage of loose heels. Becoming accustomed to weighting both feet equally takes practice. Give yourself time to strengthen the necessary thigh muscles. One difficulty I faced in learning the telemark turn was in feeling comfortable with my feet separated and equally weighted. It was only through practice and repeated attempts that I mastered the position.

From a straight downhill run, practice sinking into the telemark position. Hold the position momentarily, then switch lead skis like you did while practicing on the flat. Experiment with standing tall and making the switch, staying low, and even jumping into the new position while moving. Try skiing across the slope and do the same thing. Feel the edging needed to prevent side slipping.

The turn develops from the half wedge, which looks like a sliver rather than a full piece of pie. As an exercise, begin from a straight run on a gradual slope with both skis parallel. With weight over the straight running ski, stem the other ski out into a half wedge. Then let it come back parallel again. Try it to the other side, then repeat. Without turning, the exercise emphasizes maintaining body weight over the straight running ski.

Next begin to change direction by applying just enough pressure to the stemmed ski to cause a slight direction change. Try making small turns in both directions. Feel that the turn is accomplished with most of the weight on the flat inside ski.

Make a run to the bottom linking half wedge turns. Keep the turns fairly close to the fall line or the centrifugal forces tend to throw the body weight over the downhill ski. Remember, the exercise is primarily to practice weighting a flat inside ski. Keep speed down so the sensation can be fully realized. If you go too fast, the turn ends in a christie. The forces of inertia take over and you're pitched to the downhill ski.

Now, with the groundwork laid, the turn begins to take shape. Ski across the hill and begin to stem into a half wedge—but instead of moving the ski sideways, move it forward and out. Pressure the stemmed ski enough to cause a direction change and, as the skis move through

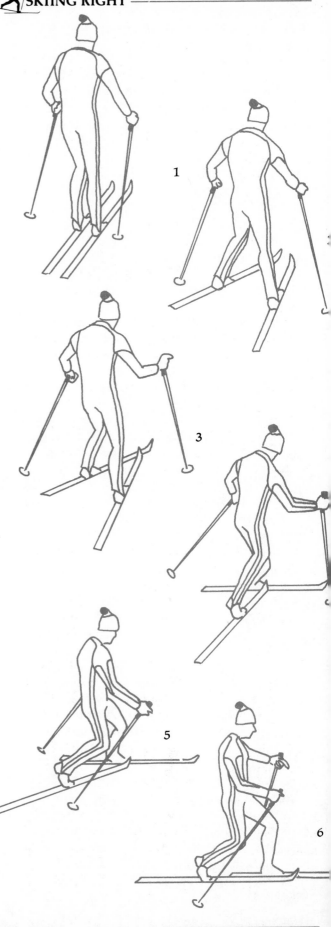

the fall line, sink into the telemark position to finish the turn. Equalize the weight between front and back feet. Continue into another turn by moving the new uphill ski forward, then push it out in front and sideways to initiate turning. The body stays low throughout the stem and ensuing telemark position, and it may straighten up only momentarily as the feet come together during the lead change.

When practicing half-wedge telemarks, emphasize keeping the weight over the inside ski and adding just enough resistance (or pressure) to the outside ski to begin the turn. Use gentle slopes at slower speeds for quality practice, where weighting both feet equally is stressed. I've found this to be a crucial feeling to develop. The tendency is to apply total weight on the lead ski, which causes overturning, where the tails slide downhill too much and you end up finishing the turn uphill. Sensing the weight on the ball of the back foot, not the toes, is vital. Review the straight-run telemark and slow half-wedge turns to reaffirm the weight commitment. Facing the upper body and hands downhill throughout the turn will help to weight the rear foot. Start with a forward-stemming, half-wedge into a telemark position. The half-wedge position provides stability and the initial direction change before the telemark position is assumed. Practice linking several turns until a good equal weight distribution is obtained.

To refine the turn, smooth out the transition between lead changes by dropping into the telemark position as the foot moves forward. With practice and speed, the stemming motion can be diminished, allowing the foot to move directly forward into the telemark. The efficiency of such fluid motions adds to the overall graceful nature of the turn.

Aside from the body mechanics of creating a turn, a more aggressive skier will combine speed, pressure, and edging to his benefit. With proper equipment—heavy, supportive high-topped boots, metal edged skis— the telemark turn becomes very dynamic. Within the confines of high-speed, medium-radius turns, the ability to edge both the front and back ski adds tremendous control. Using both uphill edges takes practice. A good focal point is to concentrate on feeling pressure on the big toe of the downhill foot and the little toe of the uphill foot. Pressure both feet equally at higher speeds and a downhill-facing upper body will definitely twist the waistline, facilitating equal pressure. The hips stay square to the skis or turn slightly inward to the slope. This type of twisting ("anticipation") stretches and contracts muscles, adding an aggressive edge set to the end of the turn and a rebound or untwisting into the next.

STEP TELEMARK

I've often used step telemarks to start turning while on tours in the back country. A case in point was an all-day tour breaking trail through a foot of new snow. All three of us had our sights on what we thought would be exquisite downhill runs from the top. After two hours of slogging through the powder, we reached the top. We flipped a coin to see who would have the honors; I won and quickly prepared to shove off. The first two turns felt great. The snow was light and turning was easy, but then it hit—wind crust from the western exposure had developed halfway down. My abrupt forward fall let the others know what to expect. From there on down, I lifted my uphill ski up and stepped it out, converging to the downhill ski. This maneuver helped start the ski turning. Then I followed through in a low telemark position. Because the snow made sliding the skis difficult, stepping into the turn was a sure way down.

A converging step is closely aligned to the half-wedge telemark, except that the ski is lifted off the snow. The advantage is an assured commitment to the new turning ski (downhill). When used in bumps, the converging step acts as a quick move into the turn. The body weight, depending on the terrain, completely moves to the forward stepped ski as the rear foot and ski are lifted and set down parallel with the front ski. This type of complete step-over telemark develops a cadence of 1, 2,—1, 2. The rhythm is helpful for quickly turning skis on steep, packed slopes or bump runs.

A separate step into the telemark can be used when accelerating into the turn. For instance, skating into the turn places the skis at divergent angles to begin with. Racers skate for speed at the start of the race and on any flat sections along the course. Stepping skis parallel to the side is also used to initiate turns. Besides racing, the parallel step is a great way to miss rocks or stumps. Just step to the side and keep going.

CONTINUOUS MOVEMENT

This idea centers around the concepts of static and dynamic motion. Like the diagonal stride, which is never static, the telemark turn can become a continuous motion.

Instead of sinking into the telemark position and holding firm throughout the turn, try speeding up the lead change to the point of starting the rear ski forward just as the skis pass the fall line. Continue the movement forward and right into the next turn. As the skis pass each other, the feet come together briefly in a momentary parallel stance. A good skier will use this fleeting position for speed control or for projecting the body into the new turn.

The movement from one turn to another is a constant flow. Apply pressure to both skis and edges equally throughout the lead change. Feel constant movement while turning, never remaining in a static position. Try it for a new sensation and feel the difference.

Analogous to the continuous movement idea is what I call the "two P's" of efficient telemarking. "Perpetual pressure" describes a continual application of pressure to both skis' uphill edges as early in the turn as possible, until the release or edge change into the new turn. One way this pressuring may be accomplished is a gradual flexing of the knees. At the finish of the turn, flatten the skis, change to the new uphill edge and slowly begin to extend the legs throughout the turn. To achieve more edge bite on harder snow to minimize skidding and maximize carving, increase the pressure over the "big toe, little toe." By starting the turn in a low, bent-knee position and extending throughout the turning arc, pressuring both skis can be increased. It is a type of down-unweighted turn, where the edge change is made at the skier's lowest point, when the pressure on the skis lessens and a new turn is started.

Practice with thoughts of rhythmic nature: turning to a song with a heavy drum beat, running a slalom course making smooth turns. This type of mental image creates the mode for more edge engagement and increased pressure.

TELEMARK POLE PLANT

Body position is a contributing element to a more edge-biting carved turn. As in the body position of parallel christies, the upper body and arms face downhill. The hands control the poles

and, at this stage, the pole is planted forward and downhill of the body, as in the parallel turn.

Emphasis should be placed on reaching downhill for the pole plant. In this way, the body mechanics counter with the lower leg, the knee in particular moving into the hill. To feel how the pole plant helps edging, practice standing on the hill and reaching downhill to plant the pole. Feel how the ankles, knees, and hips move into the hill naturally to maintain your stance. Practice linking medium-radius turns on moderate to increasingly steeper slopes. Notice the fine tuning that takes place to control speed and prevent excessive skidding. The upper body twists downhill while, from the waist down, the hips, knees, and ankles twist into the hill.

To feel how the pole plant helps edging, practice standing on the hill and reaching downhill to plant the pole. Feel how the ankles, knees, and hips move into the hill naturally to maintain your stance. Practice linking medium-radius turns on moderate to increasingly steeper slopes. Notice the fine tuning that takes place to control speed and prevent excessive skidding. The upper body twists downhill while, from waist down, the hips, knees, and ankles twist into the hill. It's a real wind-up motion, contracting and stretching the muscles involved. But, when this torque is released, it can be used to initiate another turn—like releasing a wound-up rubber band.

Skidding, however, is a necessary element of speed control in short-radius turns on steep slopes—and there is a certain amount of skidding in every turn. The performance skier, by virtue of his expanding skills, will appreciate the rounded turns created by minimal lateral ski displacement. Racers are, of course, concerned about speed, and the faster turn is one that employs more carving and less skidding. A skiddy ski is slower because its path is lateral across the hill rather than closer to the fall line. But, in actuality, there is a certain amount of skid in all turns. Learning to control that depends on individual preference and need. Back country powder skiers have little use for carving, but to the packed-slope skiers and racers intent on exploiting the telemark turn to its fullest potential, carving is a vital part of this realization.

DESCENTE STAR TEST

GO FOR THE GOLD

"The indefatigable pursuit of an unattainable perfection . . . is what alone gives a meaning to our life on this unavailing star."

Logan Pearsall Smith

How do you rate yourself as a skier? Novice? Intermediate? Advanced intermediate? Expert? Better-than-average-but-not-that great? The Professional Ski Instructors of America (PSIA) has the answer to this question in its Descente STAR Test. Patterned after a similar testing system (called Test International) that has been in use in Europe for some time, and more recently in Japan and Canada, the Descente STAR (for "Standard Rating") Test is a standardized rating system for recreational skiers to evaluate your ability. It tells you how good you are in all kinds of conditions and on all kinds of terrain.

Descente STAR Test is designed for all levels of skiers; the bonus is, no matter how good you are, Descente STAR Test can help you improve. It's a three-level evaluation; novice and intermediate skiers will want to start with the bronze level, which works on five basic

maneuvers on fairly easy trails. Once you've passed the bronze test, and won the distinctive bronze award pin, you'll want to try the silver test (more advanced maneuvers on more difficult trails), and ultimately, on to the gold.

The system works like this: You decide which of three tests you'd like to take, either novice (bronze), intermediate (silver), or advanced/expert (gold); pay a fee; and go with a specifically trained instructor/tester to a particular trail that has been designated the official Descente STAR Test trail for that level. Once there, the instructor has you perform the five basic maneuvers. The tester will rate each maneuver from 1 to 5. For the gold, a passing score is 15 points or better.

If you receive a passing score in four out of five maneuvers, you receive a pin in the appropriate color—bronze, silver, or gold. You also recieve a STAR Test passport signed by the tester, verifying your results, and you receive a scorecard with the tester's comments.

According to Mike Dolan of the PSIA, the bronze test will be "easy," the silver "moderately difficult," and the gold "very, very difficult, the highest standard." Dolan says that only about 50 skiers a year will obtain the gold pin, making it a very prestigious award.

You will be allowed to practice before taking the test on the Descente STAR Course. Modeled after the popular parcourse exercise trails found in many parks, Descente Star Course is a free guide through the various Descente STAR Test skills. At most areas, the bronze, silver, and gold trails will be marked with signs that allow you to practice the Descente STAR Test at your own pace. It's as simple as skiing from one sign to another, practicing each manuever as you go.

In fact, most participating Descente STAR Test ski schools will offer Descente STAR Clinics and Lessons, specifically designed for you to work on the basic maneuvers needed to pass Descente STAR Test. Not incidentally, these Descente STAR skills will turn out to be the technical building blocks of competent all-around skiing ability.

BRONZE TEST DESCRIPTION

1.) The candidate must adequately perform the skill to the standards set by the PSIA.

2.) The technique used must be in harmony with good sound skiing technique even though it may differ from the technique taught by PSIA.

3.) The skier must show a certain consistency in technique, along with a good basic stance and show of balance.

4.) Scoring for Bronze is: A minimum score of at least 3 on four of five events. Therefore a minimum passing Bronze score is 13.

$$4 @ 3 = 12$$
$$1 @ 1 = \underline{\ 1\ }$$
$$13$$

Scale

5 excellent
4 very good   PASS
3 satisfactory-good
....
2 unsatisfactory-fair
1 poor   FAIL

In the bronze STAR Test a skier has two chances at each skill. In all levels, a skier may take the STAR Test as many times as desired.

PERSONAL TEST RECORD

DATE	SKILL #1	SKILL #2	SKILL #3	SKILL #4	SKILL #5	TOTAL POINTS

BRONZE PROFICIENCY SKILL #1

S NOWPLOW: A technique to slow down or stop on a downhill run. Push your ski tails out like squashing a grape with your heel while keeping equal pressure on the inside edges.

BRONZE PROFICIENCY SKILL #2

STRAIGHT RUNNING: Skiing straight down a gentle hill. Look ahead and use your knees as shock absorbers. Stay loose.

BRONZE PROFICIENCY SKILL #3

HERRINGBONE: A technique used to climb relatively steep hills. Imagine walking like a duck or penguin while keeping skis in a "V" position. Keep head up.

BRONZE PROFICIENCY SKILL #4

DIAGONAL STRIDE: The fundamental Nordic technique for skiing efficiently on flat terrain. Combine the stride of jogging with the gliding grace of ice skating for a perfect diagonal stride.

BRONZE PROFICIENCY SKILL #5

UPHILL DIAGONAL STRIDE: A diagonal stride technique modified to climb hills. Use quicker strides, keeping hands low when poling. Look up the hill.

SILVER TEST DESCRIPTION

1.) The candidate must adequately perform the skill to the standards set by the PSIA.

2.) The technique used must be in harmony with good sound skiing technique even though it may differ from the technique taught by PSIA.

3.) The candidate must show stability and consistent control.

4.) Scoring for silver is: a minimum of at least 3 on four of five events. Therefore a minimum passing Silver score is 13.

$$4 @ 3 = 12$$
$$1 @ \underline{1} = \underline{1}$$
$$13$$

Scale

5 excellent
4 very good   PASS
3 satisfactory-good
....
2 unsatisfactory-fair
1 poor   FAIL

On the Silver Test, the skier *does not* get a second try on a skill; however, he may take the STAR Test as many times as desired.

PERSONAL TEST RECORD

DATE	SKILL #1	SKILL #2	SKILL #3	SKILL #4	SKILL #5	TOTAL POINTS

SILVER PROFICIENCY SKILL #1

S NOWPLOW TURN: A safe, stable technique to make a controlled turn. Keep a good "V" wedge and pressure one ski more than the other.

SILVER PROFICIENCY SKILL #2

STEP TURN: An easy way to turn a corner at slow speeds. Take small steps to the side while maintaining edging and balance.

SILVER PROFICIENCY SKILL #3

KICK TURN: A way to turn around while standing still. Plant poles behind, chorus-girl kick, pivot ski around and follow with the other one. (Caution: requires limber knees and hips.)

SILVER PROFICIENCY SKILL #4

DOUBLE POLE: A maneuver to move on flat or slight downhills using only the pole push. Hinge at the waist. Push with both poles.

SILVER PROFICIENCY SKILL #5

DIAGONAL STRIDE WITH GOOD WEIGHT TRANSFER: A way to ski efficiently on the flat. Shift the weight from one ski to the other as the feet pass one another, then continue gliding on one ski only.

GOLD TEST DESCRIPTION

The gold is the standard of success to this program. Therefore it must be worthwhile and made to be very prestigious.

1.) The candidate must adequately perform the skill proficiency events to the standards set by the PSIA.

2.) The technique used must be appropriate and efficient, in harmony with PSIA techniques. One does not simply get a Gold. He/she must be an expert and earn the Gold.

3.) The candidate must be aggressive, show skiing know-how and good skiing judgment relative to speed, terrain, and snow conditions, as well as consistent control.

4.) Scoring for the Gold is: A minimum of at least 3 *on all five events*. Therefore a minimum passing score on the Gold is 15.

5 @ 3 = 15

Scale

5 excellent
4 very good   PASS
3 satisfactory-good
. . . .
2 unsatisfactory-fair
1 poor   FAIL

PERSONAL TEST RECORD

DATE	SKILL #1	SKILL #2	SKILL #3	SKILL #4	SKILL #5	TOTAL POINTS

GOLD PROFICIENCY SKILL #1

D IAGONAL STRIDE TIMED
CORRECTLY: The key to achieving the
graceful, fluid motion of the racer.
Coordinating the sequence of poling, pushing off
from one ski, and gliding on the other ski requires
balance, timing and practice.

GOLD PROFICIENCY SKILL #2

TELEMARK TURN: The classic Nordic turn. Drop into a semi-kneeling position, and steer the front ski into the turn while edging both skis to make them curve.

GOLD PROFICIENCY SKILL #3

PARALLEL TURN: Used to turn or slow down using both skis together. Use a strong up motion to unweight the skis so they can be turned and edged together.

GOLD PROFICIENCY SKILL #4

ONE-STRIDE DOUBLE POLE:
A combination of diagonal stride and double poling. Bring both hands forward while pushing off with one leg. Then finish with a double-pole push.

GOLD PROFICIENCY SKILL #5

S KATE TURN: A way to maintain
or increase speed on a turn. Spring
off a well-edged ski onto the other one in
the new direction.

COMPETITION

HOW THE RACERS SKI

"Genius is one percent inspiration & ninety-nine percent perspiration."

Thomas Alva Edison

It's often said "to be a good racer is to be a good poet." The flowing, seemingly effortless movements of cross-country skiing transcend purely physical effort, bordering on the edge of consciousness. There have been days when I wished the track would never end and the smooth, fluid motion would never cease. But as with all good things, the feeling must end. It is that burning desire to recreate those special days that keeps me coming back.

Track skiing exudes efficiency. The equipment is light and those skinny skis—oh, how they move! I feel so complete when I slip into my one-piece stretch nylon suit, my every movement corresponding to the stretch quality of the thin nylon thermal layer. The track unfolds like a rolled-up carpet; muscle effort becomes forward momentum. My arms move forward and back, giving me a little more glide for my efforts as I move down the track. Wasted movements are eliminated as all energy is directed forward. Continuous movement, that alternating rhythm, keeps the mind free of thoughts, establishing a oneness with the track. The track, the guiding light, is the source of life-giving mental relaxation and freedom.

Racing, or what some call performance skiing, can give such an elevated feeling. Racing is nothing more than going fast on skis. If your technical skills as a recreational skier are developed, the groundwork is laid for racing. The techniques used are the same; the difference lies in the amount of effort or energy expended.

Think about how you move when you are late for a meeting or for school. You begin walking fast, maybe even moving into a little jog to quicken the pace. Notice what is actually happening. You quicken the pace (or tempo), pushing more forcefully from each foot. The body moves forward and the arms swing at the sides, in time with the legs. The faster you want to go, the more power you put into pushing off the ground. When you reach a jog, the push projects your body briefly off the ground before you land on the other foot. The arms swing forward and back in time with the legs. Momentum is maintained until you reach your goal. The same movements apply when you're learning to ski faster. Once a certain level of proficiency is reached, it seems to be human nature to want to test yourself and see how fast you can move around a marked course.

Citizen racing is the wintertime equivalent to summer fun runs. The challenge is between yourself and the course. Individual effort is rewarded by finishing, not by beating the competition. Races vary from three kilometers to fifty kilometers and are open to everyone sixteen years of age and older. The United States Ski Association (USSA) has developed different race series. Some are ten-kilometer races; others, like the Great American Ski Chase, are a series of eight 50-kilometer races spread over the entire winter. There is a class for every age group, so competition is with peers. On the whole, races are low-key events with a friendly social atmosphere. I've seen skiers sign up for a long race just to enjoy the feed stations. Citizens' racing is for the local duffer as well as the hot young star of tomorrow. The name "citizen" says it all—we *all* qualify for entry.

Some of the Colorado citizens' races have been staged for years and attract 500 to 1,000 skiers. Races like the Frisco Gold Rush, Governor's Cup, Rabbit Ears Race, Keystone Caper and the Copper Derby are just some of the many races available for testing your ability to move fast on skis. Check at your local ski shop or touring center for details of races in your area.

THAT POWERFUL KICK

In racing, the push-off becomes the "kick," the powerful push down and off the ski that functions like the main thruster on the space shuttle. The legs provide the main thrust in the diagonal stride. To a great extent, the larger leg muscles determine how fast you move. Push off (or kick) from the ski forcefully and the resulting glide carries you far down the track before another kick is needed.

The mathematical formula used by the United States Cross-Country Ski Team (Charles Dillman, 1978) for determining speed is velocity = stride length × stride rate. A stride is the complete sequence of movements beginning with a pole plant and ending with the opposite pole plant. Stride length is defined as the distance covered between one kick and the next kick. Stride rate is defined as the time taken between one kick and the next kick. The faster skier is the one who goes as far as possible with each stride while taking less time per stride.

How this formula is transferred to muscular effort constitutes efficient technique. It is the most efficient technique—with no wasted movement—that is the ideal. That is not to say that you'll always win races when your form is picture perfect. There are too many variables. Differences in body build alone allow some skiers to ski faster in spite of their technical errors. The important thing to recognize is that all of the fastest skiers have learned how to apply force effectively to allow them to go faster. Individuals vary in the way they apply that force, and so does their visual appearance. In other words, to learn by imitation alone may not be the answer. The emphasis should be on *you*, your particular body build and style. Some skiers are very strong in their upper body and arms; others may rely on their stronger leg muscles.

I remember a college racer who was short and stocky—watching him ski was a real lesson in locomotion. He would start pumping those strong, muscular legs and poling with his big arms and I'd swear there would be steam coming out the top of his hat! There was no real finesse or grace to his skiing; you always felt he'd never make it around the whole course. He seemed to be working so hard at it. But when the first skiers began to finish, there he would be, right up front. I think he skied on pure determination, but, boy, did he win! If I were to imitate his choppy, short stride, I'd tire quickly.

To learn how to ski efficiently, transferring your muscle effort into forward motion is an individual discovery. However, certain guidelines have been noted after careful analysis of the world's best racers. These skiers all display similar positions and movements that maintain their high rate of speed. Here is a closer look at those optimum techniques. How you apply these mechanics to your own skiing is a matter of style. Going fast is the ultimate equalizer.

DIAGONAL STRIDE

I f you can ski a good diagonal stride, then adding more energy into your movements will make you go faster. But here is the catch—for how long? Cross-country races are usually longer than one mile. To sustain efforts for the entire six miles (ten kilometers) or thirty-two miles (fifty kilometers) requires a minimum of wasted motion. If your upper body has a tendency to sway excessively from side to side as you ski, covering one mile may not even tire you. But continue for six miles and the extra muscle expenditure may run your energy level low. In cross-country skiing, "wasted movements" refers to any movements that do not contribute to your forward progress. In racing, wasted movements are compounded over the entire course and energy reserves are taxed unnecessarily.

If you watch good racers ski, you will notice two important visual cues: (1) they stretch out more (their leg and arm movements are more extreme) and (2) their torsos (upper body) lean forward. If you look further, you'll also notice the directness of their efforts. The arms swing parallel to the sides, the legs swing behind and forward to support the body. There is a feeling of flowing, effortless movement. What muscular effort is there is woven intrinsically into the entire stride. The untrained eye may not be able to tell where the power is originating. But power it is, and it is originating from two main thrusters—the legs and arms.

The diagonal stride is defined in three phases (courtesy of the United States Cross-Country Ski Team biomechanical research).

(1) The *kick phase* starts when the legs come together and ends when the foot lifts off the snow.

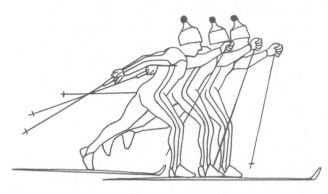

(2) The *free glide phase* starts at lift-off and ends when the pole is planted.

(3) The *poling phase* starts at the pole plant and ends when the legs come back together.

Breaking the stride down into these distinct phases will simplify our discussion and focus attention on our power sources.

THE KICK

T he kick is the primary mover. Without an explosive kick, momentum is thwarted and the resulting glide is squelched. In no other phase of the diagonal is there such powerful acceleration. The poling phase maintains speed and the glide phase loses speed. The kick needs to be quick and explosive to generate speed in the first place. I can still recall the fifty-kilometer race when I was skiing behind a member of the United States team, trying to imitate his motions and timing. I noticed the tremendous glide he had for each kick. He was kicking fewer times per minute and was gliding farther on each kick. It didn't take long before he was out of sight. In a fifty-kilometer race, the savings in energy didn't hurt, either. I realized then that it was the quick, powerful kick that helped him glide farther.

The timing of the kick occurs when all the weight is on the kicking ski. The body is in a forward-leaning position with the hips over the balls of the feet. Thighs are vertical at the moment of kick. The kicking foot is flat on the ski; legs are flexed so when the kick occurs, the body is projected forward.

A flexed leg has better potential for power. Think of jumping straight up in the air as high as you can, like you would to stuff a basketball through the hoop. Would you jump from straight legs, from a slightly bent position, or would you really get low and spring like a cat? I think you would agree there is power in bent (flexed) legs.

As the kicking leg extends to the rear, the leg should line up straight with the rest of the body. By keeping the whole foot on the ski during the kick, it helps pressure the ski flat to the snow and prevents kicking backwards too much, which can cause you to slip. This is sometimes called a "late kick." When your skis are slipping, try the whole foot idea. It may just give you the hold you need without adding more wax. Technique and waxing go hand in hand; you can't have one without the other. It is often said, "put an instructor on any ski and he'll make it work." A better skier can adapt his technique to fit the ski and wax he is using.

At the end of the kick phase, the rear leg is extended. The front, or gliding leg supports the body. The forward knee and ankle remain flexed, maintaining a constant angle to help balance and prepare for the next kick. As the skier glides, the weight moves from the heel to the ball of the foot in preparation for the next kick. Better skiers will slide the forward foot ahead of the knee to maximize glide, taking the pressure off the grip wax momentarily, like the way a racer in a tuck rocks back on his heels to reduce pressure on the grip wax, facilitating speed.

GLIDE PHASE

During the free glide phase, all weight is transferred to the forward gliding leg. At this point (which is actually a very momentary position), the forward foot is ahead of the knee with the weight on the heel to maximize glide. When gliding, more than fifty percent of your weight should be on your heel, with the balance distributed over the rest of your foot. Weight transfer (or weight shift) is important to good glide. Rather than a side-to-side movement of the upper body, a weight transfer is made through a forward movement of the hips and upper body moving down the track. The knee angle remains constant when the leg comes

through, holding rigid in a flexed position during the glide.

Any excessive movement while gliding will absorb energy and slow the glide. For instance, pushing the knee forward puts weight on the front part of the ski, pressuring the grip wax and slowing the ski. The glide is the only time in the diagonal stride when there are no forces acting to accelerate, so try to avoid excessive body movements that will defuse the glide. Except for the arm swinging forward in preparation for the pole plant, there is little other bending or flexing.

POLING PHASE

The glide phase ends when the pole is planted. The pole should go in ahead of the gliding foot when moving fast, somewhat closer to the gliding foot at slower speeds, and even behind the gliding foot on uphills. The exact pole plant location varies with speed, but it should be as far forward as strength and pole length allow. Better skiers plant the pole immediately after the kick and before the trailing leg has begun to swing forward. Pressure is applied to the pole strap to help maintain momentum on the gliding ski for as long as possible before a decrease in acceleration. The poling arm should be advanced near the body when the feet come together. The trailing leg may start to move forward before the pole is planted, but this is usually a natural relaxation, not a forceful swing.

As the arm swings forward to plant the pole, the upper body or torso may rise slightly. This is a natural movement and does help initiate poling with the larger muscle groups of the stomach, shoulder, and back, before the smaller arm muscles take over.

The pole is planted with a flexed elbow. The angle is maintained as power is initially applied, but the arm is totally extended as the hand passes the hips. As the pole is planted, the pull is first down toward the knees, then a push-off as the arm extends to the rear. The importance of fully utilizing the poles is evident in stride lengths. Better skiers have a longer stride length, partly because they are kicking quickly and explosively, but also because they maintain this momentum into the poling phase with a strong use of the arms and poles.

Poles supply almost forty percent of some racers' power. That's a high percentage; have you been neglecting this critical area for increasing speed? The poles play a major part in the more proficient skier's technique, helping keep the gliding ski moving a little farther on each stride.

In order to transmit this power from the arms into forward motion, the body must be held rigid. Once the pole is planted, the arm angle must remain the same while power is initially applied. The arm extends only as the hand passes the hip, and ultimately straightens behind.

When the poling hand moves down near the knees, the legs should be moving together as another kick is occurring. The poling will even continue into the kick phase of better skiers. They use it to get just that little bit of extra push.

L earning to ski efficiently is a result of continued practice, and a good diagonal stride will continue through all other aspects of cross-country technique. Knowing how to walk or run are similar movements, but their application to skiing takes precise timing and balance. Kicking from one ski when all the body weight is over it is different than walking on firm pavement. The ability to balance over a gliding ski involves a dynamic equilibrium unfamiliar to walking or running. The coordination of arms and legs is altered slightly to maintain proper timing.

Some skiers may have a tendency to ski with their backs too straight, an unnaturally tense position. A more comfortable position is to stand with a relaxed, slightly rounded back. A forward-leaning attitude aids balance and keeps the hips a bit farther forward of the center of gravity during the kick phase.

When skiing, the arms and legs should swing forward, taking advantage of the relaxed pendulum action of an object in motion. The laws of physics tell us that an object in motion will continue in motion unless acted upon by an external or internal force. The rhythmic nature of the diagonal stride lends itself well to continuous motion. The self-perpetual nature of flat skiing is obvious to performance skiers.

As the arms and legs move forward, the relaxed, easy swing should not be interrupted by lifting the limb. Use this time to release muscle tension and allow the muscle tissue to experience (ever so briefly) a moment of unrestricted blood flow that permeates the excess buildup of any lactic acid (a physiological trait of constant muscle tension without normal blood circulation). A good cross-country skier takes advantage of the forward swing to relax. If you haven't ever focused attention on this brief phase of the total stride, try to think about relaxing as the arm and leg swing forward. The benefits may surprise you.

The power of the diagonal on the flat is enhanced by fully extending the poling arm and kicking leg to the rear. At the end of the pushing phase (either of the arm or leg), everything should be extended in a straight line. The upper body and rear leg should line up straight without a bent leg or cocked elbow. To practice, try slowing the stride and exaggerating the leg extension and arm push so that the knee and elbow joints open, fully utilizing the entire range of movement.

T iming is relative to when the kick occurs. The exact timing must be such that the body weight is centered over the kicking ski..This allows maximum pressure on the ski for wax grip. The term "late kick" means that the skier is kicking *after* the body weight has moved ahead of the kicking foot. Therefore, not enough pressure is being applied to make the grip wax stick. Because the skier's weight is too far forward, the body weight has already been moved to the new forward ski before the kick has occurred. The kicking force tends to be backward rather than down. The hips drop back instead of moving forward and the power of the kick is lost. A self-test you can use to determine if your timing and balance are correct is auditory. If you can hear the tail of the rear ski slap the snow after each kick, it means your timing is off and your body weight back. The tail slaps because the hips are back. The body needs to be forward, balanced over the gliding ski. The timing is correct when the kick starts before the feet come together and force the ski down into the snow rather than backwards. The rear ski should swing forward and meet the snow with a "swoosh" and long glide.

The scooter exercise is a good way to really feel the exact timing. Without poles, place both hands on your right knee. That ski will act as your wheels. Scoot along the track using your left ski to push. The push from the scooting foot must be timed so that all the body weight is over the scooting foot. Short quick scoots (pushes) will move you better than longer ones. Be sure and switch legs as you practice, and if you're moving well along the flat, try a gradual uphill. This is the best exercise I've seen for developing proper timing. You must have it to move.

DOUBLE POLE WITH AND WITHOUT A KICK

The double-poling techniques are used whenever speeds are too fast for effective diagonal striding. Double poling means, simply, using both poles simultaneously for propulsion or combining the power of a kick with a double pole push. The technique is particularly useful on gradual downhill sections of track that are too fast for the diagonal and too slow for a low, aerodynamic tuck.

The decision to double pole is usually based on velocity, not necessarily on terrain. A strong skier may be moving fast enough to use double poling effectively on flat trails, whereas a slower, less skilled skier may still be using the diagonal stride. If grip wax is worn off, double poling might be the only alternative for propulsion—although it won't win races, unless the skier is very strong in his upper body. Bill Koch (U. S. Cross-Country Team member) set a record for skiing fifty kilometers in one hour and fifty-nine minutes on a flat course with little kick wax, mostly skating and double poling the entire distance. As equipment and waxing are refined, skis become speed machines to carry racers who best transfer their muscular energy to them. Today, racers even use the double pole with a kick up gradual hills.

As your skill at double poling improves, where you once used a diagonal stride, you'll now kick double pole. It is only natural to get from the start to finish as fast as possible. When the diagonal doesn't move you any faster, it's time to change to double poling. When and where this transition takes place varies according to wax, strength and proficiency. Watch the better skiers and notice how smoothly they make the transition from diagonal stride to double pole. Notice how the poling is altered slightly as one pole misses a beat, staying forward, waiting until the other pole and hand are forward, then moving into a double pole plant. The same hesitation with one pole is used when switching back to diagonal skiing. This move from one technique to another, or "change-up," is made with such a flowing, effortless flair that rhythm is continuous, momentum sustained.

Practice changing from diagonal stride to double pole on flat terrain. Move slowly at first, trying to develop a feeling of continuous movement. Experiment with a slight hesitation with one arm and pole, before the double pole. The legs continue kicking until the arms are ready. Find a particular section of track where you can repeat this "change-up" again and again. Remember: continuous movement will maintain momentum during transitions.

DOUBLE POLE WITH A KICK

The skills involved in the double pole with a kick (or, as some racers call it, the kick double pole) are similar to those used in the diagonal technique. The kick from one foot is combined with a double pole push.

At the initiation of the kick, the feet are together, weight forward, hips over the feet. At faster speeds the forward lean is greater. Arms and poles begin to swing forward at the kick, in preparation for the double pole push.

For greater speed, the power will come from the kick, accomplished by kicking with a flexed leg where leg extension, combined with a forward-reaching arm movement, project the skier forward. The upper body then collapses over rigid arms to begin the poling: first a pull down then, as the hands pass the hips, an extension to the rear. The upper body bends at the waist to help supply power to the poling motion. Rather than just standing erect and using only the arms, the forward hinging of the upper body at the waist contributes additional power to the poling forces.

The upper body moves down to a point where body weight is no longer contributing to pole push. This should be somewhere above a horizontal position (90°). Any more bend is a tiring, wasted movement. Poles are planted as far forward as strength will allow and, depending on speed, angled for immediate use.

At the termination of the kick phase, the rear leg is extended and all body weight is on the forward or gliding ski. At this time, the poles should have been planted and power applied in an attempt to keep the gliding ski moving as long as possible before another kick. Remember, it is these extra inches of glide (stride length) that determine the winners. Milk the glide for as much as you can get.

As the rear leg swings forward, the poles are finishing their push to the rear. The skier moves into a period of free glide with feet together or slightly apart. To create the best possible gliding situation, the feet should precede the hips, with weight back on the heels, reducing pressure on the grip wax. During the free glide, body motions are minimized to facilitate forward momentum. The knee angle should stay rigid, only beginning slightly before the kick to load the muscles for a powerful kick.

The arm recovery forward begins as speed lessens and another kick is needed to maintain momentum. The hands should again be at their lowest point while the kick is occurring to contribute their downward momentum into the kick force. Then, as the arms swing forward, the upper body rises to a forward-leaning position (not vertical) to accommodate poling.

DOUBLE POLE

As speed increases or technique improves, the double pole with a kick will seem useless. At this point, the kick is eliminated and the poling is continued. The straight double pole technique is the fastest available to the cross-country skier. When speed is such that momentum can be maintained with just the poles, the legs take a rest and the upper body does the work. This is why training the upper body has taken on such importance in racing. It is easy to see why the stronger racers do well at double poling and why some racers double pole on sections of trail while others must continue the diagonal stride and then double pole longer before changing back to diagonal.

As both poles are planted at an angle, the body is in a forward-leaning position. Pressure is applied immediately, keeping a rigid arm angle. The angle between the upper and lower arm should remain constant during the initial phase of poling to better transmit muscular force to the ski. As the hand passes the hip, the arms are extended straight. The knees are slightly flexed and remain so throughout the poling motion, keeping extra movements to a minimum.

At the completion of the poling phase, when arms are extended to the rear, the feet should precede the hips, weight on the heels. To keep the rhythm going, the arms swing forward in a straight pendulum motion. The body weight moves toward the ball of each foot as the arms reach forward as far as strength will allow for another double pole push. For added body extension forward to help with poling, one leg can act as a counterbalance by moving slightly backward at the moment the arms are extended forward.

Without the legs, it's the upper body and arms that do all the work. To make full use of the upper body muscles, you need strong abdominal muscles to supply the initial power. To get the feeling of how the stomach muscles help, try using only one pole.

Stand in place and hold your free hand on your stomach. Keeping a rigid arm angle, begin to apply force to the pole. You should feel the abdominal muscles tense up. The shoulder and larger back muscles continue the power until the smaller arm muscles (the triceps and wrist) finish with the push behind.

At the completion of the poling phase, the back is slightly above horizontal. The effective use of the body in poling has expired. Any more downward movement is just extra work. The head should be up, eyes focused down the track in anticipation of upcoming terrain changes and other skiers.

Without a kick, the double pole is only useful if speed can be maintained with the arms only. Sensing when to add a kick to the double pole or when to change back to diagonal is an individual decision. Better skiers won't really make a conscious choice, but will automatically change back and forth as required, to hit their optimum speed.

REVIEW

When double poling becomes ineffective, it may be because of excessive squatting (bending the knees) while poling. The extra work for the legs is tiring and the bending doesn't help you go forward.

Bending the arms too much when applying power to the poles is also a loss of potential energy. The power is lost by not holding a rigid arm and pushing toward the knees. The idea is to transfer muscle energy to the ski through the poles.

Some skiers extend their arms too high in front, as if they are going to stab something when they plant their poles. Again, this is wasted motion and is time consuming. Move the arms and poles forward just enough to get the pole planted at an angle; then begin to supply power.

Practice the double pole on terrain where maintaining momentum is not a problem. You will not have to muscle your way through, but will actually be able to feel your efforts working. If the opportunity presents itself, hop in behind a faster skier. Watch his moves and try to determine what you might do differently to stay with him. And by all means, don't give up. It might not be your day; give your technique time to mature. The road to better skiing is a process. It doesn't happen all at once, but is slowly realized through constant practice and attention to detail. Usually when recreational skiers begin to think about going fast, improvements come quickly. Then a plateau is reached and it may seem like little, if any, progress is being made. At this point it may be time to get together with a professional instructor or coach for some constructive feedback about technique. Lessons aren't just for beginners; they should continue at all levels. To get off that plateau, keep the professional instructor in mind next time you have questions about your technique.

UPHILLS

"Races are won or lost on the uphills." This often-heard statement reflects the value of negotiating hills effectively and powerfully. The proper technique for skiing up hills is just as varied as the many different types of hills. Skiing from flat to uphill sections of trail should be viewed as an opportunity to gain, not lose, time.

Efficient technique on the uphills is a continuation of flat technique, with modifications. Better skiers maintain their normal flat technique on uphills as far as possible. Even as the hill gets steep, they try to maintain a long stride. Dr. Charles Dillman found stride length to be the most influential factor in increased speed in the U.S. Ski Team sports medicine program, 1980. He said after film analysis at the 1980 pre-Olympic competition, "The stride rate of the American racers studied was equal to that of the top Europeans who were filmed, but their stride length was shorter. This conclusion with stride length confirmed an earlier German biomechanical study, which showed that better citizens racers in Europe had stride rates which were equal to those of top international skiers, but their stride lengths were considerably shorter."

The arms play a big role in keeping the gliding ski moving. The pole is planted further behind, and force is applied immediately, pulling down, and then pushing off. Arm strength is crucial if one is to fully benefit from proper poling. Practice skiing hills with powerful arm movements, and the training will pay off on race day.

Because of the angle of the hill, the kick is not as forceful but the tempo (pace) is increased to maintain momentum. The kick is quick and explosive to eliminate time spent on a stopped ski. The forward foot is pushed ahead farther than on the flat, in an attempt to move the ski as far forward as possible, and it puts the weight towards the heel. To practice this idea, as the rear foot swings forward, try thinking of setting the heel down on the snow first, then let the foot slide ahead of the knee. This also applies maximum pressure on the gripping ski.

Those helpful herringbones. When the hill becomes too steep to effectively use the diagonal stride, one ski is stepped out of the track and placed at an angle (half-V position) as the diagonal motions are continued.

The half herringbone is the next fastest uphill technique. When the skis are slipping just a little, the half herringbone keeps you from having to use extra arm strength to get you up the hill. I've had to resort to this technique many times for that little extra bit of hold to get over the hill. If you keep the tempo going, you'll find this technique has the extra punch to get up and over. Practice on a gradual hill and develop a feel for the ski position. Try it on both sides; you never know when a side hill or gully may dictate which ski must be used.

When hills become steeper and the half herringbone is slipping, angle both skis to the side (V position) and keep that tempo going. For racing, the full herringbone is the last resort to get up steeper hills. The speed of top racers climbing a hill in the full herringbone is amazing. Their quick, powerful steps and strong pole use move them up hills like whirlwinds.

To properly ascend hills in the full herringbone, body position is forward with the weight over the feet, poles planted behind for a diagonal push. Take quick, small steps, keeping up the tempo. The less time you spend in the herringbone, the better.

Practice the herringbones on a gradual to steep hill. From a diagonal stride move into a half, then a full herringbone without pausing. Try to make your movements continuous, without hesitation. The smoother the transition in techniques, the less wasted motion and, consequently, the faster the time. For better hold, turn the ankles and knees into the hill. This sets the edges, providing a firm platform to push from. The steeper the hill, the wider the V.

Some courses at the upper levels of competition are groomed to leave a mound of snow in the middle of the hill to ease knee and ankle pressure, making the climb easier.

TRANSITIONS

If you ever have the chance to watch racers ski from a flat to an uphill section, notice how they make the transition. There is no wasted movement, no stopping to change technique. A certain flow characterizes these skiers, one that is noticeably lacking in the ones who are farther behind. These transitions from flat to uphill, from diagonal to double pole, contribute to the rhythm and continuous movement of cross-country skiing. Watch good skiers make these changes in terrain and technique. See if you can imitate their moves. Keep in mind that you want to FLOW into the next technique, adjusting to the terrain effortlessly.

DOWNHILL TECHNIQUES

When speed increases past the effective double pole range, the body needs to be in a position to present the least wind resistance. Like the bicycle racer bends low over the bike to cut drag, so the ski racer crouches over his skis.

The tuck is the most aerodynamic and streamlined position for skiers, ideal for slicing through the passing air. For a racer, the advantage is obvious. Less resistance equals more speed on sections where gravity does the work. This is also a time to rest—the only time in a race when the skier is not poling or kicking to keep up speed. All tucks are speed facilitators, but they vary depending on terrain and the skier's strength.

Low tuck. The low tuck is the fastest tuck position; it presents the least wind resistance. Alpine racers use this tuck for their fast downhill runs. To assume the low tuck, think of making the body into a small bullet. The knees bend, the stomach rests on the thighs, the back is straight, arms are in front of the knees with hands out in front of the face. As you pick up speed, try to keep the skis flat to the snow. The more surface area contacting snow, the faster you go. Keep the head up, looking down the track. On a smooth track with no bumps, maximize speed by sitting

back, weighting the heels and therefore minimizing pressure on the grip wax, which is slower than the glide wax on the tips and tails. The low tuck is the ideal streamline position, but requires the most strength to maintain.

High tuck. When you encounter bumps or change tracks to pass a slower racer, simply extend the arms forward and down. This modification increases stability and enables the legs to work independently as shock absorbers.

If you anticipate bumps, ice, or turns, the high tuck adds greater stability in exchange for increased drag. The back remains parallel to the skis; hands are extended in front of the face to slice through the wind. The legs are then freed to respond to the terrain.

Resting tuck. When a long, exhausting uphill is followed by a downhill, the resting tuck allows time for recovery. A low crouch is maintained, but the elbows rest on the knees, supporting the upper body. Hands sometimes cross. The position is held only long enough to rest the muscles; then a more aerodynamic tuck is assumed.

There may be times when the downhill section is quite short or, when following a double pole, the skier simply leaves his hands behind him and keeps the upper body parallel with the track. Ski jumpers use this position to gain speed before they take off and soar. The upper body can be lowered to rest above the thighs or the legs can remain fairly straight. This tuck is used for short periods of time, whenever a lowered position will cut drag.

Drafting. If you've ever been in a bike race, you are aware of the air space created by the rider in front of you that makes is easier for you to ride. In this air pocket, you can apply less force to the pedals and still maintain speed. The same effect holds for cross-country downhills. Following close behind someone on a downhill, it won't be long before you have to step out into the other track. The strategy behind "drafting," as it is called, is interesting and should not be totally neglected when racing. It may be just the final touch needed to pass a competitor.

At the 1982 World Championships in Lati, Finland, Norwegian Odivar Braa was pushing hard to the finish off the 4 x 10 kilometer relay, with the Russian Alexander Zavjalov right on his tail. Not more than thirty meters from the finish, after following Braa for the last half kilometer, Zavjalov broke out around Braa and made a bid for the win. The finish was exciting, as Braa and Zavjalov came across the line in a dead heat—the first time in racing history that a World Cup event had ended in a tie. So drafting does have its place—and don't think the better skiers aren't using drafting to their advantage. They are!

Cornering. Using the tuck to round corners requires a fine sense of balance and confidence. There is no need to break out of the tuck for certain turns (i.e. long rounded turns). In a good track, hold the tuck throughout the turn. Steer the skis, with minimal edging, to follow the tracks. Turn the hands and upper body to the outside, while moving the hips to the inside. By placing the weight to the inside and leaning in, you can maintain balance against centrifugal force. By leaning in, more weight is over the inside ski, allowing you to stay in the tracks at high speeds.

Transition. Carrying speed from the downhill to the flat is the key to improved times. Try to ski the course prior to the race to learn where the steep downhills are and where speed should be carried from them to the flats. Stay in the tuck as long as possible to save time; don't stand up too soon. Change smoothly from tuck to double pole or diagonal, trying to maintain speed during the transition.

Speed control. To control speed on downhills, the wedge is the racer's in-track braking tool. Use the half wedge for slight resistance. Pick one ski up and place it to the side, tips together, tails apart. Apply pressure to the angled ski as needed to control speed. On steeper sections of trail without tracks, the full wedge is the racer's lifeline. The wedge slows the skier's speed when he's approaching a sharp corner or where trail conditions are dangerously fast. Some skiers use the wedge as a brake when they are not sure what is coming up along the trail. For whatever reason, the wedge is the racer's best technique for controlling and staying on top of the skis. Ski areas are a good place to try your hand at downhill skiing on your skinny racing skis.

STEP TURN

Those sharp turns along courses may require a high-speed step turn or skidded turn. On certain downhills, snow conditions and speed determine which technique will be used. On sharp turns where speed is manageable, the step turn is faster than a wedge, especially in soft-packed snow where an edge set allows a firm platform from which to step off. On icy or hard-packed tracks, the step turn may give way to a lateral side slip, so the turn is completed as a parallel christie.

The decision to step turn or skid turn is a last-minute evaluation. Defined step tracks may already exist on the trail. One step or several may be needed to round the corner. The key to a good step turn is a complete weight shift from ski to ski. Lift and angle the inside ski, either for one or two big steps if speed is slow, or for a series of short quick steps at higher speeds. Quick reflexes and movements are a plus when step turning. Timid skiers find themself out in the powder if they do not step from one ski to the other with a real commitment of weight.

To practice, pick a turn you have skied before and try to perfect edging and body position, two important concerns for successful step turning. A definite edge set to the inside of the turn will

prevent the outside ski from slipping sideways. Angle the ankles and knees into the turn for more edge angle. The body is in a low crouch with legs well flexed throughout the turn. This lowered position is a must for balance and stability when shifting weight. The arms reach forward, poles pointing behind, to provide additional control.

SKIDDED TURNS

At higher speeds, the step turn gives way to a lateral side slip. When the tracks have been wiped out on a sharp turn, turning both skis together is an alternative to stepping. However, the skidding ski is slower than the flat or carving ski. Try to minimize time spent on a skidding ski by quickly rounding the corner and getting back on track.

To start a skid, use an upward extension of the legs, unweighting the skis, followed by foot steering to turn. When turning on icy hard-pack, keep your weight divided between both feet, and your hands low and forward. Ride the turn out with a solid stance on both skis. In soft snow, move the weight over the downhill ski for better carving and less skid.

REVIEW

Any successful downhill maneuver requires supple leg action, even when under stress. Racers must build self-confidence by skiing a variety of terrains. Practice on familiar trails that can be skied, again and again, taking a particular section faster each time. Try to experiment turning in and out of a tuck. Try a fast step turn on sharp corners, a half wedge to slow you down just enough to round the corner. Don't worry if you fall. Better in training than on race day! Falling is a real time-waster and should be reserved for practice!

Only after racers have experienced many downhill runs will their knees loosen up and react to the irregularities of tracks. The shock-absorbing flexed legs are a racer's support system, but only if used within their ability. Skiers must know their own limitations. Blasting down an unknown trail to make up time is foolhardy; it's not worth gambling on a fall. In these sections, it is worth the time to angle one ski in a half wedge until the hill looks skiable, then let 'er rip.

If at all possible, ski the course before the race to familiarize yourself with the unknown. If you ski the problem hill before the race, you know

what to expect and fears are squelched. Better racers pick the fastest line through the turns or the fastest track to carry them the farthest.

As confidence builds through training and practice, the faster speeds of downhills become an asset. With course preparation improving, race organizers strive to lay out courses where maximum speed is attainable. Tracks are groomed to perfection. The only limits are in the competitors themselves. According to FIS rules, all cross-country courses should have a mixture of terrain that includes one-third flat, one-third uphill and one-third downhill. From these figures alone, you can see the downhill needs attention, if winning times are your goal.

TERRAIN UTILIZATION

Skiing on touring trails without cooperating with the terrain is like driving a boat directly into a choppy sea. The boat bounces, pitches, and slows to a crawl as the engine works just to keep the bow pointing into the wind. Energy is squandered fighting the waves, rather than working with them, and using their innate power to expedite forward progress.

Paying attention to the small irregularities along ski trails can work to your advantage, complementing your efforts. Like the waves, the terrain presents its own kind of resistance. Skiing through a series of small washboard-like undulations requires a relaxed, flowing style. Hitting the bumps stiff-legged and tense will work against you, slowing your momentum. Think of heavy cream flowing from a pitcher as you fluidly ski rough sections of trail. Use a downward push on the back side of the bumps and you will even increase your speed.

The skilled racer works the terrain to his advantage continually along the race course. He goes for every bit of speed he can get. Small terrain features may be put to your advantage; next time you are out skiing, notice them and use them to increase your speed.

CHANGING TRACKS

Moving around other racers during a race is a part of a good racer's repertoire strategy. Even if no other racers are on the course, you still may want to change tracks, just to ski in the better one. Moving from one track to the other may be used for strategy purposes or simply to pass a slower skier.

You may change tracks in a sudden push to lose

the skier behind you or to move in behind another skier for pacing. Sometimes following another skier on a downhill (drafting) will increase your speed, making a track change necessary.

Mass starts seem to be a time to jockey for position, moving from track to track to gain a better position in the crowd.

Plan your move where the track is smooth and free of bumps or excess snow. Use a skating or stepping motion to make the change without breaking rhythm.

Practice by moving back and forth on a flat section of trail, using the double pole combined with a skate. The timing is "skate–double pole." When the skate occurs, it should stretch all the way over into the new track. Then the ski that was pushed off from should center itself into the new track while the skating ski is brought in alongside. The motions should be continuous. Try to develop a feeling for making the change that incorporates the smoothness of the skate turn with the rhythm of the double pole. The move should at least maintain speed, if not accelerate it down the track.

MARATHON SKATE

The marathon skate is a move perfected by the United States Ski Team for use on flats and gradual uphills. As in our scooter exercise, one ski is left in the track; the other is angled to the side and pushed off powerfully, making this technique a form of half-skate combined with a double pole. Use of a leg extension and double pole push allows more muscular energy to be transmitted to the ski, which creates more speed than straight kick or double poling. The marathon skate uses different muscles than either the diagonal or the double pole muscles that need to be trained. This is a demanding technique for the untrained skier.

Racers have found the marathon skate especially helpful to maintain speed along the long flat courses of the World Loppet Marathon Series, as well as on flat sections of any race course. In fact, Bill Koch has won races including the 1982 World Cup using the technique. Its use in the Engadin Ski Marathon in Switzerland by Bill Koch sparked Europeans to take a closer look. However you look at it, the marathon skate is a valid technique. If it's the fastest way to ski certain types of terrain, then why all the fuss?

This type of skating was used before Bill Koch popularized it, but the fact that he and other team

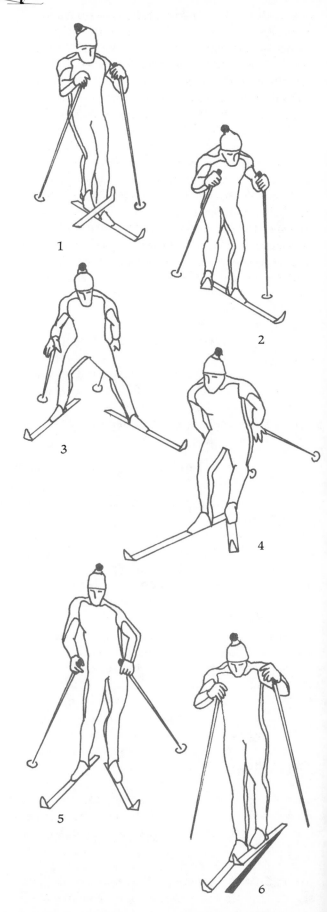

1

2

3

4

5

6

members used it for long sections of trail, and won races, started an international stir. Was the skate a valid technique, or an advantage for early racers around the track and a disadvantage for later skiers? The jury is still out, but for now, the marathon skate may be used in international racing anywhere throughout the course.

Practice the marathon skate on hard-packed trails with a slight downhill for speed. As in the double pole with one kick, the double poling begins just before the skating starts. Skating from a flexed leg provides more potential for power than skating from a straight leg. Try to imagine the speed skater using a strong leg push for acceleration, lowering the body to spring like a cat capturing a mouse. Over long distances, alternate the skating leg. For example: a sequence of seven skates, then five straight double poles as the skis come together, then seven skates with the other leg will distribute the work load.

When skating, the tail of the skating ski crosses slightly over the track and the tail of the straight running ski. Between skates, the skating ski is brought back over the track for another push. At this time, the gliding leg can be straightened slightly for a brief moment of rest.

The energy demands are great, but training will develop the muscles necessary for the marathon skate. Give it a try when you feel your speed on certain sections could be faster. Watch the track for telltale signs of other racers who are speeding along in the marathon skate when you are in the diagonal. It may be just the thing to liven up your bag of tricks!

THE NORDIC EVENTS

"'The game,' he said, 'is never lost till won.'"

George Crabbe

From the first informal competition on skis, the instinctive nature of man's quest for excellence has blossomed into the full venue of present-day competitions. From the ultimate in man's physical trials, the Olympic Games, to the local Bill Koch Ski League, competition lends itself well to the pursuit of excellence.

Cross-country ski racing is an individual sport. The race is against the watch and yourself, not against the other racers. Each racer is involved in his own personal struggle to master the many variables. The thrill of cross-country racing has a captivating quality for all ages.

THE BILL KOCH LEAGUE

The Bill Koch Ski League is a series of fun races for children 13 years of age and younger. It is designed to give young competitors and their families an introduction to cross-country skiing and ski jumping. The emphasis is on participation; winning is secondary. Associated with the league are memberships, special club activities, and audio-visual aids for use by group leaders and competitors. Local ski clubs are the best contacts to put you in touch with the league nearest you— or how about forming your own league? For information on the Bill Koch Ski League organization, contact the United States Ski Association, U.S. Olympic Training Center, 1650 East Boulder, Colorado Springs, Colorado 80909.

CLASSIFIED AND CITIZEN RACING

Classified and Citizen are the two main categories used to separate the varieties of cross-country races.

Classified. The Classified races are open to racers who belong to one of the national or international race organizations endorsed by the FIS (International Federation de Ski—the universal organizing body for all international races). The FIS rule book governs all these meets. The USSA (United States Ski Association) Competition Division is the national organization of the FIS. They keep track of point standings among all classified racers throughout the United States and the world. In order to determine rank, each classified race carries a point value based on the quality of the competitors and the racers' individual finish order.

Many junior high, high school and college races are reserved for specific age classes and divisions. Competition is keen. Racers vie for spots on divisional and national teams. The USSA Junior Olympics, held annually, allows the best USSA competitors nineteen years old and younger to compete for divisional titles.

College ski teams compete within their region to win the opportunity to ski as a team for national prominence in the NCAA (National Collegiate Athletic Association) or NAIA (National Association of Intercollegiate Athletes) meets.

The USSA-licensed competitor is eligible to compete in any USSA-sanctioned meet, such as divisional and national championships and Class I events. Class I races are the highest caliber events offered by the USSA. However, they are limited to competitors with a valid USSA Competition Membership and License. Junior Olympic prospects and senior racers wishing to ski in the National Championships must be licensed competitors. Citizen racers are not allowed to enter Class I events. Other USSA events are open to all members, and many of these races are held on courses that are not as demanding or rigorous as the ones selected for Class I events.

The USSA Master's Program has been adapted to fit the evolving needs of this lifelong skiing activity. The Master's Program provides races for the competitor who is 30 or older. Serious racing is not just for the younger crowd, but is finding its way into the older athlete's winter agenda.

Initiated in 1978-79 season, the Nordic World Cup is the race for international standings among the world's best competitors. Racers take their five best results out of nine races. The most prestigious trophy, aside from the Olympic Gold Medal, the World Cup has been held by Bill Koch and (unofficially) by Nordic Combined Skier Kerry Lunch.

United States Ski Association Age Classes

AGE	CLASS
13 and younger	Bill Koch League
14-15	Junior I
16-19	Junior II
20-24	Senior I
25-29	Senior II
30-34	Master I
35-39	Master II
40-44	Master III
45-49	Master IV
50-54	Master V
55-59	Master VI
60-64	Master VII
65-69	Master VIII
70 and older	Master IX

FIS Age Classes and Events

Cross-country male	20 and younger	FIS Junior
	21 and older	FIS Senior
Cross-country Female	19 and younger	FIS Junior
	20 and older	FIS Senior

Races are run over distances of 15, 20, and 50 kilometers (1 km = .62 miles) for men and 20 kilometers for women. In addition to these individual races, men have a 3-x-10 km relay (3 skiers race 10 km each) and women have a 3-x-5 km relay. In all cases, race courses are laid out with approximately one-third flat, one-third uphill, and one-third downhill terrain. Most race courses are prepared to a width of 3 or 4 meters with two sets of parallel tracks laid in the snow, packed and set by machine. In most classified races, skiers start one at a time, at 30-second intervals. In larger fields, two racers may start at once in parallel tracks. In relay races, the first leg skiers have a mass start, each skier with his own track. When the first skier finishes, he tags the second, and so on until all three have finished.

Race times are difficult to record because the changing characteristics of each race, such as snow and weather conditions, cause speeds to vary. However, at the top levels of international competition, good times for the various distances would be:

Men	15 km—50 minutes
	30 km—1½ hours
	50 km—2 hours and 40 minutes
Women	5 km—19 minutes
	10 km—38 minutes
	20 km—1 hour and 13 minutes

Citizen. Considered a Class II event by the USSA and open to any age or ability, the Citizen Race is for everyone. The race is as much a social happening as a competition. The racing element is definitely deemphasized and the competitive barometer is turned toward fun and camaraderie.

Citizen racing has captured the spirit of "Fun Runs" and local marathons, covering the same distances on skis. There is no better time to improve your technique than while skiing with and observing others.

The fastest growing segment of cross-country competititon, Citizen Races, are increasing in popularity (and in the number of events) throughout the United States and the world. The 10-km Citizen Race Series, popular in the United States, has developed a large following of devoted participants. The number of participants can range from 50 to the 10,000 that the American Birkebeiner attracts every February in Wisconsin. At some events, the awards are good incentives to ski your best race, especially when the prize is a free trip to a European World Loppet Race. The organizers of the American Birkebeiner did, at one time, make such an award to the winners of the citizen class (male and female), presenting them a trip to the Norwegian Birkebeiner. That's a nice reward for your efforts!

The larger Citizen Races of 40 to 100 km have formed a national alliance called "The Great American Ski Chase Series." Comprised of eight or more major ski marathons throughout the country, these races are a great test of stamina and technique. The Ski Chase is the ultimate cross-country marathon experience in the United States. Some racers have made it their goal to ski all eight races during one season.

The international equivalent to the American Ski Chase Series is the World Loppet Series. These are ski marathons that span the European and North American continents. The long-established race series begins in January with the 60-km Dolimetenlauf in Austria and ends eight races later.

January	60 km	Dolimetenlauf	Austria
January	70 km	Marcialonga	Italy
February	90 km	Konig Ludwig Lauf	Germany
February	76 km	Transjurassienne	France
February	55 km	Riviere Rouge	Canada
February	55 km	American Birkebeiner	United States
February	75 km	Finlandia Hiihto	Finland
March	85 km	Vasaloppet	Sweden
March	42 km	Engedin Ski Marathon	Switzer-land
March	55 km	Birkebeiner Rennet	Norway

The following classes are designated for USSA Citizen Races.

Age as of December 31:

MALE	AGE	FEMALE
M-1	13 and under	F-1
M-2	14-15	F-2
M-3	16-19	F-3
M-4	20-29	F-4
M-5	30-39	F-5
M-6	40-49	F-6
M-7	50-59	F-7
M-8	60 and over	F-8

Courses should be marked very explicitly to avoid any wrong turns. Appropriate kilometer markers placed along the trail indicate distance traveled.

FIS COMPETITION RULES

The rules governing the conduct of a competitor in a race are those set forth by the FIS. They are quoted here in full for the Race Committee's reference.

Competitors During the Competition

1. The competitors must follow the flagged track from the Start and pass through all controls. The competitor must complete the course on at least one (marked) ski, using only his own means of propulsion. The help of pacemarkers along the course or other pushing on uphill sections is not allowed.

2. During the race, both poles may be exchanged, but only one ski, without outside assistance. A competitor may wax his skis in the race, but without assistance from any other persons. He has the right, however, to make use of a blow torch and wax provided by others, in the same way as refreshment (either his own or supplied by others).

3. A competitor who is overtaken by another competitor must give way on the first demand, even if the course has two tracks.

4. Accidents or racers giving up should be reported to the next control or at the Finish.

5. The competitors must comply with the directions of race officials and stewards and must not intervene in the organization of the competition.

Editor's Note: A no tracking rule is desired in huge mass start races where double tracks exist the entire length of the course.

Any protests should be referred to the Protest Committee, which is comprised of the Chief of Race, Technical Delegate, and any other representatives from the race committee assigned a position on the Protest Committee.

PERSONNEL NEEDS

NAME	RESPONSIBILITIES
Race Committee	Acts as overall coordinating body for race; appoints officials, defines subcommittees, etc.
Chief of Race	"Director" of race committee, official liaison with USSA/Rocky Mountain, member of race jury, starts race
Chief of Course	Preparation of course and maintenance, refreshment areas, start and finish areas; attends inspection of course; coordinates work of course personnel
Race Secretary	Paperwork for race, coordinates work of personnel in registration, bib assignments, results, fiscal arrangements
Chief of Equipment	Collecting, designing, building, transporting, maintaining all equipment for race
Chief Timer	Oversees all timing equipment, checks proper function, makes timing checks during the race
Finish Judge	Notes bib numbers as racers cross finish line
Time of Day Announcer	Announces hours, minutes, and seconds in finish area
Marker	Announces when racers cross the finish line
Recorders (2 or 3)	Records time of finish
Transcribers	Transcribes finish time onto entry cards
Assorted Others	Assist in registration, course, finish, results, awards ceremony, first aid, photography, cleanup, etc.

SKI JUMPING

Ski jumping is one of the most spectacular of spectator sports. It employs speed and power, combined with aerodynamic control. Flying is one of the jumper's practiced skills, and he will learn to control drift, angle, and air resistance in order to fly far down the hill.

Ski jumps range in size from small, five-meter hills to the huge ski-flying hills where jumpers soar more than 170 meters (525 feet). For the purpose of Olympic and World Championship competition, athletes jump on 70-and 90-meter ski jumps. The size of any ski jump is determined by the distance along the ground from the point of takeoff to an engineering point on the landing hill known as the norm point. This is approximately two-thirds of the way down the hill, where the landing begins to flatten out.

Junior jumpers compete in a variety of meets, depending on age and ability. They jump on 15-meter to 70-meter hills, with gradual increases in size, based on their coaches' knowledge of their individual strengths and weaknesses.

Ski jumping equipment has evolved with the technological changes in ski and boot construction. Skis range in length from 230 to 255 centimeters and are twice as wide as a touring ski. Each ski weighs from 9 to 14 pounds and is made like alpine skis, using wood cores, fiberglass epoxy, and polyurethane bottoms. Ski bottoms have five to six grooves for stabilization when landing and to keep them running straight. Boots are similar to the old leather-lace alpine boots. They have a flexible sole and a high back. An old-style cable binding holds the boot into a metal toe piece. The heel is free to raise off the ski to accommodate aerodynamic flight and telemark landings.

A ski jump consists of the inrun (the approach), the takeoff (the end of the inrun, where the skier actually makes the jump), the landing, and the transition (where the landing hill begins to flatten out, slowing the skier). The landing area has three lines to afford visual control. The line farthest up the hill is the norm point, marked in blue. The norm point on a well-designed jump should be where the landing hill reaches its maximum steepness. The bottom line, in red, is where the landing hill ends and the transition begins; it is called the critical or "K" point. On modern ski jumps, landing beyond the K point is possible, but not safe. The middle line, halfway between the norm and the K point and marked in green, is the table point. It is used strictly for scoring purposes.

If you have ever watched a ski jumping competition in person or on television, the jumpers look like they are really sailing off into the sunset. But in reality, they are usually not more then ten to twelve feet above the snow at any one time. Their flight curve follows the curve of the landing hill, so a mishap or fall is eased by the steepness of the hill. A fallen skier is really moving with the hill, not landing on the flat, which has always cut down on serious injuries.

NORDIC COMBINED

At the international level, Nordic Combined Competition is a single event, combining the individual score of a 70-meter ski jump with the time in a 15-km cross-country race the next day. The Nordic Combined is often referred to as the most difficult combination of athletic events, because of the demands placed on the athlete. Training is twofold: cross-country is the endurance event, jumping is a speed/power event. Physiologically these qualities are in opposition to one another. A competitor must train like a cross-country skier to develop endurance and cardiovascular efficiency; yet this is detrimental to the development of speed and power. Thus, Nordic Combined skiers, in most cases, are not quite as capable of the kinds of performances that individual specialists can produce. However, gaining the coveted trophy is the mark of a truly unique athlete.

BIATHLON

The biathlon is another combined event; it mixes cross-country ski racing and marksmanship. The biathlete combines two events for a total score, although both events are performed during the same race. The biathlon began in the military, where shooting and skiing competitions were frequent. It was in 1960 that the biathlon first appeared in the Winter Olympic Games, followed, in May 1968, by the introduction of a relay race. In Olympic competiton the biathlon event consists of four shooting rounds along a 20-km cross-country race course. Penalty loops are added on for missed targets, to make the winner the one who skied the course the fastest while missing the fewest targets. The relay event includes four people, each one skiing a 75-km loop with two shooting rounds.

Skiing with a .22-caliber rifle is no easy task. A specially designed harness carries the rifle on the competitor's back when he is skiing and is easily released for shooting. Biathletes must shoot from one of two positions—standing or prone—depending on the requirements. Before the trigger is pulled, the racer must stabilize himself, first taking deep breaths to relax, then holding his breath as he pulls the trigger. Imagine, if you will, running a 200-yard dash, then stopping on the spot, taking aim, and firing on a target that is sometimes 100 meters away. Maintaining accuracy with a heart rate of 180 to 200 beats per minute is no easy matter.

Biathletes' training is specific. They spend time on shooting skills, cross-country conditioning, and technique. Unlike the Nordic Combined skier, whose results are based on his physical performance in two events, the biathlete must be in good physical condition and able to execute a very precise skill that requires total concentration and accuracy.

SKI ORIENTEERING

Map and compass skills are what you need to find your way in the woods. Combine the use of a map and compass with skiing, and you have the sport of ski orienteering. The Scandinavians were the early pioneers, forming competitions as a carryover from summer meets.

The object of orienteering as a sport is "finding your way." Using the map and compass as tools for determining direction, competitors navigate around specific courses of varying length and difficulty. There are many types of orienteering meets, each differing in format and scoring.

"Point orienteering" is one of the easier forms of this type of competition. Competitors ski a course marked by streamers or a specific ski trail set off the beaten track in the powder. Following the marked trail, competitors indicate on their maps the exact location of physical markers (controls) they come across. Point orienteering is excellent for developing your capacity to follow directions on a map and make decisions with respect to your own position. It is also a good race for the general public because there is no danger of anyone losing their way. All participants follow the same trail so route selection is not a problem; the ability to pinpoint your location on a map from the surrounding terrain is the key.

In such a meet, you are penalized for mismarked control points by the addition of time; for example, the judges might add two minutes for every error on your map. In addition, you might be required to answer questions about the environment, trees, terrain, and wildlife at the finish. Incorrect answers may cost competitors an additional two minutes. Usually the questions to be answered will be posted at the start of the race. Point orienteering does not require compass skills; competitors need to know how to orient their map and follow a route back to civilization.

Another form of ski orienteering is called "line orienteering." Competitors follow a line marked only on their map. If they succeed in staying on this line, they will ski upon controls placed along the line in a certain order.

This type of ski orienteering is for the advanced outdoorsman who is confident of his map and compass skills. The ability to follow a line drawn on the map while in the actual terrain takes a precise ability to read contour lines and to keep track of features, such as valleys, rivers, knolls, and ridges.

Orienteering is always fascinating. The ability to find one's way in the remote reaches of the wilderness is a joy to the mind and body. Ski orienteering is something we all do when we go skiing. We follow the touring center's trail map and we even follow road signs to locate the trailhead. Next time you go out skiing, make sure you take a map and follow along, using a compass to orient yourself to directions. In other words, take time to know where you are and don't become a victim of the terrain.

TRIATHLON

The combination of three events, such as skiing, running, and bicycling, comprises a type of triathlon. The events may vary, but the winner is the competitor who completes all three events in the least amount of time.

Many ski areas have developed team competitions where three different people compete in one event each. This type of relay allows specialization and, therefore, the game of skill is who is the faster team.

Meets are run using a mass or interval start. Once the gun goes off, participants vie for the lead, tagging off to a teammate at the completion of each leg. The order and type of events may vary from race to race. That is the fun of triathlons.

Unlike the decathlon, triathlons are not yet recognized as an Olympic event. The future of these combination events, however, is bright. National publicity has supported the idea wholeheartedly. The Ironman Triathlon, held in Hawaii each year, attracts thousands of participants. They compete in three events: (1) a two-mile ocean swim, (2) a 106-mile bike ride, and (3) a 26-mile foot run—all in the same day! The winner of that race is truly an Ironman!

Training for these events is a full-time job. The weekend racer would be hard pressed to stay on the heels of the elite triathletes. Maintaining a diversified training program adds variety to an otherwise one-man show. There is never a dull moment in preparing for a triathlon. But don't let the heavies scare you away. Local triathlons that include skiing cast a whole new light on multi-event sports. Like in soccer, participation is not just for the big and strong. Triathletes can be small and quick, also. Triathlons open up opportunities for diversified talents to compete for a combined title. The well-rounded athlete is given his shot at victory.

TELEMARK RACING

The turn invented by Sondre Nordheim more than 100 years ago has become a separate form of competition in the modern world. Telemark racing, born in the early 1970s, has developed its own equipment, technique, and following. Races are held at alpine areas served by lifts. Contestants ski dual slalom/giant slalom courses under the watchful eye of gatekeepers who penalize them (with additional time) for improper telemark positions.

A relatively new type of event, telemark slaloms/giant slaloms are run like alpine pro skiing formats. Racers are paired with the competition on courses set exactly alike, so the winner is the first one through the finish line timing light. Elimination rounds eventually determine the overall champion.

The excitement builds as competitors battle through the gates for the leading edge, that split-second difference separating the racers. Spectators can easily follow the action from the finish or along the course. The leader is the racer who consistently beats the competition.

Another type of event combines the times of a downhill telemark slalom with a cross-country track race—a truly challenging opportunity for the well-rounded skier.

Telemark racing has taken full advantage of the loose heel and combined the two facets of cross-country skiing to encourage the personal best in each of us. Skills involved incorporate downhill turning with the dynamics of track racing. Depending on individual race organizers, racers may or may not be able to change equipment.

SKI TOURING

THE ALL-DAY TOUR

"One's complete awareness is absorbed by the skis and surrounding nature."

Fridtjof Nansen

Touring is synonymous with terms like voyage, jaunt, journey, trek and expedition. Taking a trip on skis is when the fun begins, when technique, waxing, and pleasure meet for a truly enjoyable winter experience. Ski touring allows the little kid in each of us to break out of its hardened shell, to have fun exploring new terrain, playing with friends and relishing moments of exhilaration and the sense of accomplishment at day's end.

This chapter is not intended to be a step-by-step guide to ski touring, but an introduction to the variety of experiences awaiting the adventurous skier in the backcountry. From photography to telemarking, the information herein will help make your tours safe and hassle-free. Setting out on your own into the back country, like setting sail across an ocean, is a step into the unknown. Once you leave the safety of the warm car and the mountain trail wanders

from civilization, survival rests with the head on your shoulders and the pack on your back. There are no warming huts serving hot chocolate and offering a cozy bed for your frozen body. No, whatever happens along the trail must be dealt with individually, using the acquired knowledge of backcountry safety.

Ski tours can range from a half-day excursion to a full-blown five-day trip. The decision is up to you. For the summer backpacker, the desire to visit a favorite fishing hole in winter may require a night out. An overnight trip requires a slightly different plan of attack. Personally, I have enjoyed the all-day tour on many unforgettable trips. Spending the day skiing into remote areas, finding a nice downhill, socializing with friends, enjoying a pleasing lunch in the shelter of a tree and skiing out by nightfall is one of the truly worthwhile experiences of my skiing career. The camaraderie of a small group is an ideal way to get away from the hustle and bustle of the workaday world, a great way to release tension and physically exert the entire body. As Sven Wiik would say, "You should ski at a pace where you will feel pleasingly tired at day's end." Ski touring can be a very relaxing way to spend a day, returning to the comforts of civilization, a hot shower, dry clothes and a warm meal when the sun goes down.

The variety of places to ski to and explore is limitless. This text is designed for the tour leader, whoever that may be. It could be you. Someday you may be in charge of organizing and leading a ski tour. The training a professional tour leader receives prepares him for every eventuality of the back country. The real emphasis of a tour leader's training relates to the five "P's."

THE FIVE "Ps"

"Prior Planning Prevents Poor Performance" is the tour leader's motto. Good tours do not just happen; planning and preparation are prerequisites. Preparation is crucial on tours of any length. I have heard of people getting lost only half a mile from the car. It can happen and, unless you are prepared, the results can be devastating. I do not mean to throw a scare into you, only to point out that self-reliance is necessary on back country tours. You are on your own. It is you and the woods when trouble develops. Be prepared; prevent problems before they become real.

PLANNING

Airline pilots would never take off before consulting their checklist. The tour skier should do likewise. The organized PSIA certified tour leader plans ahead and eliminates problems before they happen. Certified guides are skilled leaders; they have studied and trained extensively to provide their clientele a safe, enjoyable experience. When touring, though, it is the sense of mutual responsibility for each other's safety that can make or break a tour. Each person should take an active part in the tour and be conscious of waxing changes, weather conditions, how others are feeling and moving. The guide leads by knowledge and experience, but everyone along is actively involved. Who knows? Someday you may be the leader and it is good to know the responsibilities that go with the job.

Here are a few considerations any tour group should address prior to and during every tour.

The tour leader should first decide who to include and where the tour will go. The number of people and their particular abilities are decisive factors in determining appropriate tour length and trail difficulty A group of friends starting out will remain friends if the route is carefully selected to suit all abilities. Care is required to keep the group together, not outdistancing a disgruntled, slow skier who finds the pace too fast or the route too difficult.

Transportation is another integral part of good tour organization. Who is driving whom and where is the trailhead? Plan transportation accordingly.

Determine if the tour is going to be an out-and-back trip or a point-to-point trip. An out-and-back trip is no problem. Just park the car at the trailhead and hope the snowplow has not buried it by the time you return. If the tour is a one-way journey, you will need to spot a car at the other end of the trail or find a willing volunteer to meet the group at the trail's end. The problem with this system is maintaining a time schedule. When the weather is great, people would rather ski a little longer than meet their ride on time!

Be sure of each person's physical condition and skiing ability before leaving. If there are unfamiliar faces in the group, do a quick warmup loop to determine skill levels. It is better to spend time doing this at the beginning of the tour than having the whole group suffer because of someone who overestimated his own ability.

I have seen too many skiers overrate themselves because they underestimated the extent of the tour. It is better to say "no" to an eager skier in the morning than to have an exhausted basket case by evening. If you are the tour leader, be sure to check your group and actually see how they ski first.

The size of the group may vary, but three is a good minimum number. If a problem does arise, one can stay with the injured skier while the other goes for help. Groups of ten or more are sometimes good when there is new snow and trail-breaking up front. Skiing alone is not recommended.

Check each skier's equipment. Make sure it is in good working condition. Bindings should be tight, heel plates attached, skis on the correct feet, boots laced (and waterproofed). Time spent will be saved on the trail. Run down clothing items such as hats, gloves, insulating layers, hooded jacket. The leader should be carrying an extra wool sweater, extra hat, socks, gloves, and sunglasses for unexpected emergencies.

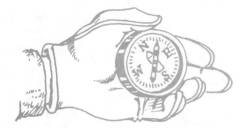

Knowing the route is the leader's responsibility. The trail should be reviewed by the entire group prior to leaving so everyone is familiar with specific names of peaks, meadows, and highways in the area. This could be helpful in an emergency. Remember to file a "flight plan" with the lodge or with friends. If the group is not back by its check-in time, a rescue group is activated. Usually a rescue party will ski your route from end to beginning, if it is point to point, or follow your tracks on a loop tour. Stick with your intended route or the rescue may never happen.

Take along a map and compass. U.S. Geological Survey (USGS) maps are the best. They are detailed, accurate, and provide the most descriptive picture of the terrain. The 7.5-minute series is standard for outdoor use. Its scale is about 2.5 inches to the mile or one inch for every 2,400 feet. The entire map covers approximately 54 square miles—about seven miles across and eight miles from top to bottom of the map.

Knowing the route is one thing, but being able to follow it on the map is another. The map is no good if no one can read it. The compass is but a toy to the untrained person. Knowledge of how to use map and compass is a prerequisite for PSIA certification. Take the time to study how to read a map and compass. Learn the few simple fundamentals and practice, practice, practice. Check the bibliography for good books on the subject. Most are designed with self-help aids and exercises that give you practice situations and practical tasks.

No animal has an easier time getting lost than a human. We have no reliable, innate ability to orient ourselves. Sure, we can tell when we are downwind of a bakery, but in a flat, tree-covered forest without the sun, we are lost. The map and compass give us direction, enabling us to venture farther with less chance of getting stranded.

Even with all of our knowledge and confidence, becoming disoriented can happen. It usually catches you off guard, when you least expect it. If you realize you are off track, take time to analyze the situation. Getting lost is not usually the problem. It is how we handle being lost that causes problems. Here are some ideas to keep in mind if that moment comes and you find yourself disoriented.

- First, accept the fact you are off-course. Do not push on stubbornly. There is no shame in facing reality.
- Stop and try to determine your postion on the map from recognizable features. Take a cross bearing (two compass bearings off distant features on the map); the intersecting lines drawn on the map indicate approximate location.
- If it is cloudy and the map is useless, use a compass safety bearing (a compass heading 180° from the direction from which the tour started). Follow the bearing until you hit a highway or town.
- Backtrack for a sure way out, but only if your ski tracks have not been covered by blowing snow.
- Ski along a stream or down a valley to find civilization.
- Try to determine direction from natural indicators. Drifts and leaning trees indicate prevailing wind direction. Vegetation is usually thicker on north-facing side. At night, the Big Dipper is roughly north. The three stars in Orion's Belt are in the eastern sky.
- Take a guide who knows the area.

PACK SUPPLIES

The leader's pack is the security bundle containing everything the group needs to use in an emergency. Anything that might go wrong, from sunburned cheeks to a broken ski tip, the leader should be able to fix in five minutes or less. This rule is strictly adhered to by certified tour leaders. My years of tour-leading at the Scandinavian Lodge in Steamboat Springs, Colorado taught me this courtesy. The entire group is affected when they have to stand around waiting because of a problem, and on cold days this can be a nuisance. Avoiding these unnecessary delays and discomforts is the goal of good tour leadership.

The Boy scout motto "Be Prepared" is very much a part of winter safety. The chance of a serious problem occurring on a tour is slim, but do not play with the odds. Take precautions *before* the tables turn.

Pack supplies vary within the group, but the leader should carry what others do not. Take time to consolidate essentials the night before. Eliminate excess weight in repeated items. Be sure someone in the group is carrying each item of essential gear.

REPAIR KIT

(1) **Flathead Screwdriver.** Most binding screws are now using posi-drive Phillips screws. Take along extra screws, some oversized, to replace ones that have worked loose. Steel wool or toothpicks will help to fill an enlarged hole.

(2) **Pliers.** These are the all-purpose tool for a variety of duties. Combination sets exist that include pliers, screwdriver, crescent wrench, etc. It's the kind of tool you may not use at home, but is very useful on the trail.

(3) **Drill.** A small hand drill can be used to move binding on a broker ski or redrill a binding that pulls out.

(4) **Knife.** A combination knife like the Swiss Army knife is best, even if it is only used to cut the sausage for lunch. They can come in handy!

(5) **Spare Tip.** Take one along for security. It is not likely to happen, but if a ski tip does break, it is a long walk out. Some models double as snow scoops and saws, adjusting to fit skis of different sizes. Be sure the plastic or metal tip fits the skis being used in the group.

(6) **Spare Pole Basket and Strap.** Skiing without these can be difficult and tiring. An extra basket can be easily slid on the tip, or taped on if it is too big. A spare strap can be attached with wire or taped to the handle. A tour guide I know has a spare pole strap made of canvas that fits entirely over the handle. All you do is slip it on, tighten the Velcro around the pole shaft and you are off! A very clever idea.

(7) **Spare Binding or Bail.** The security of knowing you are prepared is, again, a comforting thought.

(8) **Tape.** This all-purpose remedy can solve a number of problems. For example, use it on the person behind you who will not stop talking.

(9) **Wire and Rope.** Include a flexible thin wire that can be wound for broken bails, pack straps, sunglasses, pole strap attachments, etc. Pliers and bailing wire have been known to keep a tour on the move. Extra rope is great for broken pack straps or for lashing extra clothes to packs. In an emergency evacuation, making a ski sled by lashing skis together and supporting the victim on crossed ski poles is a possibility.

FIRST AID

It is one thing to be prepared for any eventuality, but it is another to actually deal with a medical emergency. First aid gives immediate attention to injuries until a doctor arrives. In the back country, unless there is an M.D. on the tour, medical help can be hours away. The tour leader must be equipped with first aid supplies to handle most all potential problems. I say "most all" because if you were to carry every conceivable first aid item, your pack would be chock-full and then some. A few commercially made kits are compact, lightweight and contain adequate supplies. Here is a list of some of the first aid supplies I have always carried on ski tours:

(1) **Band-Aids**—a variety of sizes and shapes, round, rectangular and butterfly.
(2) **Ace bandages**
(3) **Compresses and gauze**
(4) **Triangular bandages**
(5) **Disinfectant**
(6) **Moleskin and safety pins**
(7) **Wire mesh splints**
(8) **Athletic tape**
(9) **Tweezers and scissors**
(10) **Aspirin**

Every outdoor recreationist can benefit from taking an American Red Cross first aid course. The knowledge gained is invaluable and will stay with you for life. PSIA-certified tour leaders have had extensive training in practical first aid for the specific problems associated with winter recreation. For a look at specific cold-related problems, refer to the section on Winter Safety. A good book for further study is *Mountain Medicine* by James Wilkerson (The Mountaineers, Seattle, 1967) for a complete description of back country first aid. This book has been a constant source of reference in the diagnoses and treatment of mountain ailments.

EMERGENCY KIT

Although day tours are planned for about five to eight hours of skiing, tour leaders prepare for the worst—an emergency overnight. Without prior planning, an overnight stay because of weather or injury is not the most enjoyable experience. A certified tour leader is trained and equipped for the night.

Emergency kits are made up of the essential items needed to stay overnight. They also contain a good dose of altitude readjustment pills. The necessary items in an emergency kit can all be contained in a small coffee can. The can, itself is an intrinsic item in the kit, is used in heating water for hot tea and soups. Here are some ideas for developing your own emergency kit:

(1) **Waterproof matches** and a candle for starting fires. A candle also helps once you're inside shelter, out of the wind. The heat of bodies plus a candle can keep the temperature near or above 30° F.

(2) **Space blanket** or large plastic tarp to cover up the entrance of a snow pit or similar quick shelter. (A snow pit is simply a hole dug in the snow large enough to shelter the entire group and just deep enough for every one to sit out of the wind (either on branches or packs).

(3) **Food**—Hard candy, bouillon cubes, dehydrated soup mixes, teabags, sugar, all to keep the energy level up and calories available for burning. Salt or salt tablets will help fight fatigue.

(4) **Signal mirror**—you never know when the flashing of a mirror could be used to catch someone's attention, or to individually inspect a frostbitten nose.

(5) **Whistle**—the sound is far better than yelling and carries much farther in a snowy amphitheater. Snow is sound deadening. Three short blasts on a whistle is the universally recognized emergency signal.

(6) **Flashlight or head lamp**—this is necessary for night travel and map reading. It is a good idea to tape the on-off switch to prevent accidental tripping.

(7) **Shovel**—in addition to the items in your can, a lightweight, sturdy shovel is a must for digging shelters. The amount of snow one can move with a good shovel will far extend the group's hands, and digging is wet business. Carry a dry pair of gloves to change to when done. (Refer to the overnight tour section for specific snow shelter construction.)

(8) **Avalanche beacons**—by far the best rescue technique going. Using radio signals transmitted by the victim bured in a slide, the person above may be able to zero in on a covered skier. There's no guarantee, because batteries can go dead and even if someone is found, it may be too late. Take precautions to avoid potential slide paths, and do not think because you have beacons you can take chances.

ROUTE SELECTION

Your route to the local grocery store is as familiar as the back of your hand. You can anticipate stoplights and stop signs and come up with a fair time estimate for the trip. In other words, when you know the route, determining time is easier. Professional tour leaders have a similar rule; they must ski every route before taking a tour on it. Knowing the actual route is a must and an important safety factor. The leader then is aware of shortcuts back when time is running out, approximate time required in different snow conditions, and alternate routes for different abilities.

If skiing the route beforehand is not possible, study a topographical map of the area. Pay careful attention to altitude differences, which indicate climbs or downhill runs. "Guesstimate" how long it would take to comfortably ski the route, then add time for lunch, rest breaks and waxing stops. If snow conditions are powdery, trail breaking is a consideration. Skiing one kilometer may take 20 to 30 minutes when breaking a foot of new snow. Allow time for these variables.

The certified tour leader is responsible for the safety of the entire group and takes great pains to avoid any potential problems. It is often easier to ski a group uphill than it is to get the same group back down. The considerate leader will, therefore, select a route up and down that is suitable for the weakest skier in the group. This may mean traversing down your favorite powder run in favor of the group's safety. A good teacher knows that students need a challenge to reach their potential, but a safe tour leader knows that when you are five miles from the nearest road, it is no time to be experimenting. A good tour leader keeps skiers within their comfort zone, not at their limits. They save the experimentation for trails closer to home, and take the easy route down rather than risking a fall.

When selecting a route, consider snow conditions, wax, wind and any other factor particular to the day's tour. If possible, ski in snow best suited for the wax the group is using. If this is not possible, when waxing problems develop, either reroute the tour or spend a little time explaining the technique adjustment necessary to make the skis work.

On cold, windy days, route the tour through the trees so people do not become cold and uncomfortable.

PACE

An enjoyable touring pace covers about one mile per hour. This is a good rule of thumb to follow when planning tours. Chances are this pace will average out by day's end, once the lunch break, picture stops and afternoon tea are taken into account. When touring, I always leave enough tea left in my thermos for the two o'clock tea break.

A ski tour is not a race. The pace should be such that every skier is moving at a comfortable speed. It is better to be moving slowly and consistantly, like the tortoise, rather than fast, like the rabbit who always must stop and wait. A continuous steady pace keeps the group together and requires less energy. You will still reach your destination.

A well-planned route should have you back at the car or lodge by 3:30 p.m. If it is December or January, darkness falls at approximately 5:00 p.m., so you leave yourself a 1½-hour margin of safety. When problems arise, it is a welcome feeling to have extra time before dark in which to find a solution.

SAFETY PLAN

If a member of the tour group falls and twists his knee, the leader needs to have an alternate route. A safety plan is like a contingency fund; it is not used unless there is an emergency. I always ski with the thought in the back of my mind of such an accident happening and I think about what I would do to solve it. A problem like this may never happen, but if it does, be prepared!

If a "flight plan" is filed with the ski school, lodge, or friends, when the group is overdue, a rescue procedure should be followed. Know the phone numbers for the search and rescue organization, the local snowmobile club and the emergency evacuation helicopter. When we toured from the Scandinavian Lodge, we always carried a portable communications radio for just such an emergency.

Evacuation from the snowy reaches of a back country tour is nothing to take lightly. Every effort should be made to help the injured skier out under his own power. Hauling someone out on a makeshift sled is no easy job, even for the best skier.

The snowmobile and the cross-country skier may not be the best of friends, but when an evacuation is necessary, the machines are lifesavers. The speed and ease with which a snowmobile can reach the scene of an accident is unsurpassed.

PRACTICAL WEATHER TIPS

Knowing how to forecast possible weather conditions is helpful and fun. Anticipating weather developments before they occur is part guesswork, part study and part intuition, but there are certain weather signs that may guide your decisions when on the trail. This section is offered to give the tour skier some ideas of weather forecasting for safety's sake.

Listen to the daily weather forecast at the beginning of the tour. Find out existing road conditions and the likelihood of incoming storms. If you are planning an all-day tour and it is already snowing hard in the morning, and the weather report sounds uninviting, enjoy the safety of skiing at your local touring center. When the weather turns nasty, cross-country skiers are usually prepared to cope with adverse conditions, but surprise storms can catch people off guard, and present unexpected problems.

Most tour groups can survive the high winds and blowing snow by simple route selection tactics, but all-day tours usually begin with a car trip to the trailhead. Here is where the real danger exists. Sometimes high mountain roads and passes are the most dangerous elements of ski tours. Take the necessary precautions when driving to and from tours. Make sure you have adequate snow tires or chains. If the storm is just beginning when you leave the parking lot for your tour, your car may be snowed under when you return. Always park your car with the engine facing away from the wind, to keep it from becoming packed with blowing snow.

Once the tourers have left the warmth of the car, they are on their own, with no radio or television to give them local weather reports. Storms and inclement weather patterns that could develop are now the tour group's inherent responsibility.

How can you, as a tour leader, be more conscious of weather developments before they happen? Here are a few tips for on-trail weather forecasting that can be an interesting sidelight the whole group can involve itself with.

Weather develops from masses of air, each containing its own characteristics of temperature and humidity. These masses are referred to as "fronts," either warm or cold. It is the meeting of these air masses that can cause storms. Warm air masses are lighter than cold air masses. When the prevailing winds blow a cold air mass down from the north, it slices under the warm air and, if there is enough humidity present, clouds form and precipitation develops. The same thing happens when a warm air mass from the south moves north, riding up and over the cold air and causing a storm.

The weight difference of each air mass creates a pressure gradient that is read by meteorologists as the barometric pressure. The amateur weather forecaster needs to remember that snow is condensed from the lighter, warm air masses rising over the heavy, cold dry air masses. A general rule in forecasting is "A falling barometer signals a storm; a rising barometer means fair weather is on its way."

On the trail, moving air masses are best studied in the wind and clouds. If the skies are clear with little wind present, look for continued good weather. But if the wind starts to pick up and high, wispy clouds start developing, a storm may be forming in the next 12-24 hours. Winds out of the north usually forecast clearing, colder weather. West and northwest winds are favorable and can mean warmer temperatures. Winds from the southwest to southeast indicate a likely storm situation.

Wind shifts are an early sign of approaching storms. The winds asociated with a low-pressure (or warm, moist air) mass move counterclockwise, and winds associated with a high-pressure (or cold, dry air) mass move in a clockwise flow. Careful observers can tell where they are located in relation to the front by wind speed and direction. The wind blows faster near the center of the low or high pressure system, and if it continues to blow after dark, it is a sign of an imminent weather change. High winds also are present when there is a large pressure gradient between air masses. Usually, high winds are signs of either clearing or worsening weather conditions.

The appearance of the sky, whether cloudy or clear, is a visible sign of impending weather. When a warm air mass moves over a cold air mass, usually well in advance of any storm, thin, windblown, wispy-looking cirrus clouds are formed. If the cirrus clouds are followed by thicker, lowering cloud formations, a storm is brewing. A cold front is usually preceded by warning clouds called "alto cumulus" clouds.

These look like clumps of cotton, are evenly spaced and may develop into thicker, lower clouds as the storm develops.

Have you ever noticed the rings around the sun before? Halos around the sun or moon indicate the presence of a thin layer of ice crystals in the upper atmosphere through which light is refracted. The upper-atmosphere ice crystals, called cirrostratus clouds, usually follow the high cirrus clouds and, therefore, give less warning of an oncoming storm.

Fronts move at varying speeds, but a good average rate is 600 to 800 miles every 24 hours. Looking at the newspaper weather map where warm and cold fronts are indicated by markings, you can make predictions of when they will reach your area. Storms sometimes follow fairly predictable paths. It is a good idea to check on such local weather patterns if you're venturing into a new area.

Have you ever noticed how the animals along the touring trail sometimes disappear for no apparent reason? The birds suddenly make themselves scarce. The squirrels who frequent your lunch site are no longer around. Wildlife is much more sensitive than humans to changes in the atmospheric pressure. But have you heard of the person who feels impending weather changes in his knee joints? A slight air pressure change can affect these sensitive joints in mature adults. Changes in your normal perspiration levels could mean high humidity, indicating a low barometer and unsettled weather. Even having to rewax your skis often during the day has been a sensitive skier's signal that a change in weather is coming.

A little attention paid to weather forecasting clues may just save you an uncomfortable tour or, possibly, an unexpected night out. Losing your bearings in a fast-moving blizzard is not what constitutes the perfect trip. Next time you are outside, become a weather watcher rather than a weather victim.

NIGHT TOURING

Whenever the full moon comes out on a clear night, we try and schedule a moonlight tour. Once a month the opportunity presents itself to ski at night with nothing but the light of the moon illuminating the trail, a truly intriguing experience that has prompted many a social event. Skiing at night holds a special appeal. Blazing a trail through darkened timber with the moon's glow as our guide, the back country opens its otherwise silent night to the few adventurous skiers who brave this new frontier. Just like the depths of the ocean hold a special appeal for the deep sea diver, so does the back country at night appeal to a skier. The terrain you are familiar with during the day changes its appearance when the sun goes down, transforming your frequented trails into a new skiing dimension.

If you can't wait for a moonlit night, a headlamp expedites the situation, allowing night tours whenever you are in the mood. The nighttime skier fastens the lamp around his head and, if the batteries are contained in the lamp itself, all he has to do is switch on the lamp. Some models use a separate battery pack that is affixed to a back pocket or coat pocket. Whatever type of lamp you use, be sure the batteries will go the distance. Battery life in cold weather is reduced, whether you are using a size C dry cell or size AA. It is challenge enough to ski your favorite downhill at night, let alone trying it when your headlamp begins to dim as the batteries fade.

Take precautions when skiing at night. Slow down on hills to below normal daytime skiing speeds. Use caution when skiing next to streams or lakes. Reduce skiing speed in unfamiliar terrain. Watch out for dips, cliffs, and barbed wire fences.

When offered an opportunity to try a night tour, accept it. The hour or more you spend skiing will stick in your mind as one of life's unique experiences. You have to try it before you can realize what the night tour has to offer.

THE OVERNIGHT TOUR

"Don't let being lost take the fun out of not knowing where you are."

Lars Larsen

When the "call of the wild" beckons and the all-day tour ends too soon, adapt summer backpacking gear to the demands of winter and an extended tour can become a reality. Whether staying one night or several, winter camping opens up the magnificent splendor of the total winter environment. Properly equipped, the experienced winter camper will stay within his comfort range (barring an occasional bone-chilling morning, when even the simple tasks of heating water, dressing and staying dry become major efforts).

The organization of overnight tours is similar to that of all-day tours, but with the added demands of preparing sleeping quarters, cooking and dressing. It is a long night when the wind is howling and you are huddling together because that extra parka and down booties were left home to cut pack weight. Preparation is the key to overnight enjoyment.

The back country tour skier must carefully plan for every eventuality, asking "what if?" to determine responses in an emergency. Self-reliance must be the winter camper's answer. What if someone forgets his sleeping bag? What if someone breaks a ski in half at the binding? What if someone has severely frostbitten feet? What if a bad fall twists a knee and immobilizes a skier? These questions could go on and on, but the point is that familiarity with the different situations that could arise is crucial, as well as finding solutions. Mentally prepare yourself for any eventuality beforehand. Discover how self-reliant you really are.

PREPARATION

As the necessary supplies start to add up, the typical day pack may become too small. Plan to use a larger pack. The best bet are the large, soft packs designed for active climbers or skiers. These allow the weight to ride lower on the back, not up toward the shoulders which makes skiing difficult and top heavy, to say the least. Plan on skiing with more weight than you would on your all-day trips. This may take a little getting used to, but with practice you will soon adjust to the added load. A well fitted pack will do wonders to alleviate problems when skiing. Select a pack that will mold to your body. A chest or waist strap helps minimize slippage and bouncing.

The pack supply list for the all-day tour will include all of the equipment necessary for an overnight tour, with the addition of

(1) **Expanded first aid kit.** Compresses, ace bandages, wire mesh splint and ropes, salt tablets, eye medication, antibiotics medicines, and altitude sickness medication (Diamox). (For further reference, consult James Wilkerson's book on *Medicine for Mountaineering*.)

(2) **Food and cookware.** Here is where prior planning prevents an empty stomach. Sit down before any trip and carefully outline each main meal, especially breakfast and dinner. Packing all ingredients in separate plastic bags labeled "Friday's Dinner" or "Saturday's Breakfast" eliminates your having to rummage through all the packs on a cold night. Preferably, foods should be prepared hot. Plan on taking a lightweight backpacking stove. An open fire may be a great way to warm up and dry clothes but, in bad weather, a stove can be used in the confines of a tent or snow cave. Menus should lean heavily toward carbohydrates. Use dehydrated foods to cut weight and if there is not a stream nearby, the camp stove will be a constant workhorse, melting snow for meals, drinking, and washing.

(3) **Extra clothing.** When winter camping, it is better to be overprepared than to skimp on such essential items as warm clothes. If your inner layers become wet, the chill is teeth-chattering. Take dry clothes to slip into at night when the work is done. Take along extra socks, hats and mittens should your other ones become wet. After a long day of trail breaking, the comfort of a dry turtleneck is an uplifting thought. If you plan on digging any kind of snow shelter, then bringing extra clothes is a must. A waterproof or Gore-Tex snowsuit is great.

(4) **Sleeping bag and pad.** Once the kitchen area is cleared and that last cup of warm drink is working its way into your system, the sleeping bag takes on a certain individual importance. The thought of slipping into a warm bag is comforting

at day's end. Select a sleeping bag to suit your needs. Some heavy expedition bags may be more insulation than you will ever need. A lighter weight bag may be more adequate. Goose down is by far the best insulator and compresses nicely into a small stuff sack. Dacron or fiberfilled bags, however, will still insulate even when wet. Because of the condensation in a tent, a synthetic bag may be preferable for a multi-night tour.

The use of a sleeping pad is a must. Snow is a good insulator but will also rob you of valuable heat. A full-length pad will keep the entire body off the snow. When rolled, they are small and easily transported, and they make a good lunch seat, too. Several styles are available, but one caution: ask about compressibility. Some of the ensolite varieties tend to mat down after use and lose their insulating value.

(5) **Tents and shovels.** Finding shelter on winter camping trips is crucial to survival. Decide at the start whether the group will use tents or dig snow shelters. Tents are great for spring trips when the snow is consolidated. The variety of lightweight backpacking tents makes tenting a real possibility. In the middle of winter when the snow is soft and powdery, a platform can be packed out (with skis first then boots) to firm up the snow for setting up the tent.

If the group is small, a snow cave is an excellent winter shelter. The insulating properties of snow makes sleeping in one quite comfortable. There may be a raging blizzard outside, but inside sound is muffled and the temperature will stay around freezing. If you opt for a snow cave, be sure to take along a lightweight shovel or two for digging. Plan on at least 1½ to 2 hours to dig a four-man cave. Snow shovels with large scoops are best and there are many good commercially made ones on the market.

Besides adequate preparation, the back-country skier needs to be aware of winter first aid, avalanche problems, and snow shelter construction.

WINTER FIRST AID

This is in no way intended as a first aid text, merely as a discussion of the common medical emergencies associated with winter travel. Pay particular attention to the causes and symptoms for each malady. This kind of checklist will help on-trail diagnoses.

Most medical problems encountered on a ski tour will be cold induced, such as hypothermia or frostbite, but altitude-related problems like mountain sickness and pulmonary edema, as well as heat-related problems, can all crop up.

HYPOTHERMIA

The silent killer, hypothermia is a constant threat to the unwitting skier. Have you ever been out in winter weather when you were poorly dressed or wet from sweating and you could not stop shivering? Shivering is the body's way to produce heat. It's also one of the early signs of hypothermia.

Technically, hypothermia is the lowering of the body's core temperature to below 98.6° F. In hypothermia, the body loses heat faster than it can produce it. The balance is tipped in favor of heat loss. Consequently, the body shuts off blood flow to the extremities. Before you are aware anything is happening, you may begin to fumble with your ski poles needlessly; you may also slur your words. All skiers in the group should watch out for the early signs of hypothermia, such as poor coordination, fatigue, thickness of speech, and shivering. These symptoms are mild at first, but uncontrollable in later stages.

Hypothermia is not a specific, localized feeling of cold in the hands or feet, but a total bone-chilling cold throughout your entire being. The cold takes away good judgment and even the simplest of tasks, like zipping your coat, becomes difficult. The hands do not respond normally. Their fine motor control is lost. Many cases have been reported of well-prepared skiers, equipped for overnights, found dead without even their extra clothing on because they were too disoriented and uncoordinated to put it on.

The group leader should be aware of these symptoms, and each person should watch his partner closely on cold days. When the skier in front of you begins to stumble, stepping out of the track to catch his balance, stop and analyze the situation. Talk to the skier. See if he is coherent and ask him to he would like to slip on your extra coat or have a drink of hot tea.

The treatment for hypothermia is warmth. Warm the entire body by taking off any wet clothes and adding dry insulating layers. Warm liquids and food help keep the calories burning, producing heat. External heat from a fire or stove will help. In extreme cases, the victim should be evacuated quickly to a warm car. The best rewarming process is soaking in a warm tub of water. However, if evacuation is out of the question, warming must be done on the trail.

To fully rewarm someone may take six to eight hours, so work accordingly. Use your stove to heat hot water bottles. Placed on crucial arteries (the neck, groin, under the arms), these will heat the inner body. If a sleeping bag is handy, place the victim and partner together for direct heat transfer. Quick action is necessary to raise the body's temperature. If it falls into the 94°-90° F. range, the results can be serious. Below 90° F. the body stops shivering, the muscles stiffen and the mind is on the edge of consciousness. Without adequate warming, the victim may become comatose and total cessation of life is not far behind.

Acting early, while the tour is still a happy, smiling group, may seem premature, but once the victim loses core temperature, things move fast. Take precautions early. Make sure the group has hats and gloves on. Ensure that extra clothing is added when outside temperatures drop. Plan frequent rest stops to drink and snack. Keep the group mentally active by giving each person a responsibility to occupy his thoughts.

With modern clothing, nutritional information and common sense, the prepared tour skier should not encounter anything but mild symptoms of "exposure," the old term for what skiers and hikers have come to know as the silent killer—hypothermia.

ALTITUDE SICKNESS

Altitude sickness is another invisible enemy of every wilderness adventurer. The heights we enjoy so much can cause undue pain and discomfort. When skiing mountain trails above 10,000 feet, its symptoms may affect even the experienced mountaineer.

The main cause of altitude sickness is lack of oxygen, particularly when ascending quickly from lower elevations. Plane rides, car trips, and, of course, ski trips all involve this phenomenon. Any sudden rise in elevation affects the body's ability to adjust to the lessened oxygen content of the atmosphere. Given time, the body will make the adjustments naturally. Unfortunately, this may be impractical on a short weekend trip. The compromise means living with the symptoms until descending to a lower altitude.

Studies have been done on the effects of hypoxia (lack of oxygen) on humans. An excellent book on the subject is *Going High* by Dr. Charles Houston. His studies on high-altitude physiology have determined that body functions such as blood chemistry (red blood cells and hemoglobin increase), water retention, and salt and hormone balance all are altered by sudden changes in elevation.

The best prevention allows an "acclimatization" period. This is why the climbing expeditions to the Himalayas and Alaska's high mountains schedule rest days at certain elevations to let the body adjust naturally. A climber's saying goes, "Climb high, sleep low"—body physiology is facilitated by acclimatizing.

Acute Mountain Sickness (AMS) is the common name for this form of altitude sickness. The outcome is not life threatening, but in extreme cases it can lead to other ailments. It may have even happened to you before, but may have been written off as just a headache or flu.

Typically the ski tour begins with a drive to snow, usually at a higher elevation. Starting late, you get out of the car, wax, and take off. By lunch your head aches but you don't pay much attention to it. Maybe it is just dehydration, so you drink an extra gulp of water. By evening the headache is still there and you just keep climbing higher. You feel a little nauseous as you set up camp. By morning, after a sleepless night, you still feel a little uncomfortable but as you start to ski out, you feel better and better.

If you have spent any time in the mountains you probably have felt these AMS symptoms but have learned to live with the inconvenience. The symptoms first noticed are tiredness and headaches, developing into nausea and loss of appetite. During the night sleep may be interrupted by nightmares and erratic breathing. AMS may affect the younger members of your party more than the older set, especially those under 20 years. Prevention through drinking and eating are the two main ways to combat the illness—besides descending to a lower altitude, which is the cure-all, but unfortunately may cut the weekend short.

Drinking plenty of fluids will alleviate the potential for dehydration, which is a common concern in preventing AMS. Water loss when skiing happens through perspiration (sweating), respiration (breathing) and urination. Keeping the body hydrated is, therefore, a constant process. Take time to drink and snack often. Stick to high-carbohydrate foods—noodles, rice, breads, etc.— which provide nutritional protection against AMS. Treating symptoms with drugs may be of temporary help. Aspirin or Diamox may be used

if recommended by a doctor familiar with altitude sickness.

High Altitude Pulmonary Edema. AMS is an unpleasant feeling that will go away when descending to lower altitudes. High Altitude Pulmonary Edema (HAPE), however, is not as forgiving and can lead to death. HAPE results from extended stays over 10,000 feet where rapid ascents and heavy workloads combine to produce an oxygen deficiency. When the oxygen supply lessens, the body tries to compensate by sending more blood to the lungs in an attempt to pick up more oxygen. In the process, there is a tendency for people to spring a leak in the small capillaries surrounding the lung, thus filling the lung (or small air sacs, alveolae) with fluid. The only treatment is to move the victim lower and administer a drug called Diamox to stimulate breathing.

The symptoms you want to be aware of that are different from AMS are a persistent cough and a faint gurgling sound heard when breathing. This may be accompanied by shortness of breath, restlessness, and a feeling of pressure on the chest. If any of these symptoms are suspected, evacuate the victim to a lower altitude immediately, preferably four to five thousand feet lower if possible. Learn to recognize the early signs of altitude sickness and do not be the tough guy putting up with the discomfort. It may just backfire.

DEHYDRATION

Acommon wintertime problem among cross-country skiers, water loss is prevalent when engaging in a physically active outdoor winter sport like skiing. When the muscles begin working, water is expelled through

the tissue in what we commonly call sweat. If this loss of water is not replenished, muscle effectiveness is eventually reduced and other symptoms can develop—such as headache, a greater susceptibility to cold, loss of judgment, and eventually collapse. Susceptibility to frostbite is increased as peripheral vessels are constricted, a cause of excessive water loss.

Skiers lose water not only through perspiration, but through respiration or breathing. Seeing your breath vaporize in front of you may look intriguing, but that vapor is made up of tiny water droplets. Have you ever watched a ski racer come to a stop on a cold January day? The steam rises like a hot geyser in Yellowstone.

The prevention is, of course, drinking liquids. Drink often, and for all-day trips plan on two to three quarts per person. Some people may get by with less, but be sure to take extra water with you. Even though you are surrounded by snow, extracting the bound-up water molecules from it is difficult. After the first hour of skiing or training, stop for liquid refreshment. Keep the liquids flowing into the body on long trips. Some touring centers even plan for such rest stops along the trail. Small snack bars, while serving a functional role, are ideal for conversation and taking part in the social aspect of skiing.

Make sure that you drink mostly water with a diluted mixture of flavoring. High sugar content may upset the stomach and slow the body's ability to absorb the liquid quickly. The idea is to replenish lost liquids in the most natural form available. This is why plain water works best.

Racers may be seen drinking other concoctions devised by nutrition experts as they stop for feeds spaced at intervals along the course. New research is always being conducted by nutritionists to find the most easily assimilated fluid for optimum performance. A good rule to follow when actively participating in an outdoor activity such as skiing is "drink before thirsty; eat before hungry."

THE SUN

Effects of the sun are often overlooked, until evening when the skier's face may look like a bright tomato on a white plate. Protecting against the sun's harmful rays in winter is easily accomplished by sun creams or lotions. Even on cloudy or hazy days, the sun's ultraviolet and infrared rays continue to penetrate. The constant reflection from the snow around you on some days may make you feel like you are in a big reflector oven. Any open areas of skin can be affected—the top of your nose and head, the back of your ears, even the underside of your chin at times.

Apply sun creams or lotions to the susceptible areas of open skin before you go skiing. Most products indicate whether they are for tanning or providing a total sun block. People with sensitive skin should consider using a sun block rather than a tanning product. The combination of oils and moisturizers used in most sun creams or lotions will either prevent the sun's rays from penetrating or screen them out. The baseball cap in spring will protect the top of the head as well as shading the face from direct sun.

Sunglasses are a must on sunny days any time during the winter. Going without is damaging to the eye and may cause what is known as "snow blindness." The corona of the eyeball burns, becoming red and irritating every time you blink. It feels like having sand in your eye that does not rub away. The only cure is a lot of cold damp washcloths and time.

Usually when the eyes get sunburned the skin surrounding the eye is affected also. It is not unusual for extremely sunburned eyes to swell shut. Let me tell you, it is a very uncomfortable feeling, and once you have had it you will never go without your sunglasses again. Once you have burned your eyes, they are susceptible again and more sensitive to bright lights, but vision should not be affected. Consult your doctor if irritation persists for more than four or five days.

FROSTBITE

The easiest ways to sabotage your warmth are wearing the wrong clothes and eating the wrong foods. Dress lightly and the cold will penetrate you deeply. Eat lightly and the furnace may go out prematurely. No matter how hard you try to protect against the cold, that frequent enemy of winter travelers can catch you off guard. When areas of skin such as your face, ears, hands, and feet become very cold, so cold that blood circulation is restricted, exposed tissue begins to freeze. Just like germs attack the teeth in dental decay, so will the cold attack the vulnerable areas of the body.

The early signs of frostbite are a numb, tingling feeling and white patches of skin, referred to as "superficial frostbite." One fairly reliable symptom of continuing frostbite is the sudden and complete cessation of cold or discomfort in the affected part. Some people report pleasant feelings of warmth and thoughts like "I will be all right now; it is going numb." Take heed of such feelings. Act immediately to rewarm the affected part. Take your boot or glove off and place your extremity inside a partner's coat where rewarming can occur. Early detection can save you the pain of further advancement. A warm hand placed over the white skin should quickly turn it back to cherry red. Fingers can be rewarmed by tucking them into the armpit and applying light pressure. Without blood circulation in the small peripheral blood vessels and capillaries, the skin will actually freeze.

Be aware of the wind chill factor when touring. Protect open areas of skin such as the face and ears. If the air temperature is 10° F. and the wind is blowing 30 miles per hour, the actual temperature on exposed skin is –29° F. It won't take but a minute to freeze exposed skin.

Avoid giving a frostbite victim alcohol. That warm feeling a person may get from drinking alcohol is deceptive. Alcohol actually dilates the blood vessels on the skin's surface, causing the body to lose heat more quickly. Smoking cigarettes, on the other hand, causes the blood vessels to constrict, limiting blood flow. Rewarming is a very uncomfortable feeling, like being burned. The affected area will blister and sting, and medical care will be required to avoid infection.

Superficial frostbite is the first sign of freezing tissue. The skin is numb and has a white, waxy appearance. After thawing, the area turns a mottled blue or purple and swelling begins. Blisters may form in severe cases between 24 and 36 hours after rewarming. The blisters slowly dry up and turn black in about two weeks. The skin eventually peels away and the new skin is tender and red for several weeks. An itching, prickling feeling may persist for some time afterward. The blood vessels will remain somewhat constricted, leaving the affected area extremely sensitive even to mild cold in the future.

Deep frostbite is a much more serious injury. It results in amputation in extreme cases, although every attempt is made when rewarming to eliminate tissue damage and possible infection. Two concerns are primary when dealing with deep frostbite. Unlike superficial frostbite, which involves only the epidermal layer of outer skin, deep frostbite penetrates deeply into the tissue, possibly to the bone. It is accompanied by huge blisters that take

Chill Factors or Effective Temperatures at Various Wind Speeds

Wind Velocity	35	30	25	20	15	10	5	0	–5	–10	–15	–20	–25	–30
5 mph	33	27	21	16	12	7	1	–6	–11	–15	–20	–26	–31	–35
10 mph	21	16	9	2	–2	–9	–15	–22	–27	–31	–38	–45	–52	–58
15 mph	16	11	1	–6	–11	–18	–25	–33	–40	–45	–51	–60	–65	–70
20 mph	112	3	–4	–9	–17	–24	–32	–40	–46	–52	–60	–68	–76	–81
25 mph	7	0	–7	–15	–22	–29	–37	–45	–52	–58	–67	–75	–83	–89
30 mph	5	–2	–11	–18	–26	–33	–41	–49	–56	–63	–70	–78	–87	–94
35 mph	3	–4	–13	–20	–27	–35	–43	–52	–60	–67	–72	–83	–90	–98
40 mph	1	–5	–15	–22	–29	–36	–45	–54	–62	–69	–76	–87	–94	–101

Temperature (Fahrenheit)

from three days to a week to develop. Usually severe frostbite attacks the feet or hands, which are most susceptible to the cold on extended trips. In extreme cases when frostbite hits, swelling of an entire limb may persist for a month or more. The pain and throbbing may persist for two to eight weeks; when the blisters fall off, a reddened area very sensitive to touch and permanently sensitive to cold remains.

Treatment for deep frostbite should be evacuation, if possible, to the nearest hospital or camp where rewarming of the frozen part can occur. Rewarming on the trail is discouraged. Once a foot is thawed on the trail, the victim becomes an immediate litter case, and cannot assist in his own evacuation. It is better to leave the part frozen until reaching adequate rewarming facilities. Dr. William Mills, Jr. of Anchorage, Alaska, who has dealt extensively with cold injuries, states:

Unless you have an adequate method for transporting the patient down either by sled or helicopter so that he himself need not use his hands or feet, I think I would discourage thawing at 18,000 feet. He would be wise to stump his way down with frozen, unthawed feet even if it took 12-18 hours as long as the objective was adequate shelter, reasonable comfort and a spot from which he could be flown or carried to a hospital. We have had a half dozen patients who have walked for three to four days with completely frozen extremities, some of whom have sustained no loss at all. Others lost toes only. In no case did any of them lose any more of the foot than toes. There appears to be an opportunity even to preserve all of the digits, provided that as soon as the patient reaches a place where thawing can be managed, it is done by the method of rapid rewarming followed by the regular routine of aseptic hospital care.

Water rewarming is the accepted method, placing the affected part into water of 108° to 112° F. in a tub large enough to hold the entire foot. The entire room or tent should contribute to total body warming. Give the patient warm liquids and make active attempts to warm the body, because even if he is insulated by heavy coats, the patient will not be able to generate enough internal warmth. If a tour group succumbs to such a problem, it is preferable to seek out professional assistance. For the day tour group the problem is not as much a concern as it is for those on overnights or extended trips. Take the necessary precautions;

prevention is worth the time. Here are a few guidelines to follow from *Frostbite* by Bradford Washburn:

Prevention of Frostbite

Overall physical well-being, good clothing and intelligent operations in the field are by far the best insurance against frostbite. When you are exhausted, hungry, ill, injured or hypoxic, your chances of frostbite injury are increased. A few basic tips for prevention follow:

1. Dress intelligently to maintain *general body warmth*. In cold, windy weather, don't forget to protect your face, head and neck adequately. Enormous amounts of body heat can be lost through these often-neglected parts of the body, despite ample protection everywhere else.

2. Eat plenty of the right sort of appetizing food to produce maximum output of body heat. Diet in cold weather at low altitude should tend heavily toward fats, with carbohydrates next and proteins least important. As altitude increases above 10,000 feet, carbohydrates are most important and proteins least. Experiment with fats. If members of the party digest them readily, they are excellent, but don't count on everyone liking them at high altitude.

3. Don't climb under too extreme weather conditions, particularly at high altitudes on exposed terrain. Don't get too early a start in cold weather. Use the configuration of the mountain to help you find maximum shelter and maximum warmth from the sun. In short, use your head—and use it more and more the higher you climb!

4. Avoid all tight, snug-fitting clothing—particularly on the hands and feet. Socks and boots should fit snugly, with no points of tightness. In putting on socks and boots, carefully eliminate all wrinkles in socks. Don't use old matted insoles.

5. Avoid perspiration under conditions of extreme cold. Wear clothing which ventilates adequately. If you still perspire, remove some of your clothing or slow down! Keep your feet and hands dry. Even with vapor-barrier boots, you must not permit your socks to get too wet. All types of boots must be used with great care *during periods of inactivity, after exercise* has resulted in damp socks or insoles.

6. Wear mittens instead of gloves in extreme cold, except for specialized work like photography or surveying, where great manual dexterity is required for short intervals of time. In these situations, wear a mitten on one hand and a glove temporarily on the other, if possible. If bare-finger dexterity is required, use silk or rayon gloves or cover with adhesive tape all metal parts which must be touched frequently. Remove

thumbs and holds fists in palm of mittens occasionally to regain warmth of whole hand.

7. Always be careful while loading cameras, taking pictures or handling stoves and fuel. Remember that the freezing point of gasoline is near –70° F., and its rapid rate of evaporation as well as its extreme chill make it very dangerous. Never touch metal objects with bare hands in extreme cold—or even in moderate cold when the hands are moist.

8. Mitten-shells and gloves to be worn in extreme cold should always be made of soft, flexible dry-tanned deerskin, moose, elk or caribou—not horsehide, which dries out very stiff after wetting. Removable mitten inserts or glove linings should be of soft wool. Never use oil or greased leather gloves, boots or clothing in cold-weather operations. Under many conditions it is wise to tie mittens together on a string hung around your neck or to tie them to the ends of your parka sleeves.

9. Always carry extra socks, insoles and mittens in your pack.

10. Keep socks clean—at least those which are worn next to the skin. The use of light, smooth, clean socks next to the skin, followed by one or two heavier outer pairs, is good practice.

11. Keep toenails and fingernails trimmed to reasonable length.

12. Don't wash your hands, face or feet too thoroughly or too frequently when living under rough-weather conditions. Tough, weatherbeaten face and hands, kept reasonably clean, resist frostbite most effectively.

13. Constant use of wet socks in any type of boot will soften your feet, make the skin more tender, greatly lower resistance to cold and simultaneously increase the danger of other foot injury such as blistering.

14. *Wind and high altitude* should always be approached with respect. Either of them makes otherwise moderate conditions more dangerous. Both together can produce dramatic results when combined with cold.

15. Don't exercise too strenuously in extreme cold—particularly at high altitude where undue exertion results in panting or very deep breathing. Very cold air brought too rapidly into the lungs will *chill your whole body*, and under extreme conditions may even damage lung tissues and cause internal hemorrhage.

16. Once you have been thoroughly chilled (without any injury whatever), it takes *several hours* of warmth and rest to return your body to normal, regardless of superficial feelings of comfort. When recovering from an emergency cold situation, do not venture out again into extreme cold too soon.

17. Do not smoke or use alcohol, even in moderation, at high altitude. Never use either tobacco or alcohol *at any altitude* under conditions when the danger of frostbite is present or after it has occurred.

18. If you have ever been frostbitten, great care must be taken to protect the once-injured area from future damage.

19. Much outdoor work in really cold weather cannot possibly be performed in warmth and comfort. Learn carefully how cold you can get while still working safely—then never exceed this limit.

20. If you are frostbitten or otherwise injured in the field, *keep calm*; panic or fear will result in perspiration, which in turn will evaporate, causing further chilling which will intensify the crisis and aggravate the injury itself.

21. Always keep your tetanus boosters up to date. They may give you valuable added protection in the event of frostbite or any other injury in the field.

SNOW SHELTERS

The planned night out is far preferable to the impromptu overnight, but ski tourers are sometimes faced with unplanned overnights. They are challenging situations that can be mastered. Climbers or mountaineers call their unplanned nights on rocky ledges bivouacs. An important aspect to survival when skiers are faced with an unexpected night out is finding shelter. An emergency bivouac may not be comfortable, but at least you can survive.

Removing yourself from direct exposure to the elements in winter is much easier than in summer because of all the snow. We have talked about snow as a great insulator because of the large amount of dead air spaces in the snowpack. Snow also exhibits structural properties when densely packed, allowing a variety of below-snow shelters. The best insulation on a cold night is the snow around you. Here is where your imagination can run rampant, discovering the many types of possible shelters. Whenever you build a snow shelter, keep these points in mind: (1) time available before dark; (2) digging utensils (shovels, skis, etc.); (3) manpower to help dig; and (4) snow consistency, snow depth and terrain.

Dig in using shovels, skis, even a spare tip, to form a windbreak or cave. The idea is to remove yourself from the wind, rain, snow, etc. If time is limited and there is no shovel, look for natural alcoves—a deep hollow below a tree, a large rock outcropping, or a depression. With a little sculpturing these natural retreats provide asylum from the open air.

In flat, open areas, dig a snow pit or trench just deep enough for sitting room. A long, narrow trench can be covered with skis, poles, branches, or plastic tarps for warmth. Use packs or branches to sit on to avoid direct contact with the snow.

Digging a long shaft into a side hill can serve two or three skiers quite comfortably. Packs and snow can function as doors, sealing off the night air.

The creative shelter is waiting to be discovered on every tour. The ingenious skier will find it, whether the night outside is planned or not. Emergency bivouacs are not the end of the world. Sure, it might not be as warm as you would like, but *you can survive.*

The total snow cave provides the best insulation and is the ultimate in winter accommodations. Surrounding himself with one to three feet of snow, the winter camper is free to design the snow castle of his dreams. Taking one or two hours to build a two- to four-person structure, the snow cave is not the fastest shelter to build. But when completed it provides warmth and comfort beyond your wildest dreams.

A suitable site is the leeward side of a hill where snow has drifted, forming a solid snowpack. Fresh, loose snow makes a poor cave. The snow will give way easily and will not hold its shape. If this is a problem, try piling up a mound of snow and letting it sit momentarily. The denser snow will provide better support for hollowing out a cave. This is also done in early-season caves when snow depth is a problem.

Locate your cave on a hillside to take advantage of the warmest air in a valley. About one-third of the way up a mountainside is the warmest layer of "still" air. The coldest night air settles in the valley floor. Plus, when digging, the snow tailings will roll downhill and save extra shoveling.

A snow cave is begun in one of two ways:

(1) Dig a small hole horizontally into the drift and then angle up two or three feet, hollowing out a room large enough for sleeping benches and packs. Move all the snow down and out the small entrance hole.

(2) Dig out the entire entrance, exposing a solid front wall. Now dig out the internal structure, shaping the domed roof and elevated bed benches to allow the cold air to flow down and out the lower cave entrance. Once the inside is formed and packs moved in, the front is then closed, using snow blocks cut from the compact snow shoveled out of the cave. The blocks are placed in layers from the bottom up to form the outer wall. A small hole is then carved in the bottom for the entrance.

"When I'm in a snow cave, won't I eventually run out of air?" Because snow is very porous and the entrance is never closed tight, an air vent is only needed if you are using a stove or burning a candle all night. Otherwise, a vent allows the warm air to escape. A vent is easily made by poking a ski pole through the cave ceiling if air movement is needed.

Digging a cave is like sticking your gloves in a bucket of water. They become quite wet, as do other clothes you have on. Using a rain suit and plastic gloves is not a bad idea. Be sure to carry extra dry clothes, or else waterproof coverings if you plan to dig a cave.

The size of the cave may depend on the amount of gear you are packing. Plan to bring all supplies inside to prevent freezing or burial in a snowstorm. You may even want to tuck your boots inside your sleeping bag for that little extra touch of warmth.

The inner cave takes shape with time. A cave with shelves for candles or a small food storage cache for refrigeration is hard to leave. Candles will warm a cave and supply plenty of light. After all the effort of building a cave you may want to make it your base camp and enjoy the day tours you can take in the area.

With these thoughts in mind, you should never have to face a cold night out in the open. The shelter you make is left up to your own imagination. Comfort is a matter of preference and preparation.

AVALANCHE!

"We are dancing on a volcano."

Comte de Salvandy

An avalanche is the fall or slide of snow down a mountainside. To the cross-country skier, avalanche is a nine-letter word and a constant hazard on most all back-country tours. The avalanche is not restricted to certain times of the winter or only after a heavy snowstorm. They can happen anywhere, any time, given the prerequisites for an unstable snowpack.

This section on avalanches presents a synopsis of some of the extensive research on the subject. It is intended to make you aware of the "whys and hows" of avalanches and their effect on the back-country skier, and is in no way all-inclusive. If anything, I hope it encourages you to study further.

Snow, unlike rain, is precipitation with structure. Each snowflake is unique. No two are the same. The variety is infinite, the forms intricate. Depending on temperature and humidity, moisture forms into rounded balls or elaborate crystals. Once on the ground, snow continues to undergo transformation. As the snowpack increases from fall to spring, the well-formed crystals are constantly changing. This transformation is referred to a "metamorphism" by snow physicists. Two main types of metamorphism are reported by the U.S. Forest Service, "ET" and "TG." Knowledge about each type is important to the winter traveler.

Have you ever skied in fresh powder snow? Did you notice how light and fluffy it is? That same powdery snow after two or three days becomes a much denser, more consolidated mass. Each individual crystal is compressed by weight of the snowpack, creating a stronger snowpack as individual crystals undergo structural changes, bonding together in ice grains. This common occurrence is called "equitemperature metamorphism," or ET metamorphism, an interlocking of snow crystals to form a more cohesive solid structure. It is called equitemperature because it takes place with no great difference in temperature among the different layers of snow involved.

The second type of metamorphism involves a great temperature variance between the top and bottom layers or between layers within the snowpack. This is called "temperature gradient metamorphism" or TG metamorphism. The Eskimos have known of the insulating properties of snow for a long time. Inside igloos or snow caves, air temperature stays between 29 and 34° F., even when it is below zero outside. This same temperature difference occurs between the warmer ground level and the outer layer of snow. For example, early in the fall, when the first 12 inches of snow accumulates, ground temperature remains around 32° F. while the outside air temperature may drop well below zero. This creates a rather large temperature differential and results in a strong vapor flow from the warmer snow crystals near the ground outward, toward the colder snow layer. Because of such a large temperature difference, the lower snow crystals lose moisture, transforming into large angular shapes with very fragile bonds between them. It is referred to as "depth hoar" in advanced stages. Depth hoar is similar to ball bearings or "sugar snow" as it is known to skiers. The grains are quite large and bonding is nonexistent.

If the snow is not too deep, it is interesting to dig a snow pit and actually uncover the bottom layer of TG snow. You can see just how delicately the crystals are hooked together. TG conditions also may occur within the snowpack, given certain weather conditions. New snow falling on an old snowpack can produce a thin layer of TG snow, which may be only one-eighth inch thick but deadly. Even the trained avalanche expert may miss these very weak layers, and such layers are prime concerns for winter travelers. The additional weight of a skier crossing an open slope could easily break this delicate bonding and down comes the snow. The same thing could happen naturally from increased snow loads after storms or wind drifts that cause heavy, overhanging weight. Until that time, though, the snow acts as a visco-elastic mass, flowing and moving downhill. Have you ever noticed the small trees on slopes that tend to bend downhill? They are a sure sign of gravity's pull, or "creep" as the experts call it, which is most common at warmer temperatures (32° F.) when snow is more viscous. Colder snow remains rigid and more resistant to creep. Watch for this sign of an active moving snowmass.

Snow mechanics is an interesting study and worth your time if for no other reason than understanding why avalanches occur. Avalanches can occur on any incline but are frequent on slopes between 30 and 45 degrees.

We have seen how snow structure and weight can cause avalanches. The wind is another concern. Wind drifts on the leeward side of ridges or peaks can break loose naturally or because skiers get too close to the edge. Skiers should stay on the windward side of ridges well away from the overhang or "cornice."

Avalanche danger is particularly high immediately following storms. The new snow adds to the weight of the existing snowpack and is very unstable, sometimes resulting in direct-action sluffs. You probably have seen these types of slides driving along mountain roads. The snow gives way from the increased weight of the new, loosely packed snow. If it is snowing one inch or more an hour you can suspect trouble. Another danger sign of impending avalanche is a cracking or settling sound when skiing, indicating unstable snowpack conditions. I remember touring on Rabbit Ears Pass in Steamboat Springs, Colorado. When skiing across an open meadow the whole area would settle, and you would hear a loud crack and "whooooosh" as the air rushed out of the settling snow.

The way a slope is situated plays a role in snow stability also. Snow on north-facing slopes is usually deeper from less sun melt and more likely to slide in midwinter. South-facing slopes are slide prone in spring when the sun warms the top layer of snow, causing snow structure to change. In the spring, it is safer to cross potential slide areas early in the morning rather than in the afternoon when the snow is wetter.

As a member of the Tenth Mountain Division serving in World War II, Charles C. Bradley learned about avalanches the old-fashioned way, through experience. The many different types of avalanches are classified in two main categories, direct- and delayed-action avalanches. Here is an excerpt of his slide classifications:

DIRECT-ACTION AVALANCHES

These result from weather conditions of the moment.
Dry- or powder-snow avalanches.
Precaution: Stay off the slopes during a heavy snowstorm, especially one with wind, and for a

few hours after the storm has ended.

Wet-snow avalanches. These are sometimes the result of heavy rain on the snowpack and often the product of warm spring sun, either of which loosens grain bonding of the surface snow, producing a layer of very mobile slush. Ponderous and slower moving than powder avalanches, they can be massive and destructive. Precaution: Stay off sunny slopes in spring and any slope in a rainstorm.

DELAYED-ACTION AVALANCHES

These are really sneaky ones! They require considerable time to mature, and when they let go may have little or nothing to do with the weather conditions of the moment. Because time generally favors the development of strength in the main pack, these tend also to be slab avalanches and large, with a highly destructive potential.

Climax avalanches (usually large and all the way to the ground). Precaution: With a long pole, probe down through the snowpack for a sense of weakness at depth. Be sure to probe all the way to the ground. What you do with the information is up to you.

Wind-slab avalanches. These are difficult to anticipate. A snow surface that has experienced strong winds is usually a poor bonding surface for later snowfalls. The greater the load of the subsequent snow, the more apt it is to fracture and slide out on the old surface. Precaution: Expect the situation to exist on any slope generally exposed to wind. There are places and times when it can be tested safely by skiing. Better take an avalanche course first. If you like snow pits, dig one on the slope. Make the uphill face vertical. Cut into the pack on each side of the face and start a new vertical face one foot uphill. With each vertical increment, as you cut down note whether there is any tendency for the freed block to slide off on some well-defined plan. If you find it, there may be a hazard. If you don't, there may be none. You're on your own.

Rain- or thaw-slab avalanches. Rain or thaw at the surface can later freeze and provide a marvelously hard sliding surface for the avalanche of subsequent snow accumulations. Precaution: The probe can usually spot an icy layer at depth, but you won't know without digging whether or not it is well bonded to the snow above it.

We have defined two major types of avalanches: direct action and delayed action. Within those categories we find two principal kinds of snow slides: loose snow and slab avalanches.

(1) Loose snow slides start as a result of snow load on the upper layers of the snow pack. They can start at one point or in a small area and will grow in size and quantity of snow as they descend. Loose snow slides move as a formless mass with little internal cohesion.

(2) Slab avalanches are by far the most destructive. They can sweep cars off mountain passes and demolish anything in their path as they rush pell-mell downhill. Slab avalanches start when a large area of snow breaks loose at a weak layer of snow and begins to slide all at once. There is a well-defined fracture line where the snow breaks away. The snow is characterized by the tendency of the crystals to stick together in solid mass or large chunks of snow.

To summarize, please review the following points detailing avalanche precautions and procedure. Used with a little common sense, they may save your life.

AVALANCHE: AVOID AND SURVIVE

Terrain and field notes:
- Avalanches are most common on slopes of 30 to 45 degrees.
- Slab avalanches are more apt to occur on convex slopes, or at the turnover or a hill.
- In early and midwinter there is greater danger on north-facing slopes.
- On south-facing slopes the danger increases on sunny days and in spring.
- Leeward slopes tend to collect snow in cornices and snow pillows. These slopes are more dangerous because of increased snow loading.
- Windward of a crest may be safer because of compacted snow or less snow.
- Any hill that is open, without rocks, trees, or heavy vegetation to anchor the snow presents a greater hazard.

Weather field notes:
- Wind over 15 miles per hour can increase the danger as it moves and loads snow onto leeward slopes. Look above for wind plumes rising from peaks and ridges to indicate wind direction.
- The time of greatest avalanche activity is during or immediately following a storm; 80 percent of all slides usually occur at this time.

- The faster snow falls beyond one inch per hour, the faster danger increases.
- Snow that has already lost the six-armed star shape as it deposits on the ground indicates suspected instability. Temperature near or above freezing tends to cause the snowpack to settle and bind.
- Continued cold weather after a storm can cause snow to persist in an unstable condition.

Route selection and observation:
- Contact the local weather authority, ski patrol, or ranger—someone with information on local conditions.
- Pack and use avalanche cords (electrical transceivers are better), sectional probes, and shovels.
- Use routes on ridges and stay on the windward side. Next best is to travel on the valley flat, well away from runout areas.
- Watch for old avalanche blaze marks: fracture lines above, debris below, a lack of large trees in between.
- Avoid gullies and confined basins.
- Watch for running cracks.
- Listen for hollow sounds.

If you must travel on a dangerous slope . . .
- Do not traverse the hill; take a straight up or down route.
- Only one person at a time, with all equipment loosened, should go ahead. All others should watch and wait.
- Stay as near the top as possible if you must cross a slope.

- Use dense woods or rocky ridges as islands of safety.

If you are caught . . .
- Get rid of any equipment you can. Skis, for example, can pinion or confine you more firmly.
- Make a vigorous effort to swim, trying to move toward the top and the side of the flowing snow.
- Try to keep snow from packing into your mouth. If you can tell that things are slowing down, try to get an arm in front of your face to form an air space.
- Stay calm to conserve air and strength.

If you have just seen someone swept away . . .
- Mark the spot where the person was last seen. Search directly downhill of the marked spot in a quick "scuff" search, using a ski or pole to rake the top layer of snow for any signs.
- If you are the only person at the scene, do not leave immediately to go for help, unless it is very close by.
- If there is more than one remaining in a party and aid is within a short distance, one should leave to find rescue assistance, and the others should organize a probe line to work methodically across the debris.
- Remember, after one-half hour the buried have only a 50 percent survival rate.
- If found get to their head first, check for breathing and neck or back injuries before moving, treat for shock.

CROSS-COUNTRY KIDS

CHILDREN & SKIING

"Every child should know a hill, And the clean joy of running down its long slope with the wind in his hair."

Edna Casler Joll

Children enjoy the winter playground, too. Cross-country skiing lends itself to their playful natures. Give a pair of skis to a child and he will teach you how to ski. Have you ever watched children play, the way they turn and move? They move with complete abandon and a full range of motion. They see what's to be done and just do it. Children learn by feel; they do not need any long explanations.

Children learn by doing. Think back to your early attempts at riding a bike. No one was there telling you just how to sit and which way to turn the handlebars. You learned by feel, by trial and error, by doing. We, as adults, need to rekindle this natural way of learning without the complications imposed by our conscious, thinking mind. Let the children be our teachers for awhile; enjoy their energy and exuberance, and try to share in it.

Cross-country skiing is a true family activity. Just like summer hiking trips to your favorite lake, they allow everyone to be together and enjoy the woods. Ski tours with the whole family add a touch of pleasure to the long winter months. Ski tours can occur anywhere there is snow. If you are fortunate to live in snow country, the decision to ski on the weekend or after school is a less harried one than it would be for the citybound family—although a good four to six-inch snowfall can turn the local park into a virtual skier's paradise.

The experience children gain from watching a parent or friend ski in the back yard, sliding back and forth, may be all it takes to excite them to try it themselves. Once they catch the bug and really want to try skiing on their own, introduce it to them gradually.

Begin with a little snow play. Let them ride on

your skis as you hold them, or take off one ski and have them stand on it and slide. If you have a "pulk" or sled, let the child ride it as you ski in front. Any kind of game that gets children out of the house and involved in snowy activities eases their minds as they begin to ski.

WHEN TO START

The decision on when to start children skiing is individual. Everyone is different. If you feel your child is interested then, by all means, get him started.

You may have an old photo album with a picture of your first day on skis. Beginning a child at two, three, or four years takes patience and understanding, but two-year olds have been known to ski. The main impression a child should receive from skiing is one of enjoyment.

Take time to fit equipment and dress the child to stay warm. If you live in snow country, choose a nice day, preferably one that is sunny and warm. Limit the time on skis to half-hour sessions at the most. Do not allow the child to tire or become frustrated. At this age, your main concern is to introduce another play activity. Do not jeopardize a child's eventual skiing career by pushing too hard. Remember that cross-country skiing is a lifelong activity that lends itself to participation by all ages. Keep the child's initial attempts fun. Start his career in skiing off right.

Parents need patience when working with children. Kids may not cooperate as you would like them to or make just the right moves. Rather than teaching by talking, save your voice and just let them imitate you. Children have not developed their thinking minds yet and any talk is usually lost in translation. Besides, they don't stand around long enough to listen! Instead of talking and thinking like an adult, try acting like a kid and be the leader of the group. Lead them through the back yard obstacle course. Pay attention to what they do and try to expand on their games.

Starting children without ski poles is a safe approach. Their hands are free to swing and to help them get up after a fall. Playing a game of snow soccer is easier without poles, as they can hit the ball with their hands instead of their feet. Arm movements are not complicated by pole use. The same idea is also used in adult ski lessons when the poles are complicating the stride.

Playing games is a good way to emphasize movement with children five to nine years of age. Hide and seek is fun in the woods. One child hides his eyes and counts to fifty while the others go hide. The object is to make it back to the base without being tagged. A variation would be to hide apples, oranges, or cookies in a designated area. When they are all hidden, turn the kids loose. The reward is evident.

Follow the leader is a good game to use on trails or circle loops. Making bumps or dips will add to their fun. Fox and geese is a game where one child is the fox and the other children are geese. Staying in a confined area, the fox is let loose to capture the geese, who ski around to avoid being tagged.

Games are a great way to direct the child's energy to a desired end, even if that end is to learn how to function with other children. Learning to get along with peers is very important!

PROGRAMS FOR CHILDREN

The Scandinavians have long recognized the value of starting children to ski while they are very young. There is an organization for the promotion of skiing in Norway, Skiforeninger, which runs ski schools in sixty different locations in and around Oslo. The classes are for children up to eight years of age. Tomm Murstad, a Norwegian who created the largest children's ski school in Norway, forty years ago, says, "You cannot force a child to ski or learn. If a child is not interested or is unwilling to learn, then it is the instructor's job to evoke interest. This must be done carefully, for as soon as a child is placed under stress, even in an enjoyable learning situation, potential interest may be killed."

If it is fun, children usually want to join in. Make your family trips enjoyable and be good examples for them to follow. Then your children will have been given a good opportunity and whether the child pursues it depends on his own personality.

EQUIPMENT

As for adults, the fit of children's skis, boots, and poles affects their enjoyment of the sport. Equipping children is a constant struggle to keep up with their growth. Boots bought new one year are too small the next. A good place to get equipment is the "Ski Swap."

Usually held in the fall, "Ski Swaps" were created by skiers, for skiers, to buy and sell used equipment. Ski shops can be helpful in ski selection and boot fitting, and more and more shops specialize in the younger skier. Take advantage of their expertise. Another help in searching out equipment is your local cross-country ski school. Buying old rental gear in the spring might be another option.

Skis. No-wax skis are best for children. They eliminate the need for wax and, therefore, the frustration of slipping back when the wax is not right. Slippery skis during those first attempts is enough to frustrate anyone, let alone a child who just wants to have fun. Waxing is a needless delay at this stage. It takes time away from skiing.

Ski length for the two- to five-year-old is about the same as the child's height. As the child gets older (six to ten years) and gains experience, gradually increase the ski length, eventually using the same sizing as the adult—to the wrist of the outstretched hand. Buying long to save a few bucks as the child grows is like buying the ten-speed bike before the tricycle. It is best to learn on the proper size of ski. Long skis are difficult to turn and may have stiffer camber which the child cannot push to the snow.

Boots and bindings. Again, it is best to use regular three-pin square-toe cross-country boots. The nordic norm measures a junior boot at 71 mm. If possible, when a child grows enough to fit into a cross-country boot, use it. The added support and control are the main reasons. There is a binding called a "Balato" that buckles down on any winter boot. For small feet, these work fine, but they do not allow the child to really control the ski. Cable bindings can work with ordinary boots, but check to see if the toe of the binding and boot match. Do not make the mistake of improper boot/binding fit. Your child will never forgive you. It is frustrating to always be coming out of the binding.

When sizing new boots, using two or three pairs of socks may bulk up a boot to fit for two years (who said we couldn't economize?). Be careful not to get boots so long that the feet are swimming in them. If in doubt whether to go longer or shorter, opt for the larger boot at this age.

Poles. Children two to five years of age should learn to ski without poles. It will be one less piece of equipment to worry about and will not affect the child's skiing in a negative way. If anything, it will help.

The older group, six to nine years of age, may want to use poles because they will be skiing longer distances and could start utilizing the poles for more power. Pole length should be shorter rather than longer. You might get by two years on one pair of poles before longer ones are needed.

IN TERMS OF SKIING

"A barren superfluity of words."

Sir Samuel Garth

ARM SWING (RECOVERY, RETURN): The forward motion of arms to prepare for pole plant and push.

BASIC BODY POSITION: A neutral stance with the center of balance over the feet. Knees and ankles are comfortably flexed.

BASIC STANCE: A position in the diagonal stride where both legs are together and the skier is in a forward-flexed position.

CADENCE: A means to keep rhythm or timing.

CHRISTIES: Refers to turns that show a skidding on both uphill edges.

COMPRESSION: Using stomach muscle contraction and body weight for power in push-off and polling.

CONVERGING SKI MOVEMENTS: Displacing one or both skis to form an "A" relationship, with the tips closer together than the tails.

DIVERGING SKI MOVEMENTS: Displacing one of the skis to form a "V" position with the tips farther apart than the tails.

DOWNSTEM: Placing the ski in an "A" or converging position where the downhill edges can "bite" sufficiently to serve as the support for an extension and the initiation of a new turn. Downstemming can also serve as a means for slowing down.

EDGE CHANGE: The action of tilting the skis about their longitudinal axis from one set of edges to the other.

EDGING: A ski position with an angle between the running surface of the ski and the snow or from active application of lateral pressure by knees and ankles.

EXTENSION: The straightening of a joint by muscle contraction or by gravity.

FALL LINE: A line directly down the hill. The path of least resistance that any object will seek when released.

FLAT SKI: A ski with the running surface flat on the snow.

FLEXION: The bending of a joint by muscle contraction or by gravity.

GLIDE: The forward movement of a weighted ski.

KINETIC: In skiing, the forces and energy of the swinging motion of arms and legs.

LATERAL: Situated on, directed toward, or coming from the side.

MATCHING: The act of bringing the skis into a parallel relationship.

MOMENTUM: The motion of a skier that is a result of effort, the product of the skier's mass and velocity.

POLING: Applying force on the pole to aid in forward motion (pole push).

POSITION "A" (SNOWPLOW, WEDGE): Convergent ski tips, i.e., tips together, tails apart.

POSITION "V": Divergent ski tips, i.e., tips apart, tails together.

PRESSURE: A force to the ski created by weight, muscle action, and/or turning speed.

PUSH-OFF (TAKE-OFF): The action of pushing down and back on the weighted ski, using knee and ankle extension (push-off). This is often referred to as the "kick," with the power behind the stride, or take-off but the manual will use "push-off" as a more descriptive term.

RHYTHM: The regular repetition and natural flow of elements within a sequence.

ROTARY PUSH-OFF: The movement of pushing-off and turning one or both legs so that the body is rotated about its vertical axis.

SEQUENTIAL LEG ROTATION (SELR): The action of using one ski as a support from which, or against which, the other ski is turned.

SIMULTANEOUS LEG ROTATION (SILR): The action of turning both legs at the same time.

SKIDDING: The combination of skis moving forward and sideways through a turn.

SLIDING: The movement of the skis in the direction of the longitudinal axis.

SLIPPING: The movement of the skis sideways.

STEERING: The result of the skier's muscular effort to guide his or her skis along the desired path.

STEMMING: The displacement of one ski to a position convergent with the other ski. The stem usually results in a situation where the skis are on opposite edges.

STRIDE: A complete sequence of movements beginning with a pole plant and including a push-off, weight transfer, and glide. A new stride begins with the pole plant of the opposite arm.

STRIDE LENGTH: The distance traveled during one stride.

TELEMARK POSITION: A position where one ski trails the other. The tip of the trailing ski is midway between the tip and the binding of the leading ski or farther back.

TEMPO: The rate at which strides are performed.

UNWEIGHTING: The process of raising the body up or sinking down, creating a negative pressure from the skis on the snow surface, allowing the skis to be turned.

WEDGE: Same as the "A" position.

WEIGHT TRANSFER: Moving the body weight from one foot to the other.

SKIING DIRECTORY

CANADA

BRITISH COLUMBIA

NAME OF AREA LOCATION	TELEPHONE #	TRAIL MILES	MAINTAINED MILES	INSTRUCTION	RENTAL	SNACKS	MEALS	LODGING	CAMP
1. **ABC Adventure Tours,** Vancouver, BC V6B 2Z5	(604)687-7885	55	30	x	x	x	x	x	
2. **Big White,** Kelowna, BC V1X 4K5	(604)765-4111	15		x	x			x	
3. **Chilanko Lodge,** Kleena, Kleene, BC; Bellevue, WA 98004	(206)822-9241			x		x	x	x	x
4. **Fairmont Hot Spgs. Resort Ltd.,** Fairmont Hot Spgs., BC V0B 1L0	(604)345-6311	30	20	x	x	x	x	x	
5. **Forbidden Plateau Lodge,** Courtenay, BC V9N 54N	Radio Operator	15			x		x	x	
6. **Hemlock Valley,** Agassiz, BC V0M 1A0	(604)524-9741		4	x	x	x	x	x	
7. **Kimberley,** Box 40, Kimberley, BC V1A 2Y5	(604)427-4881	30	30	x	x				
8. **Mount Washington,** Courtenay, BC V9N 2L3	(604)338-1386	12	12	x	x	x	x	x	
9. **Kitimat,** Kitimat, BC V8C 1B4	(604)632-5558	50	10	x			x	x	
10. **North Cariboo Cross Country Ski Tours,** Quesnel, BC V2J 3J8	(604)992-7379			x	x	x	x	x	
11. **Northern Lights Alpine Recreation,** Invermere, BC Y0A 1K0		75+	50	x			x	x	
12. **108 Resort Ranch,** 100 Mile House, BC V0K 2E0	(604)791-5211	40	40						
13. **Prince George Chamber of Commerce,** Prince George, BC	(604)562-2454	40+	40	x	x			x	
14. **Ptarmigan Tours** c/o Repp Agencies, Kimberly, BC	(604)427-2221						x	x	
15. **Red Coach Inn,** 100 Mile House, BC V0K 2E0	(604)395-2266								
16. **Tod Mountain,** Kamloops, BC V2C 5M8	(604)372-5757	13		x	x				
17. **Whistler/Blackcomb,** Whistler, BC V0N 1B0	(604)932-4222			x	x	x		x	

ALBERTA

NAME OF AREA / LOCATION	TELEPHONE #	TRAIL MILES	MAINTAINED MILES	INSTRUCTION	RENTAL	SNACKS	MEALS	LODGING	CAMPING
1. **Banff/Lake Louise Chamber of Commerce**, Alberta, T0L 0C0	(403)762-3777	100+			x	x		x	
2. **Canadian Mountain Holiday**, Banff, Alberta T0L 0C0	(403)762-4531	300	13		x			x	
3. **Inuvik Ski Club**, Inuvik, N.W.T. X0E 0T0			4					x	
4. **Marmot Basin**, Jasper, Alberta J0E 1E0	(403)852-3816								
5. **Paskapoo**, Calgary, Alberta I3B 0H0	(403)288-4112								
6. **Provincial Park Branch**, Wasa, BC V0B 2K0									
7. **Ribbon Creek Hostel**, Seebe, Alberta T0L 1X0		200+	50	x	x			x	x

MANITOBA

NAME OF AREA / LOCATION	TELEPHONE #	TRAIL MILES	MAINTAINED MILES	INSTRUCTION	RENTAL	SNACKS	MEALS	LODGING	CAMPING
1. **Canadian Ski Association**, Winnipeg, Manitoba		60+	60+	x	x				x
2. **Mount Agassiz**, McCreary, Manitoba R0J 1B0	(204)835-2246	15							
3. **Riding Mountain National Park**, Wasagaming, Manitoba R0J 2H0	(204)848-2811	150+	150+					x	

ONTARIO

NAME OF AREA	LOCATION	TELEPHONE #	TRAIL MILES	MAINTAINED MILES	INSTRUCTION	RENTAL	SNACKS	MEALS	LODGING	CAM
1. Bear Trail Inn Resort,	Whitney, Ont K0J 2M0	(705)637-2662	80	13		x	x	x		
2. Calabogie Peaks,	Ottawa, Ont K2A 1T2	(613)752-2720	10	10	x	x				
3. Crazy Horse Ski Club,	Lansdowne, Ont K0E 1L0	(613)659-3058	10	10		x		x		x
4. Homestead Cross Country Ski Resort,	Duram, Ont N0G 1R0	(519)369-2725	24	20	x	x		x	x	
5. Horseshoe Valley Resort,	Barrie, Ont L4M 448	(705)835-2014	40	40	x	x		x	x	
6. Kwagama Lake Lodge,	Sault Ste. Marie, Ont P6B 5L1	(705)253-3075	31					x	x	
7. Metro Region Conservation,	Downsview, Ont M3N 154	(416)661-6600	12	12	x	x				
8. Moonstone,	Coldwater, Ont. L0K 1E0	(416)368-6900	10	10	x	x				
9. Mont Antoine,	Mattawa, Ont P0H 1V0	(705)744-2844	25	25						
10. Mont Pakenham,	Pakenham, Ont K0A 2X0	(613)624-5290	20	20	x	x				
11. Nordic Inn,	Dorset, Ont P0A 1E0	(705)766-2346	12	12				x	x	
12. 1000 Nordic Trails c/o Craiger's Resort,	Mallorytown, Ont K0E 1R0	(613)659-2266	24	24				x	x	
13. Shanty Bay Cntry. Club/Cross-Cntry. Ski Resort,	Shanty Bay, Ont	(705)726-1922	15	15	x	x		x	x	
14. Soo Finnish Ski Club,	Sault Ste. Marie, Ont P6B 5T4		30	30	x	x	x			
15. Stokely Creek Lodge,	Goula River, Ont P0S 1E0	(705)649-3421	55	45	x	x	x	x	x	x
16. Sundance,	Thunder Bay, Ont P7C 4X9	(807)622-0792	11				x	x	x	
17. Talisman Ski Resort,	Kimberly, Ont N0C 1G0	(519)599-2520	15	15	x			x	x	x

QUEBEC

NAME OF AREA	LOCATION	TELEPHONE #	TRAIL MILES	MAINTAINED MILES	INSTRUCTION	RENTAL	SNACKS	MEALS	LODGING	CAM
1. Alpine Inn,	Ste. Marguerite Station, Que	(514)229-3516								
2. Auberge Normande,	Lake Beauport, Que G0A 2C0	(418)849-4486	60	60	x	x	x		x	
3. Bromont,	CP29, Bromont, Que J0E 1L0	(514)534-2200	12			x				
4. Camp Fortune,	Old Chelsea, Que J0X 2N0	(819)827-1717	100	100	x	x		x		
5. Le Chateau Montebello,	Montebello, Que J0V 1L0 (Director of Sports)	(819)423-6341	95			x	x	x	x	
6. Edelweiss Valley,	Wakefield, Que	(819)459-2859		10		x				
7. Far Hills Inn,	Val Morin Station, Que	(514)866-2219	50	50	x	x		x	x	
8. Gray Rocks Inn,	St. Jovite-Mont Tremblant, St. Jovite, Que J0T 2H0	(819)425-2771	15			x	x	x	x	
9. Hotel l'Esterel,	CP38, Ville d'Esterel, Cty. Prevost, Que J0T 1E0	(514)228-2571	30	30	x	x			x	x
10. Manoir St. Castin,	Lac Beauport, Que G0A 2C0	(418)849-4461	125	125	x	x				
11. Mont Grand Fonds,	CP66, La Malbaie, Cte. Charlevoix, Que G0T 1J0	(418)665-2334	34			x				
12. Mont Habitant,	St-Sauveur des Monts, Que J0R 1R0	(800)363-3612	25			x	x			
13. Monte Ste. Anne Park,	Beaupre, Que G0A 1E0	(418)827-4561	100	100		x		x		
14. Mont Ste. Marie,	Lac Ste. Marie, Que J0X 1Z0	(819)467-5200	50			x	x			
15. Mont Tremblant,	Que J0T 170	(819)425-2711	69	45	x	x				
16. Villa Bellevue,	Mont Tremblant, Que J0T K20	(819)425-2734	60	20	x	x		x	x	

NEW BRUNSWICK & NOVA SCOTIA

NAME OF AREA	LOCATION	TELEPHONE #	TRAIL MILES	MAINTAINED MILES	INSTRUCTION	RENTAL	SNACKS	MEALS	LODGING	CAM
1. Mont Farlagne,	Edmundston Ski Ltd., Edmundston, NB E3V 3L2	(506)735-6617	30							
2. Poley Mountain Development Ltd.,	Sussex, NB E0E 1R0	(506)433-2201	11			x		x	x	
3. Wostawea Ski Club,	Fredericton, NB E3B 1B1	(506)455-2679	38+		x	x		x	x	
1. Canadian Hostelling Association,	NS B3J 3G6		45+	10		x			x	
2. Keltic-Cape Smokey,	Igonish Beach, Cape Breton, NS B0C 1L0	(902)285-2880	95	95						
3. Old Orchard Inn Ski Touring Center,	Wolfville, NS	(902)542-5751	15			x	x		x	x

QUEBEC

NEW BRUNSWICK

NOVA SCOTIA

ALASKA

NAME OF AREA	LOCATION	TELEPHONE #	TRAIL MILES	MAINTAINED MILES	INSTRUCTION	RENTAL	SNACKS	MEALS	LODGING	CAMPING
1. Alaska Wilderness Unlimited, Box 4-2377, Anchorage, AK 99509		(907)277-0197			x					x
2. Alyeska Resort, Girdwood, AL 99587		(907)783-2222	7	7	x			x	x	
3. Arctic Valley, Anchorage, AK 99510		(907)272-7767	5		x		x	x	x	
4. Bear Brothers Whole Wilderness Experience, Anchorage, AK 99509		(907)344-5760			x	x		x	x	x
5. Birch Hill Ski Area, Fairbanks, AK 97701		(907)479-7208	12	6	x				x	
6. Chugach National Forest, Anchorage, AK 99501										
7. Chugach State Park, Anchorage, AK 99501		(907)274-4679	25							
8. City and Borough of Juneau, Juneau, AK 99801		(907)586-3300								
9. Eaglecrest, Juneau, AK 99801		(907)586-5284	6	6	x	x			x	
10. Far North Ski Guides, Anchorage, AK 99504		(907)279-2314			x				x	x
11. Mendenhall Glacier Recreation Area, Juneau, AK 99802		(907)586-7151								
12. Hatcher Pall, Palmer, AK 99645			25	20						x
13. Mount McKinley National Parks, McKinley Parks, AK 99755			85		x	x		x	x	x
14. Municipality of Anchorage, Anchorage, AK 99502		(907)274-2525								
15. Nordic Ski Club of Anchorage, Anchorage, AK 99501					x	x				
16. Nordic Ski Club of Fairbanks, Fairbanks, AK 99708									x	
17. Nordic Ski Trails, Anchorage, AK 99502		(907)272-4485								
18. Prism Ski Touring, Girdwood, AK 99587		(907)783-2945			x			x	x	
19. Sourdough Outfitters, Bettles, AK 99726		(907)692-5252			x			x	x	x

UNITED STATES

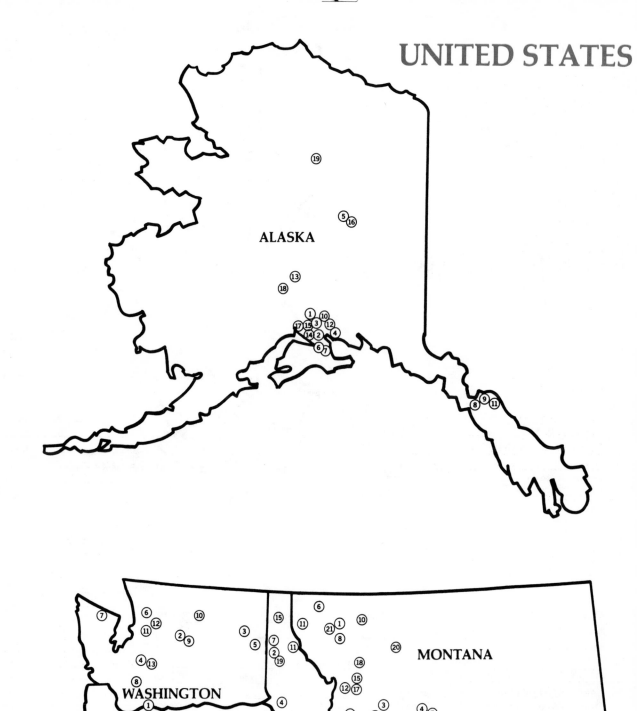

WASHINGTON

NAME OF AREA, LOCATION	TELEPHONE #	TRAIL MILES	MAINTAINED MILES	INSTRUCTION	RENTAL	SNACKS	MEALS	LODGING	CAMPING
1. District Ranger, Carson, WA 98610	(509)427-5645		12					x	x
2. Family Adventures, Inc., Leavenworth, WA 98826	(509)548-7330	30						x	x
3. 49° North, Chewelah, WA 99109	(509)935-6649	20		x	x				
4. Mount Ranier National Park, Tahoma Woods, Ashford, WA 98304	(206)569-2341	5			x	x	x	x	x
5. Mount Spokane Skiing Corp., Spokane, WA 99208	(509)238-6281	16			x			x	x
6. North Cascade National Park, Sedro Woolley, WA 98284	(206)855-1331	11					x	x	x
7. Olympic National Park, Port Angeles, WA 98362	(206)452-9236	25				x		x	x
8. Saint Helens State Park, Cougar, WA 98616	(206)238-5244	10	8					x	x
9. Scottish Lakes Cross Country Ski Area, Leavenworth, WA 98826	(509)548-7330	30			x			x	x
10. Sun Mountain Lodge, Winthrop, WA 98862	(509)996-2211	50	30	x	x			x	x
11. The Cross Country Center, Snoqualmie Pass, WA 98068	(206)434-6303	25	25	x	x				
12. Mountain Home, Easton, WA 98925	(509)656-2346	10	10	x	x			x	x
13. White Pass Co., Yakima, WA 98907	(509)453-8731			x	x	x	x	x	

OREGON

NAME OF AREA, LOCATION	TELEPHONE #	TRAIL MILES	MAINTAINED MILES	INSTRUCTION	RENTAL	SNACKS	MEALS	LODGING	CAMPING
1. Anthony Lakes Corp., North Powder, OR 97867	(503)963-6913	100				x	x	x	
2. Chiloquin Ranger District, Chiloquin, OR 97624		30							
3. Cooper Spur Ski Area, Parkdale, OR 97047	(503)386-3381				x	x	x		
4. Crater Lake National Park, Crater Lake, OR 97604	(503)594-2211	10				x	x	x	
5. Diamond Lake Resort, Diamond Lake, OR 97731	(503)793-3333				x	x	x	x	
6. Hoodoo Ski Bowl, Sisters, OR 97759	(503)Hoodoo 1/2	20		x	x	x	x	x	
7. Mount Ashland Ski Area, Ashland, OR 97520	(503)482-6406	6			x	x	x	x	x
8. Mount Bachelor/Rossignol Nordic Sports Center, Bend, OR 97701	(503)382-2442	40	21	x	x	x	x	x	x
9. Mount Hood Multorpor-Ski Bowl, Government Camp, OR 94028	(503)272-3330	12		x				x	x
10. Odell Lake Resort, Crescent Lake, OR 97425	(503)433-2540	30		x	x	x	x	x	
11. Sunriver Lodge, Sunriver, OR 97701	(503)591-1221	50		x	x	x	x	x	
12. Timberline Lodge, Government Camp, OR 97028	(800)452-1335	100	15	x	x	x	x	x	x
13. Willamette National Forest, Westfir, OR 97492	(503)782-2291	22			x				

IDAHO

NAME OF AREA, LOCATION	TELEPHONE #	TRAIL MILES	MAINTAINED MILES	INSTRUCTION	RENTAL	SNACKS	MEALS	LODGING	CAMPING
1. Brundage Mountain, McCall, ID 83638	(208)634-7462								
2. Burley Ranger District, Burley, ID 83318	(208)678-0439	3	3	x			x		x
3. Busterback Ranch, Harrison, ID 83833	(208)774-2217	20	20					x	x
4. Caribou National Forest, Pocatello, ID 83201	(208)232-1142	50							
5. Cottonwood Butte, Cottonwood, ID 83522	(208)962-3495							x	x
6. Craters of the Moon National Monument, Arco, ID 83213		100							
7. Fernan Ranger District, Coeur d'Alene, ID 83814	(208)667-2461	20							
8. Galena Lodge Touring Center, Ketchum, ID 83340	(208)726-4010	36	26	x	x	x	x	x	x
9. Kelly Canyon Ski Area, Idaho Falls, ID 83401	(208)538-6261				x	x	x	x	
10. Leonard Expeditions, Stanley, ID 83278	(208)774-3656			x	x	x	x	x	
11. Lookout Pass, Wallace, ID 83873	(208)752-1221	6			x				
12. Magic Mountain, Albion, ID 83311	(208)638-5599				x				
13. Pebble Creek, Pocatello, ID 83204	(208)234-0271								
14. Pomerelle, Albion, ID 83311	(208)638-5599	12			x				

continued ...

NAME OF AREA	LOCATION	TELEPHONE #	TRAIL MILES	MAINTAINED MILES	INSTRUCTION	RENTAL	SNACKS	MEALS	LODGING	CAMP
15. Priest Lake Ranger District, Sandpoint, ID 83864			20							
16. Skyline Ski Area, Pocatello, ID 83201		(208)775-3744				x	x		x	
17. Sun Valley Nordic Ski School, Sun Valley, ID 83353		(208)622-4111								
18. Targhee National Forest, Saint Anthony, ID 83445		(208)354-2312	50							
19. Timber Ridge Ranch, Harrison, ID 83833		(208)689-3315								
20. Wilderness River Outfitters, Salmon, ID 83467		(208)756-3935			x		x	x	x	x

MONTANA

NAME OF AREA	LOCATION	TELEPHONE #	TRAIL MILES	MAINTAINED MILES	INSTRUCTION	RENTAL	SNACKS	MEALS	LODGING	CAMP
1. Big Mountain Sky Area, Whitefish, MT 59937		(406)862-3511	50		x	x	x	x	x	
2. Big Sky of Montana Resort, Big Sky, MT 59716	1-800-548-4486	(406)995-4211	35		x	x	x	x	x	
3. Boulder Hot Springs, Boulder, MT 59602		(406)225-4272	50		x			x	x	
4. Bridger Bowl Ski Area, Bozeman, MT 59715		(406)587-2111			x	x	x	x	x	
5. Butte Beef Trail, Butte, MT 59701		(406)494-7000	6	6	x					
6. Crystal Lakes Resort, Fortine, MT 59918		(406)882-4455	25		x	x		x	x	
7. Flaming Arrow Ski Touring Centre, Bozeman, MT 59715		(406)587-2001	30		x	x	x		x	x
8. Flathead National Forest, Kalispell, MT 59901		(406)755-5401	50		x	x	x		x	x
9. Gallatin National Forest, Bozeman, MT 59715			100		x	x	x	x	x	x
10. Glacier National Park, West Glacier, MT 59715		(406)888-5441	700							
11. Libby Ranger Station, Libby, MT 59923			18		x	x	x	x		
12. Lolo Pass Winter Sport Area, Lolo, MT 59847		(208)942-3113	30		x	x	x	x	x	
13. Lone Mountain Ranch, Big Sky, MT 59716		(406)995-4644	55	35	x	x	x	x	x	
14. Lost Trail Pass, Sula, MT 59871		(406)821-3201	50		x	x	x	x	x	
15. Marshall Mountain Ski Area, Missoula, MT 59801		(406)258-6619	20		x			x	x	x
16. Maverick Mountain, Polaris, MT 59746		(406)834-2412			x					
17. Montana Snow Bowl, Missoula, MT 59801		(406)549-9777							x	x
18. Montana Sports Ranch, Condon, MT 59826		(406)754-2351	7	7				x	x	x
19. Red Lodge Mountain, Red Lodge, MT 59068		(406)466-2288	20		x	x	x	x		
20. Teton Pass Ski Area, Choteau, MT 59422		(406)466-5749	50		x	x	x	x	x	
21. Whitefish Nordic Ski Center, Whitefish, MT 59937		(406)862-5294	50		x	x	x	x	x	x
22. Yellowstone Nordic, West Yellowstone, MT 59758		(406)646-7319	200	25	x	x	x	x	x	
23. Yellowstone Rendezvous Touring Center, West Yellowstone, MT 59758		(406)646-7712								

CALIFORNIA

NAME OF AREA	LOCATION	TELEPHONE #	TRAIL MILES	MAINTAINED MILES	INSTRUCTION	RENTAL	SNACKS	MEALS	LODGING	CAMP
1. Alpine Meadows, Tahoe City, CA 95730		(916)583-4232			x	x				
2. Bear Valley Touring Center, Bear Valley, CA 95223		(209)753-2844	50	6	x	x	x	x	x	
3. Big Chief Guides Nordic Resort, Truckee, CA 95734		(916)587-4723	25	25	x	x	x	x	x	
4. Buffalo Bill's Nordic Center, Big Bear Lake, CA 92315		(714)866-5253	100		x	x	x			
5. Mill Creek Station, Mentone, CA 92359	District Ranger	(714)794-1123								
6. Dodge Ridge Ski Area, Pinecrest, CA 95364		(209)965-3474			x	x				
7. Donner Ski Ranch, Norden, CA 95724		(916)426-3578			x	x	x	x	x	
8. Echo Summit, South Lake Tahoe, CA 95731		(916)659-7154								
9. Ernie's June Lake Ski Touring Center, June Lake, CA 93529		(714)648-7756			x	x			x	x
10. Goldmine Ski Area, Big Bear Lake, CA 92815		(714)585-2517			x	x	x	x		
11. Kirkwood Ski Touring Center, Kirkwood, CA 95646		(209)258-8864	40	16	x	x	x	x	x	

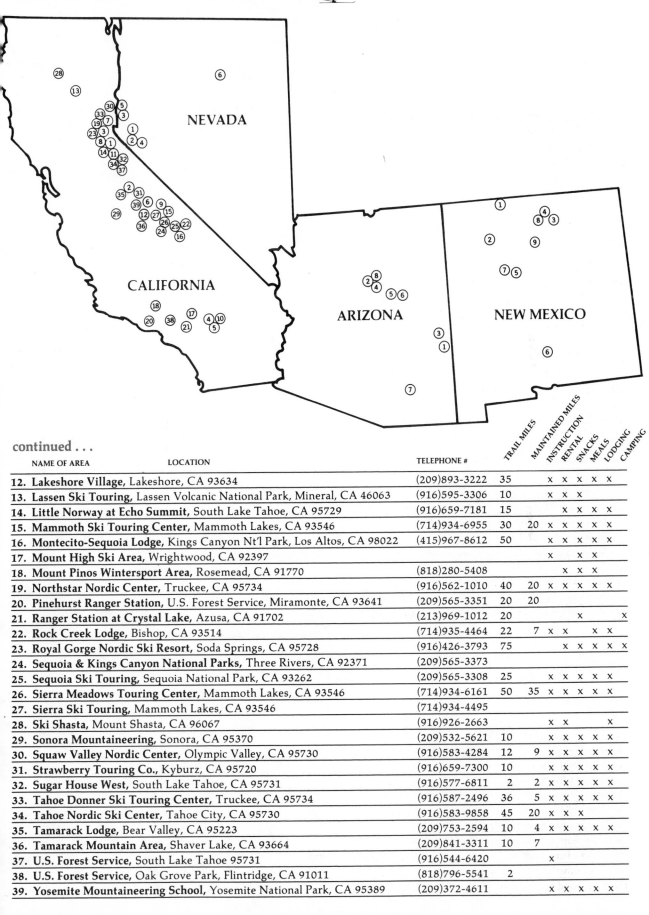

continued . . .

NAME OF AREA	LOCATION	TELEPHONE #	TRAIL MILES	MAINTAINED MILES	INSTRUCTION	RENTAL	SNACKS	MEALS	LODGING	CAMPING
12. Lakeshore Village, Lakeshore, CA 93634		(209)893-3222	35		x	x	x	x	x	
13. Lassen Ski Touring, Lassen Volcanic National Park, Mineral, CA 46063		(916)595-3306	10		x	x	x			
14. Little Norway at Echo Summit, South Lake Tahoe, CA 95729		(916)659-7181	15			x	x	x	x	
15. Mammoth Ski Touring Center, Mammoth Lakes, CA 93546		(714)934-6955	30	20	x	x	x	x	x	x
16. Montecito-Sequoia Lodge, Kings Canyon Nt'l Park, Los Altos, CA 98022		(415)967-8612	50		x	x	x	x	x	
17. Mount High Ski Area, Wrightwood, CA 92397					x			x	x	
18. Mount Pinos Wintersport Area, Rosemead, CA 91770		(818)280-5408			x	x	x			
19. Northstar Nordic Center, Truckee, CA 95734		(916)562-1010	40	20	x	x	x	x	x	
20. Pinehurst Ranger Station, U.S. Forest Service, Miramonte, CA 93641		(209)565-3351	20	20						
21. Ranger Station at Crystal Lake, Azusa, CA 91702		(213)969-1012	20			x				x
22. Rock Creek Lodge, Bishop, CA 93514		(714)935-4464	22	7	x	x			x	x
23. Royal Gorge Nordic Ski Resort, Soda Springs, CA 95728		(916)426-3793	75		x	x	x	x	x	x
24. Sequoia & Kings Canyon National Parks, Three Rivers, CA 92371		(209)565-3373								
25. Sequoia Ski Touring, Sequoia National Park, CA 93262		(209)565-3308	25		x	x	x	x	x	
26. Sierra Meadows Touring Center, Mammoth Lakes, CA 93546		(714)934-6161	50	35	x	x	x	x	x	
27. Sierra Ski Touring, Mammoth Lakes, CA 93546		(714)934-4495								
28. Ski Shasta, Mount Shasta, CA 96067		(916)926-2663			x	x				x
29. Sonora Mountaineering, Sonora, CA 95370		(209)532-5621	10		x	x	x	x	x	
30. Squaw Valley Nordic Center, Olympic Valley, CA 95730		(916)583-4284	12	9	x	x	x	x	x	
31. Strawberry Touring Co., Kyburz, CA 95720		(916)659-7300	10		x	x	x	x	x	
32. Sugar House West, South Lake Tahoe, CA 95731		(916)577-6811	2	2	x	x	x	x	x	
33. Tahoe Donner Ski Touring Center, Truckee, CA 95734		(916)587-2496	36	5	x	x	x	x	x	
34. Tahoe Nordic Ski Center, Tahoe City, CA 95730		(916)583-9858	45	20	x	x	x			
35. Tamarack Lodge, Bear Valley, CA 95223		(209)753-2594	10	4	x	x	x	x	x	
36. Tamarack Mountain Area, Shaver Lake, CA 93664		(209)841-3311	10	7						
37. U.S. Forest Service, South Lake Tahoe 95731		(916)544-6420			x					
38. U.S. Forest Service, Oak Grove Park, Flintridge, CA 91011		(818)796-5541	2							
39. Yosemite Mountaineering School, Yosemite National Park, CA 95389		(209)372-4611			x	x	x	x	x	

NEVADA

NAME OF AREA / LOCATION	TELEPHONE #	Trail Miles	Maintained Miles	Instruction	Rental	Snacks	Meals	Lodging	Camping
1. **Hope Valley Area,** Carson City, NV 89701	(702)882-2766					x	x		
2. **Lake Tahoe-Nevada State Park,** Incline Village, NV 89450	(702)831-0494	4							
3. **Mount Rose Ski Area,** Reno, NV 89505	(702)849-0704				x	x	x		
4. **Ski Incline,** Incline Village, NV 89450	(702)831-1821			x	x	x	x	x	
5. **Slide Mountain Ski Area,** Reno, NV 89505	(702)849-0852				x	x	x		
6. **Wildhorse Ranch & Resort,** via: Elko, NV 89801	Northfork 6471	30	10	x	x		x	x	

ARIZONA

NAME OF AREA / LOCATION	TELEPHONE #	Trail Miles	Maintained Miles	Instruction	Rental	Snacks	Meals	Lodging	Camping
1. **Alpine Ski Tours,** Alpine, AZ 85920	(602)339-4574	15	15	x	x			x	
2. **Arizona Snow Bowl,** Flagstaff, AZ 86002	(602)774-0562	10	10	x	x	x	x		
3. **Circle B Market,** Greer, AZ 86927	(602)735-7540	8	8	x	x	x	x	x	x
4. **Fairfield Snow Bowl,** Flagstaff, AZ 86002	(602)774-0564				x				
5. **Montezuma Nordic Ski Touring Center,** Mormon Lake, AZ 86038	(602)354-2221	15	10	x		x			
6. **Mormon Lake Ski Touring Center,** Mormon Lake, AZ 86038	(602)354-2240	50		x	x	x	x	x	x
7. **Mount Lemmon Ski Valley,** Mt. Lemmon, AZ 85619	(602)791-9721				x	x	x		
8. **Sacred Mountain Ski Tours,** Flagstaff, AZ 86001	(602)779-7809	10	10	x	x			x	x

NEW MEXICO

NAME OF AREA / LOCATION	TELEPHONE #	Trail Miles	Maintained Miles	Instruction	Rental	Snacks	Meals	Lodging	Camping
1. **Chama Pass Area,** Grande National Forest, Monte Vista, CO 81144									
2. **Cuba Ranger District,** Cuba, NM 87013	(505)289-3264	20							
3. **Drawer B,** Angel Fire, NM 87710	(505)377-2301		40	x	x	x	x		
4. **Red River Ski Area,** Red River, NM 87558	(505)754-2223			x	x				
5. **Sandia Ranger District,** Tijeras, NM 87059	(505)281-3304	5	5	x	x	x	x	x	
6. **Ski Cloud Country,** Cloudcroft, NM 88317	(505)682-2511				x	x	x		
7. **Snowfire Ski Tours,** Albuquerque, NM 87106	(505)268-4876			x	x			x	x
8. **Taos Ski Valley, Inc.,** Taos Ski Valley, NM 87571	(505)776-2266			x	x	x	x	x	
9. **Tesuque Ranger District,** Santa Fe, NM 87501	(505)988-6322								

UTAH

NAME OF AREA / LOCATION	TELEPHONE #	Trail Miles	Maintained Miles	Instruction	Rental	Snacks	Meals	Lodging	Camping
1. **Brian Head Nordic Ski Center,** Brian Head, UT 84719	(801)586-8825	10	7	x	x			x	x
2. **Brighton Ski Tour. Ctr.,** Brighton Village Store, Brighton, UT 84121	(801)649-9156	20	10	x	x	x	x	x	
3. **Bryce Canyon National Park,** Bryce Canyon, UT 84717	(801)834-5322	5							
4. **Dinosaur National Monument,** Dinosaur, CO 81610	(303)374-2216					x	x	x	x
5. **Duck Creek Ski Center,** Cedar City, UT 84720	(801)648-2495	50+		x		x	x	x	x
6. **Silver Fork Lodge,** Brighton, UT 84121	(801)649-9551				x	x	x	x	
7. **Snowbird Ski & Summer Resort,** Snowbird, UT 94070	(801)742-2222				x	x	x	x	x
8. **White Pine Touring Center,** Park City, UT 84060	(801)649-8701	3	3	x	x				x

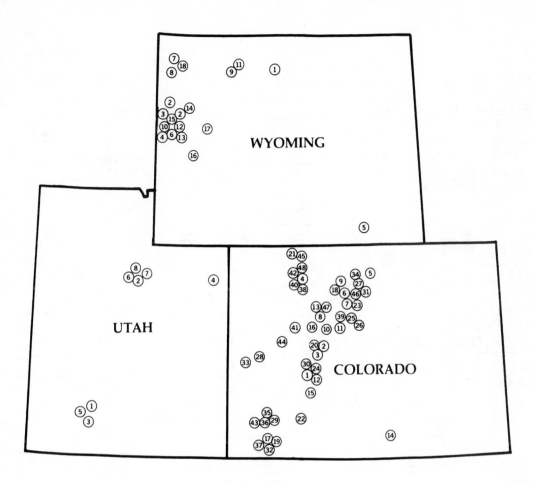

WYOMING

NAME OF AREA	LOCATION	TELEPHONE #	TRAIL MILES	MAINTAINED MILES	INSTRUCTION	RENTAL	SNACKS	MEALS	LODGING	CAMPING
1. Bear Lodge Resort, Bear Lodge, WY 82836		(307)655-2444					x	x	x	
2. Flagg Ranch, Moran, WY 83013		(307)733-4818	100+				x	x	x	x
3. Grand Targhee, Alta, WY, via Driggs, ID 83422		(307)353-2304		3	x	x				
4. Grand Teton National Park, Moose, WY 83012		(307)733-2880	40			x	x	x	x	x
5. Happy Jack Ski Area, Laramie, WY 82070		(307)745-9583				x	x	x	x	x
6. Jackson Hole Area, Jackson, WY 83001		(307)733-3316				x	x	x	x	x
7. Lankford Mountain Guides, Denver, CO 80220		(303)393-0400				x			x	
8. Old Faithful Snowlodge, Yellowstone Park, WY 82190		(307)344-7321				x	x		x	x
9. Pahaska Tepee, Cody, WY 82414		(307)587-5536						x	x	
10. Powder Hound Nordic, Wilson, WY 83014		(307)733-2181	6			x	x	x	x	x
11. Sleeping Giant Ski Resort, Cody, WY 82414		(307)587-4044				x	x	x	x	
12. Snow King Mountain, Jackson, WY 83001		(307)833-2851								
13. Sundance Ski Tours, Jackson, WY 83001		(307)733-4796				x		x	x	x
14. Togwotee Mountain Lodge, Moran, WY 83013		(307)543-2847	15	7	x			x	x	
15. Triangle X Ranch, Moose, WY 83012		(307)733-2183					x	x	x	
16. White Pine Lodge, Pinedale, WY 82941		(307)367-2913					x	x	x	
17. Wind River Ranch, Dubois, WY 82513		(307)455-2721	10	x	x	x	x	x	x	
18. Yellowstone Park Co., Yellowstone National Park, WY 82190		(307)344-7311				x	x	x	x	x	x

COLORADO

NAME OF AREA	LOCATION	TELEPHONE #	TRAIL MILES	MAINTAINED MILES	INSTRUCTION	RENTAL	SNACKS	MEALS	LODGING	CAMP
1. Ambush Ski Touring Center	Crested Butte, CO 81224	(303)349-5408	138	10	x	x	x	x	x	
2. Ashcroft Ski Touring Unlimited	Aspen, CO 81611	(303)925-1971	30	28	x	x	x	x		
3. Aspen Mountain Ski School	Aspen, CO 81611	(303)925-1220		5	x	x	x	x	x	x
4. Bearpole Ranch	Steamboat Springs, CO 80477	(303)879-0576	52		x	x	x	x	x	
5. Beaver Meadows Ski Resort	Fort Collins, CO 80524	(303)881-2450	18	18	x	x	x	x	x	x
6. Beaver Village	Winter Park, CO 80482	(303)726-5741	12		x			x	x	x
7. Berthoud Pass Ski Area	Idaho Springs, CO 80452	(303)572-8014			x	x				
8. Black Mountain Ranch	Vail, CO 81657	(303)476-1200	31						x	x
9. C Lazy U Ranch	Granby, CO 80446	(303)887-3344	10	7	x	x				
10. Colorado Outward Bound School	Denver, CO 80203	(303)837-0880			x			x		x
11. Copper Mountain Ski Touring Center	Copper Mountain, CO 80443	(303)468-2882	40	20	x	x	x	x	x	
12. Crested Butte Mountain Resort	Crested Butte, CO 81224	(303)349-6611	7	7	x	x	x	x	x	
13. Crooked Creek Ski Touring	Vail, CO 81567	(303)949-5682	70	7	x			x	x	x
14. Cuchara Valley	La Veta, CO 81055	(303)742-3661	100		x	x	x	x	x	
15. Curecanti National Recreation Area	Gunnison, CO 81230	(303)641-2336	50							
16. Diamond J Guest Ranch	Meredith, CO 81642	(303)972-3222	20	13	x	x		x	x	x
17. Diamond Lodge	Durango, CO 81301	(303)247-5098		6	x	x		x	x	x
18. Devils Thumb Ranch & Cross Country Center	Frazer, CO 80422	(303)726-8298	37	37	x	x	x	x	x	
19. Durango Nordic	Chamber of Commerce, Durango, CO 81301	(303)247-0312			x	x		x		
20. Fothergills Outdoor Sportsman	Aspen, CO 81611	(303)925-3288	100+	30	x	x	x	x	x	
21. Glen Eden Ranch	Clark, CO 80428	(303)879-3906	18	18	x	x	x	x	x	
22. Golcondo Helicopter Ski Touring Center	Lake City, CO 81235	(303)944-2256	10	3	x	x		x	x	x
23. Idlewild	Winter Park, CO 80482	(303)726-5564		20	x	x				
24. Irwin Lodge	Crested Butte, CO 81224	(303)349-5140	50	50	x	x		x	x	x
25. Keystone Resort	Keystone, CO 80435	(303)968-1234	40	20	x	x	x	x	x	
26. Keystone Touring Center	Keystone, CO 80435	(303)468-2316		13	x	x			x	
27. Lazy H Ranch	Allenspark, CO 80510	(303)747-2532				x	x	x	x	
28. Mesa Lake Resorts	Mesa, CO 81643	(303)268-5467	33		x	x	x	x	x	
29. Norwegian School of Nature Life	Silverton, CO 81433	(206)432-4233			x	x	x	x	x	
30. Nordic Adventure Ski Touring Center	Crested Butte, CO 81224	(303)349-6611	7	7	x	x			x	x
31. Peaceful Valley Lodge	Lyons, CO 80540	(303)747-2582	45		x			x	x	x
32. Purgatory Ski Area	Durango, CO 81301	(303)259-1490	45	25	x	x	x	x	x	
33. Powderhorn Ski Area	Grand Junction, CO 81501	(303)268-5482			x	x			x	x
34. Rocky Mountain National Park	Estes Park, CO 80517		50		x	x	x	x	x	x
35. Saint Paul Cross Country Ski Lodge	Silverton, CO 81433	(303)387-5494	6.2		x	x	x	x	x	x
36. San Juan Alpine Tours	Silverton, CO 81433	(303)387-5798	15	6	x	x	x	x	x	
37. San Juan National Forest	Durango, CO 81301	(303)247-4874			x				x	x
38. Scandinavian Lodge	Steamboat Village, CO 80499	(303)879-0517	1.5		x	x			x	x
39. Ski Tip Lodge	Dillon, CO 80435	(303)468-9928						x	x	
40. Sky Valley Lodge	Steamboat Springs, CO 80477	(303)879-5515	19		x	x			x	x
41. Snowmass Country Club	Snowmass Village, CO 81615	(303)923-4012	13	13	x	x	x	x	x	
42. Steamboat Touring Center	Steamboat Springs, CO 80477			9	x	x	x	x	x	
43. Telluride Ski Touring	Orphir, CO 81426	(303)728-4106		6	x			x	x	x
44. The Historic Redstone Inn/High Cntry. Ski Tour.	Redstone, CO 81623	(303)963-2526	19		x	x		x	x	x
45. The Home Ranch	Clark, CO 80428	(303)879-0469	25	13	x	x			x	x
46. Tour Eldora, Lake Eldora Ski Area	Nederland, CO 80466	(303)447-8012	24	12	x	x	x		x	
47. Vail Ski Touring	Vail, CO 81657	(303)476-5601	145		x	x			x	x
48. Vista Verde Guest Ranch	Steamboat Springs, CO 80477	(303)879-3858	50	12	x			x	x	x

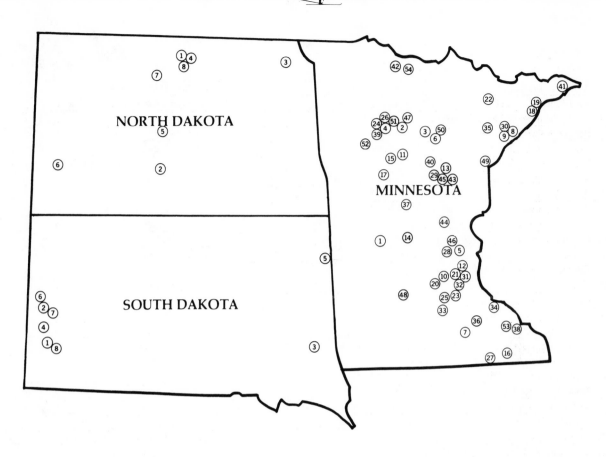

NORTH DAKOTA

NAME OF AREA / LOCATION	TELEPHONE #	TRAIL MILES	MAINTAINED MILES	INSTRUCTION	RENTAL	SNACKS	MEALS	LODGING	CAMPING
1. **Bottineau Winter Park,** Bottineau, ND 58318	(701)228-2278	3			x	x	x		
2. **Fort Lincoln State Park,** Mandan, ND 58554	(701)663-3049								
3. **Icelandic State Park,** Cavalier, ND 58211	(701)265-4561	4							
4. **Lake Metigoshe State Park,** Bottineau, ND 58318	(701)263-4561	3							x
5. **Lake Sakakawea State Park,** Riverdale, ND 58565	(701)748-2313								
6. **Theodore Roosevelt National Mountain Park,** Medora, ND 58645	(701)623-4466	25				x	x	x	
7. **Trestle Valley Ski Area,** Minot, ND 58701	(701)838-5426								
8. **Tetrault Woods State Park,** Bottineau, ND 58318	(701)228-2278	3							
9. **Turtle River State Park,** Arvilla, ND 58214	(701)343-2011				x	x	x	x	

SOUTH DAKOTA

NAME OF AREA / LOCATION	TELEPHONE #	TRAIL MILES	MAINTAINED MILES	INSTRUCTION	RENTAL	SNACKS	MEALS	LODGING	CAMPING
1. **Black Hills National Forest,** Custer, SD 57730		20					x	x	
2. **Deer Mountain Ski Area,** Deadwood, 57732	(605)578-1713	17		x	x				
3. **Great Bear Ski Valley,** Sioux Falls, SD 57101	(605)338-3516	5	5		x	x	x		
4. **Mystic Trails Cross Country Ski Center,** Hill City, SD 57745	(605)574-2809	60		x	x		x	x	
5. **Pleasant Valley X-C Ski Slopes,** Gary, SD 57237	(605)272-5614	5	2	x		x	x		
6. **Ski Cross Country Inc.,** Spearfish, SD 57783	(605)642-3851	20	20	x	x	x			
7. **Terry Peak Ski Area,** Deadwood, SD 57732	(605)578-1501	5+			x	x	x	x	
8. **Yellow Hair Outfitters,** Custer City, SD 57730	(604)673-2263	38	5	x	x	x			

MINNESOTA

#	NAME OF AREA	LOCATION	TELEPHONE #	TRAIL MILES	MAINTAINED MILES	INSTRUCTION	RENTAL	SNACKS	MEALS	LODGING	CAMPING
1	Arrowwood Resort	Alexandria, MN 56308	(612)762-1124	9	3		x			x	x
2	Bald Eagle Center	Cass Lake, MN 56633	(218)665-2241	20		x				x	x
3	Bowstring Northwood Resort	Deer River, MN 56636	(218)556-4321		9					x	x
4	Buena Vista Ski Area	Bemidji, MN 56601	(218)243-2231	15	15	x	x	x	x		
5	Bunker Hills Ski Trails	Anoka, MN 55303	(612)757-3920	13	13	x	x	x	x		
6	Camp Mishewaka	Grand Rapids, MN 55744	(218)326-5667	14	14	x				x	x
7	Cannon River Wilderness Area	N.W. Fairibault, MN 55021	(507)334-6337	6							
8	Cascade Lodge	Lutson, MN 55612	(218)387-1112	35	35	x				x	x
9	Cascade River State Park	Lutson, MN 55612	(218)387-1543	15	15						x
10	Cedar Hills Ski Park	Eden Prairie, MN 55343	(612)445-4066	2		x	x	x	x		
11	Chippewa National Forest	Walker, MN 56484		7	7						
12	Columbia Ski Touring Center	Minneapolis, MN	(612)789-2627			x	x	x			
13	Deer Acre Resort	Effie, MN 56639	(218)653-2281	8	8	x	x			x	x
14	Eagle Mountain Ski Area	Gray Eagle, MN 56336	(612)285-4567	6	6	x	x	x	x	x	x
15	Earthome Resort	Akeley, MN 56435	(218)652-2135	3	3	x	x	x	x		
16	Forestville State Park	Preston, MN 55965	(507)352-5111	6							x
17	Gloege's Outfitting	Nimrod, MN 56478	(218)472-3250	5		x	x			x	
18	Grand Portage National Monument	Grand Marais, MN 55604	(218)387-2788	9	9						x
19	Gunflint Lodge	Grand Marais, MN 55604	(218)388-2294	50	50	x	x	x	x	x	
20	Hennepin County Park Reserve District	Maple Plain, MN 55359	(612)427-4911		13						
21	Hiawatha Ski Touring Center	Minneapolis, MN	(612)724-7715			x	x	x			
22	Hidden Valley Ski Area	Ely, MN 55731	(218)365-3231	10	10						
23	Hyland Hills	Bloomington, MN 55437	(612)835-4604		6	x	x				
24	Isle O'Pines	Bemidji, MN 56601	(218)751-2783	13	13	x	x			x	
25	Jonathan Association	Lake Village Center, Chaska, MN 55318	(612)448-4700	9		x	x				
26	Kohl's Last Resort	Bemidji, MN 56601	(218)586-2251	27	5	x	x	x	x		
27	Lake Louise State Park	LeRoy, MN 55951	(507)324-5249	3	3						x
28	Lake Maria State Park	Monticello, MN 55360	(612)878-2325	5	5						x
29	Long Lake Conservation Center	Palisade, MN 56469	(218)768-4653	6	6	x				x	x
30	Lutsen Resort	Lutsen, MN 55612	(218)663-7212	19	13	x	x			x	x
31	Manitou Lakes X-C	Minneapolis, MN 55427	(612)536-5709	20	20	x					
32	Minneapolis Park & Recreation Board	Minneapolis, MN 55415	(612)348-2121			x	x	x			
33	Minnesota Valley Trail	Jordan, MN 55352	(612)492-6400	12	12						
34	Mount Frontenac Ski Area	Red Wing, MN 55066	(612)388-5826	5		x	x	x			
35	National Forest Lodge	Isabella, MN 55607	(218)323-4411	30	10	x	x			x	x
36	Nerstrand Woods State Park	Nerstrand, MN 55053	(507)334-8848	6	6						x
37	North County Ski Touring	Brainerd, MN 56401	(218)829-0900	20		x	x	x			
38	O.L. Kipp State Park	Winona, MN 55987	(507)643-6849	5	5						x
39	Old Tyme Retreat	Bemidji, MN 56601	(218)335-6604	45		x	x	x	x	x	
40	Quadna Mountain	Hill City, MN 55745 1-800-662-5796	(218)697-2303	14	14	x			x	x	x
41	Raddisson Inn	Grand Portage, MN 55605	(218)475-2401	50	50	x	x	x	x		
42	Red Lake Wildlife Management Area	Roosevelt, MN 56673	(218)783-5861	6	6						
43	Ruttgers Bay Lake Lodge	Deerwood, MN 56444	(218)678-2885	15	15	x	x			x	x
44	Saint Croix State Park	Hinckley, MN 55037	(612)384-6591	75	20						x
45	Savanna State Forest	McGregor, MN 55760	(218)426-3407	13							
46	Sherburne National Wildlife Refuge	Zimmerman, MN 55398	(612)389-3323	13							
47	Ski Tur Centre	Cass Lake, MN 56633	(218)335-8802	15	15	x	x			x	x
48	Spidahl Ski Gard	Erhard, MN 56534	(218)736-5097	18	18	x	x	x			
49	Spirit Mountain Ski Area	Duluth, MN 55810	(218)628-2891	8	8	x	x	x	x	x	x
50	Sugar Hills Ski Area	Grand Rapids, MN 55744	(218)326-9461	50	50	x	x	x	x	x	x
51	The Home Place	Cass Lake, MN 56633	(218)335-8802	15	15	x			x		x
52	Val Chatel	Park Rapids, MN 56470	(218)266-3306	8		x	x	x	x	x	
53	Whitewater State Park	Altura, MN 55910	(507)932-3007	6							x
54	Zippel Bay State Park	Williams, MN 56686	(218)783-5253	1	1						x

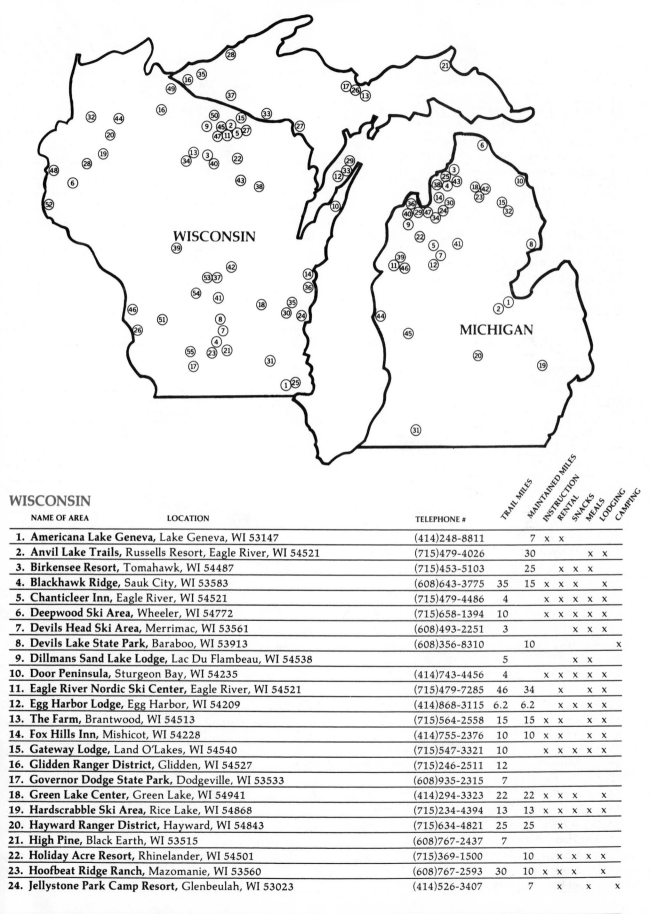

WISCONSIN

NAME OF AREA	LOCATION	TELEPHONE #	TRAIL MILES	MAINTAINED MILES	INSTRUCTION	RENTAL	SNACKS	MEALS	LODGING	CAMPING
1. Americana Lake Geneva, Lake Geneva, WI 53147		(414)248-8811	7		x	x				
2. Anvil Lake Trails, Russells Resort, Eagle River, WI 54521		(715)479-4026	30					x	x	
3. Birkensee Resort, Tomahawk, WI 54487		(715)453-5103	25			x	x	x		
4. Blackhawk Ridge, Sauk City, WI 53583		(608)643-3775	35	15	x	x	x		x	
5. Chanticleer Inn, Eagle River, WI 54521		(715)479-4486	4		x	x	x	x	x	
6. Deepwood Ski Area, Wheeler, WI 54772		(715)658-1394	10		x	x	x	x	x	
7. Devils Head Ski Area, Merrimac, WI 53561		(608)493-2251	3			x	x	x		
8. Devils Lake State Park, Baraboo, WI 53913		(608)356-8310		10						x
9. Dillmans Sand Lake Lodge, Lac Du Flambeau, WI 54538			5			x	x			
10. Door Peninsula, Sturgeon Bay, WI 54235		(414)743-4456	4		x	x	x	x	x	
11. Eagle River Nordic Ski Center, Eagle River, WI 54521		(715)479-7285	46	34	x		x	x		
12. Egg Harbor Lodge, Egg Harbor, WI 54209		(414)868-3115	6.2	6.2	x	x	x	x		
13. The Farm, Brantwood, WI 54513		(715)564-2558	15	15	x	x		x	x	
14. Fox Hills Inn, Mishicot, WI 54228		(414)755-2376	10	10	x	x		x	x	
15. Gateway Lodge, Land O'Lakes, WI 54540		(715)547-3321	10		x	x	x	x	x	
16. Glidden Ranger District, Glidden, WI 54527		(715)246-2511	12							
17. Governor Dodge State Park, Dodgeville, WI 53533		(608)935-2315	7							
18. Green Lake Center, Green Lake, WI 54941		(414)294-3323	22	22	x	x	x		x	
19. Hardscrabble Ski Area, Rice Lake, WI 54868		(715)234-4394	13	13	x	x	x	x	x	
20. Hayward Ranger District, Hayward, WI 54843		(715)634-4821	25	25	x					
21. High Pine, Black Earth, WI 53515		(608)767-2437	7							
22. Holiday Acre Resort, Rhinelander, WI 54501		(715)369-1500		10		x	x	x	x	
23. Hoofbeat Ridge Ranch, Mazomanie, WI 53560		(608)767-2593	30	10	x	x	x		x	
24. Jellystone Park Camp Resort, Glenbeulah, WI 53023		(414)526-3407		7		x		x		x

continued . . .

No. NAME OF AREA, LOCATION	TELEPHONE #	Trail Miles	Maintained Miles	Instruction	Rental	Snacks	Meals	Lodging	Camping
25. Mount Fuji Ski Area, Lake Geneva, WI 53147	(414)248-6553	3							
26. Mount La Crosse, La Crosse, WI 54601	(608)788-0044	8	8	x	x	x	x		
27. Musky Inn Trails, Saint Germain, WI 54558	(715)542-3768	30+	30+	x	x	x	x	x	
28. Nature's Way, Turtle Lake, WI 54889	(715)986-2484	20			x	x	x	x	
29. Newport State Park, Ellison Bay, WI 54210	(414)554-2500	20							x
30. Northern Kettle Moraine State Forest, Campbellsport, WI 53010	(414)626-2116	35							x
31. Olympia Resort, Oconomowoc, WI 53066	(414)567-0311	8		x	x		x	x	
32. Olympia Sports Village, Lake O'Brien, Upson, WI 54565	(715)561-4427	30	20			x	x	x	
33. Omnibus Ski Touring Center, Fish Creek, WI 54212	(414)868-3013	20	20	x	x		x	x	
34. Palmquist Farm Trails, Brantwood, WI 54513	(715)564-2558		19		x	x	x	x	
35. Pike Lake State Park, Hartford, WI 53027	(414)644-5248	2							x
36. Point Beach State Forest, Two Rivers, WI 54241	(414)794-7480		7						x
37. Ridges Inn, Wisconsin Rapids, WI 54494	(715)424-1111	5	5						x
38. Riverview Country Club, Antigo, WI 54409	(715)623-3623	8		x	x	x	x		
39. Sandhill Wildlife Area, Babcock, WI 54413	(715)884-2726	20							
40. Skiniskis Touring Center, Tomahawk, WI 54487	(715)453-4796	12	12	x	x		x		
41. Skyline Ski Area, Friendship, WI 53934	(608)339-3421			x	x	x	x		
42. Standing Rocks, Portage County Parks, Stevens Point, WI 54481	(715)822-3949	5							
43. Steeds' Wolf River Lodge, White Lake, WI 54491	(715)882-2182	50	12	x	x	x	x		
44. Telemark, Cable, WI 54821	(715)798-3811	60	60	x	x	x	x	x	
45. Thunder Lake Ski Touring Center, Eagle River, WI 54521	(715)545-2522	12	12	x	x	x			
46. Tommy's River Forest Area, Galesville, WI 54630	(608)582-2371	15		x	x				
47. Trees For Tomorrow Center, Eagle River, WI 54521	(715)497-6456	15	15	x	x	x	x	x	
48. Trollhaugen, Dresser, WI 54009	(415)755-2955	3		x	x	x	x		
49. Whitecap Mountains, Montreal, WI 54550	(715)561-2227		20	x	x	x	x	x	
50. Wildcat Lodge, Boulder Junction, WI 54512	(715)385-2421		25		x		x	x	
51. Wildcat Mountain State Park, Ontario, WI 54651	(608)387-4775	7							x
52. Willow River State Park, WI 54016	(715)386-5931	7							
53. Wood County Park Department, Wisconsin Rapids, WI 54494 x190	(715)423-3000		5						
54. Woodside Ranch Resort, Mauston, WI 53948	(608)847-4275	21	11	x	x	x	x	x	
55. Wintergreen Touring Center, Spring Green, WI 53588	(608)588-2571	15	15	x	x	x	x	x	

MICHIGAN

No. NAME OF AREA, LOCATION	TELEPHONE #	Trail Miles	Maintained Miles	Instruction	Rental	Snacks	Meals	Lodging	Camping
1. Bay Valley Inn, Bay City, MI 48706 1-800-292-5028	(517)686-3500								
2. Bintz Apple Mountain Ski Lodge, Freeland, MI 48623	(517)781-0170	4			x	x	x		
3. Boyne Highlands, Harbor Springs, MI 49740	(616)526-2171	16	16		x	x	x	x	
4. Boyne Nordican, Boyne Falls, MI 49713	(616)549-2441	25	25	x	x	x	x	x	
5. Caberfae Ski Area, Cadillac, MI 49601	(616)862-3300	9	9	x	x	x	x	x	
6. Cheboygan-Black Lake Trail, Cheboygan, MI 49721	(616)627-4547							x	x
7. Cool X-C Ski Touring Center, Leroy, MI 49655	(616)768-4624	30	20	x	x	x	x	x	
8. Corsair Ski Trails, c/o Nordic Sports, Tawas, MI 48730	(517)362-2001	30	30	x	x	x	x	x	
9. Crystal Mountain, Thompsonville, MI 49683	(616)378-2911	50	16	x	x				
10. Department of Natural Resources, Alpena, MI 49707	(517)354-2209	15	15						x
11. Enchanted Acres Campground, Irons, MI 49644	(616)266-5102	26	26						
12. Green Pine Lake Pathway, Paris, MI 49338	(616)832-2281	15	15						
13. Greenwood Campground, Alger, MI 48610	(517)345-2778	18		x	x				x
14. Hilton Shanty Creek, Bellaire, MI 49615	(616)533-8621	17	17	x	x	x	x	x	
15. Hinchman Acres Resort, Mio, MI 48647	(517)826-3991	20	20	x	x	x		x	
16. Indianhead, Wakefield, MI 49968	(906)229-5181		6	x	x				

continued . . .

NAME OF AREA	LOCATION	TELEPHONE #	TRAIL MILES	MAINTAINED MILES	INSTRUCTION	RENTAL	SNACKS	MEALS	LODGING	CAMPING
17. Ishpeming Chamber of Commerce	Ishpeming, MI 49849	(906)486-4841	10						x	
18. Kin-Mar on the Hill	Gaylord, MI 49735	(517)732-4950	15	15	x	x	x			
19. Kensington Mitropark	Milford, MI 48042	(313)685-1561	19		x		x			
20. Lake Mary Plains Pathway	Lansing, MI 48909		10						x	
21. Lost Lake Resort	Paradise, MI 49768	(906)492-3464	30						x	
22. Lost Pines Lodge	Harrietta, MI 49638	(616)389-2222			x	x	x	x		
23. Michaywe Slopes	Gaylord, MI 49735	(517)939-8800		8	x	x	x	x		
24. Mount Mancelona	Mancelona, MI	(616)587-9162		5	x	x	x	x	x	
25. Nubs Nobs	Harbor Springs, MI 49740	(616)526-2131	10			x				
26. Pictured Rocks National Lakeshore	Munising, MI 49862	(906)387-4859	8							x
27. Pine Mountain	Iron Mountain, MI 49801	(906)774-2747	6			x				
28. Porcupine Mountain	Ontonagon, MI 49953	(906)885-5798	30	30						
29. Ranch Rudolph	Traverse City, MI 49684	(616)947-9529	20	18	x	x	x	x	x	
30. Schuss Mountain	Mancelona, MI 49659	(616)587-9162	12		x	x	x	x	x	
31. Sha Ro Co Farm	Jones, MI 49061	(616)476-2464	15			x	x		x	
32. Shibui Fun Valley	Mio, MI 48647	(517)848-2250	2							x
33. Ski Brule	Iron River, MI 49935 1-800-338-7141	(906)265-4957	15	15	x	x	x			
34. Sky Valley Ranch	Kalkaska, MI 49646	(616)258-5982	20				x	x		
35. Snowcrest At Blackjack	Bessemer, MI 49911	(906)229-5115	20			x	x		x	
36. Sugar Loaf Mountain Resort	Cedar, MI 49621	(616)228-5461	13	13	x	x	x	x	x	
37. Sylvania Outfitters	Wattersmeet, MI 49969	(906)358-4766	27	18	x	x	x	x		
38. Thunder Mountain Ski Area	Boyne, MI 49713	(616)549-2441				x	x	x		
39. Timberlane Ski Touring Lodge	Irons, MI 49644		15	15	x	x			x	
40. Timberlee	Traverse City, MI 49684	(616)946-4444	18	18	x					
41. Tisdale Triangle Pathway	Houghton Lake, MI 48653	(517)422-5522	10							
42. Tyrolean	Gaylord, MI 49735	(517)732-2743	52	25	x	x				
43. Walloon Hills Ski Area	Boyne Falls, MI 49713	(616)549-2441			x	x	x	x		
44. Wiskey Creek Recreation	Pentwater, MI 49449	(616)869-8671	30	30					x	x
45. Woods & Water Campground	White Cloud, MI 49349	(616)698-6701	10				x	x	x	x
46. YMCA Camp Martin Johnson	Irons, MI 49644	(616)266-5202	10			x	x		x	
47. Yogi Bear's Jellystone Campground	Traverse City, MI 49684	(616)947-2770	7	7		x	x		x	x

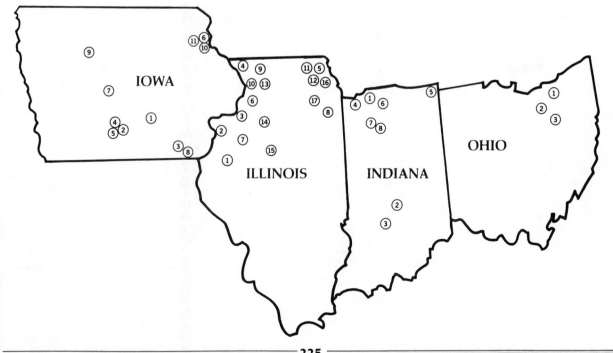

IOWA

NAME OF AREA	LOCATION	TELEPHONE #	TRAIL MILES	MAINTAINED MILES	INSTRUCTION	RENTAL	SNACKS	MEALS	LODGING	CAMP
1. **Fun Valley**, Montezuma, IA 50171		(515)623-3456				x	x	x		
2. **Iowa Conservation Commission**, Chariton, IA 50049		(515)774-5581	5	5			x			x
3. **Lacey-Keosauqua State Park**, Keosauqua, IA 52565		(319)293-3502								
4. **Lucas County Conservation Board**, Chariton, IA 50049			13							
5. **Park Ranger, Red Haw Lake State Park**, Chariton, IA 50049		(515)744-5632								
6. **Pikes Peak State Park**, McGregor, IA 52157		(319)873-2341								x
7. **Saylorville Lake**, U.S. Army Corps of Engineers, Johnston, IA 50131		(515)964-5460	4	4						
8. **Shimek Forest Headquarters**, Farmington, IA 52626			20					x	x	x
9. **Winter World**, Humboldt, IA 50548		(515)332-3329	3	3	x	x				
10. **Yellow River State Forest Headquarters**, McGregor, IA 52157		(319)586-2254								x
11. **Yellow River Station**, Monona, IA 52159		(319)539-2425	10	10	x	x	x		x	

ILLINOIS

NAME OF AREA	LOCATION	TELEPHONE #	TRAIL MILES	MAINTAINED MILES	INSTRUCTION	RENTAL	SNACKS	MEALS	LODGING	CAMP
1. **Argyle Lake State Park**, Colchester, IL 62326		(309)776-3422	6							x
2. **Big River State Forest**, Keithsburg, IL 61442		(309)374-2496	20							x
3. **Black Hawk State Park**, Rock Island, IL 61201		(309)788-9536								
4. **Eagle Ridge Nordic Ski Center**, Galena, IL 61036		(815)777-2444	24	24	x	x	x	x	x	
5. **Holiday Park**, Wooster Lake, Ingleside, IL 60041		(312)546-6444	7			x	x	x	x	
6. **Illinois & Michigan Canal State Park**, Morrison, IL 60450		(815)942-0796	15							x
7. **Jubilee State Park**, Brimfield, IL 61517		(309)243-7683	10							x
8. **Kankakee River State Park**, Bourbonnais, IL 60914		(815)933-1383		3						x
9. **Lake Le-Aqua-Na State Park**, Lena, IL 61048		(815)369-4282	7				x	x		x
10. **Mississippi Palisades State Park**, Savanna, IL 61074		(815)273-2731	8	8	x				x	x
11. **Moraine Hills**, McHenry, IL 60050		(815)385-1624	10			x	x			
12. **Norge Ski Club**, Fox River Grove, IL 60021		(312)639-5955		7	x	x		x	x	
13. **Plum Tree Ski Area**, Shannon, IL 61078		(815)493-2881				x	x	x		
14. **Saul-Trail State Park**, Kewanee, IL 61443		(309)853-5589	8							x
15. **Spring Lake Conservation Area**, Manito, IL 61546		(309)968-6197	4	4						
16. **Villa Olivia**, Bartlett, IL 60103		(312)742-5200		7	x	x				
17. **White Pines State Park**, Mount Morris, IL 61054		(815)946-3717	6							x

INDIANA

NAME OF AREA	LOCATION	TELEPHONE #	TRAIL MILES	MAINTAINED MILES	INSTRUCTION	RENTAL	SNACKS	MEALS	LODGING	CAMP
1. **Bondix Woods County Park**, New Carlisle, IN 46552		(219)654-3155	10	6	x	x	x			
2. **Eagle Creek Park**, Indianapolis, IN 46254		(317)293-4827	10	8						
3. **Gnaw Bone Camp Cross Country Ski Area**, Nashville, IN 47448		(812)988-4852	15			x	x	x	x	
4. **Indiana Dunes State Park**, Chesterton, IN 46304		(219)926-1215	25							x
5. **Pokagon State Park**, Angola, IN 46703		(219)833-2012								
6. **Potato Creek State Recreation Area**, North Liberty, IN 46554		(219)656-3490	25	25	x			x		
7. **Tippecanoe River State Park**, Winamac, IN 46996		(219)946-3213		15						x
8. **Winamac State Fish & Wildlife Area**, Winamac, IN 46996		(219)946-4422	20							

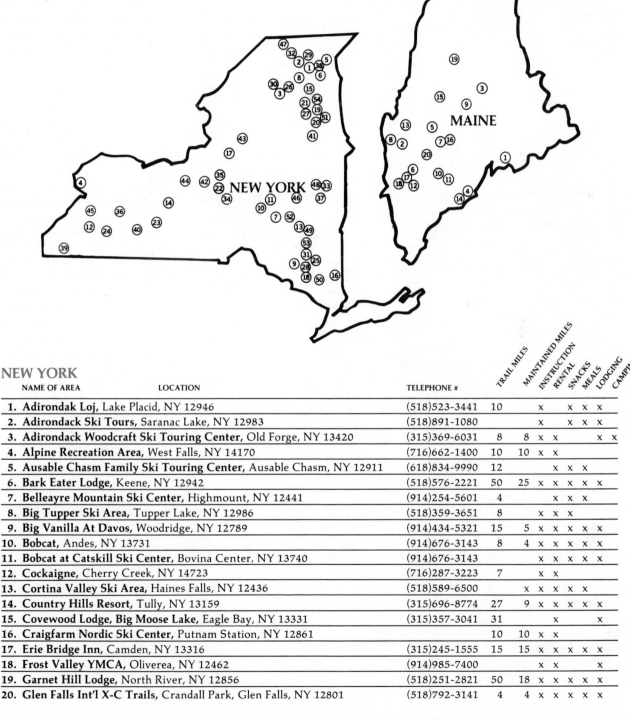

OHIO

NAME OF AREA / LOCATION	TELEPHONE #	TRAIL MILES	MAINTAINED MILES	INSTRUCTION	RENTAL	SNACKS	MEALS	LODGING	CAMPING
1. **Alpine Valley Ski Area,** Chesterland, OH 44026	(216)285-2211			x	x	x	x	x	
2. **Cuyahoga Valley National Recreation Area,** Peninsula, OH 44264	(216)653-9036	35							
3. **Towner's Woods,** Portage Cty. Park & Rec. Dept., Ravenna, OH 44266	(216)678-8851								

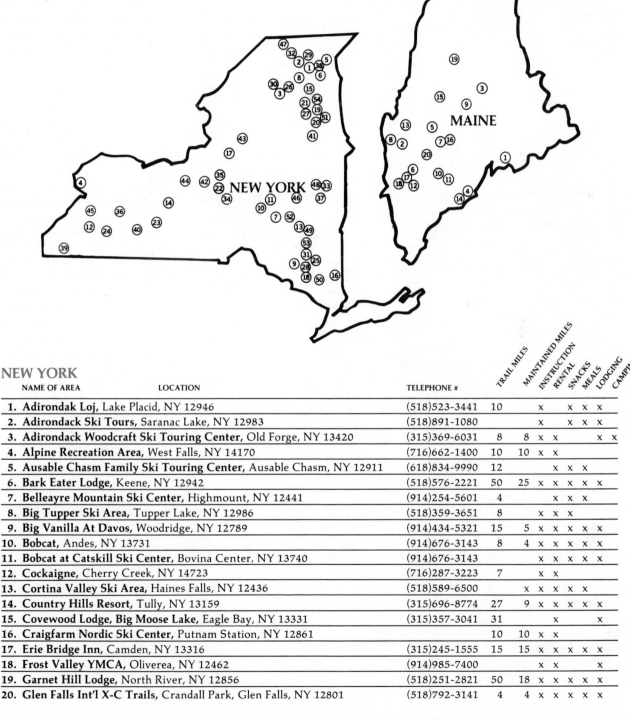

NEW YORK

NAME OF AREA / LOCATION	TELEPHONE #	TRAIL MILES	MAINTAINED MILES	INSTRUCTION	RENTAL	SNACKS	MEALS	LODGING	CAMPING
1. **Adirondak Loj,** Lake Placid, NY 12946	(518)523-3441	10			x		x	x	x
2. **Adirondack Ski Tours,** Saranac Lake, NY 12983	(518)891-1080				x		x	x	x
3. **Adirondack Woodcraft Ski Touring Center,** Old Forge, NY 13420	(315)369-6031	8	8	x	x			x	x
4. **Alpine Recreation Area,** West Falls, NY 14170	(716)662-1400	10	10	x	x				
5. **Ausable Chasm Family Ski Touring Center,** Ausable Chasm, NY 12911	(618)834-9990	12			x	x	x		
6. **Bark Eater Lodge,** Keene, NY 12942	(518)576-2221	50	25	x	x	x	x	x	
7. **Belleayre Mountain Ski Center,** Highmount, NY 12441	(914)254-5601	4			x	x	x		
8. **Big Tupper Ski Area,** Tupper Lake, NY 12986	(518)359-3651	8			x	x	x		
9. **Big Vanilla At Davos,** Woodridge, NY 12789	(914)434-5321	15	5	x	x	x	x	x	
10. **Bobcat,** Andes, NY 13731	(914)676-3143	8	4	x	x	x	x	x	
11. **Bobcat at Catskill Ski Center,** Bovina Center, NY 13740	(914)676-3143			x	x	x	x	x	
12. **Cockaigne,** Cherry Creek, NY 14723	(716)287-3223	7			x	x			
13. **Cortina Valley Ski Area,** Haines Falls, NY 12436	(518)589-6500			x	x	x	x	x	
14. **Country Hills Resort,** Tully, NY 13159	(315)696-8774	27	9	x	x	x	x	x	
15. **Covewood Lodge, Big Moose Lake,** Eagle Bay, NY 13331	(315)357-3041	31			x			x	
16. **Craigfarm Nordic Ski Center,** Putnam Station, NY 12861		10	10	x	x				
17. **Erie Bridge Inn,** Camden, NY 13316	(315)245-1555	15	15	x	x	x	x	x	
18. **Frost Valley YMCA,** Oliverea, NY 12462	(914)985-7400			x	x			x	
19. **Garnet Hill Lodge,** North River, NY 12856	(518)251-2821	50	18	x	x	x	x	x	
20. **Glen Falls Int'l X-C Trails,** Crandall Park, Glen Falls, NY 12801	(518)792-3141	4	4	x	x	x	x	x	

continued . . .

NAME OF AREA	LOCATION	TELEPHONE #	TRAIL MILES	MAINTAINED MILES	INSTRUCTION	RENTAL	SNACKS	MEALS	LODGING	CAMP
21. Gore Mountain Ski Center, North Creek, NY 12853		(518)251-2411	11		x	x	x			
22. Greandreau's Resort, Indian Lake Village, NY 12842		(518)648-5500			x	x				
23. Greek Peak Ski Area, Cortland, NY 13045		(607)835-6111	27	27	x	x	x	x	x	
24. Holiday Valley, Ellicottville, NY 14731		(716)699-2345	18	5	x					
25. Hudson Valley Wine Co., Highland, NY 12528		(914)619-7296	14	14	x	x	x			
26. Inlet Ski Touring Center, Inlet, NY 13360		(315)357-6961	75	25	x	x			x	
27. Knowlhurst Lodge, Stony Creek, NY 12878		(518)696-3335			x	x	x			
28. Lake Minnewaska Resort, Lake Minnewaska, NY 12561		(914)255-6000	150	15	x	x		x	x	
29. Lake Placid Club Resort, Lake Placid, NY 12946		(518)523-3361		12	x	x	x	x	x	x
30. McCauley Mountain Touring Trails, Old Forge, NY 13420		(315)369-6983	9		x	x			x	
31. Mohonk Mountain House, New Paltz, NY 12561		(914)255-1000	24		x	x	x	x	x	x
32. Mount Pisgah Ski Area, Saranac Lake, NY 12983		(518)891-1990			x	x	x			
33. Mount Van Hoevenberg, Albany, NY 12233		(518)457-2500	100	30						
34. Mystic Mountain, New Woodstock, NY 13122		(315)662-3322	10	3	x	x				
35. 90 Acre Ski Center, Fayetteville, NY 13066		(315)637-9023	9	7	x	x	x	x	x	
36. The Nordic Way at Coldon Langlauf Trails, Holland, NY 14080		(716)941-6675	7	5	x	x	x	x		
37. Old Wilderness Lodge, Albany, NY 12210		(518)449-5098	120	7	x	x		x	x	
38. Paleface Lodge & Ski Center, Jay, NY 12941		(518)946-2272	25	25	x			x	x	x
39. Peek n' Peak Ski Center, Clymer, NY 14724		(716)355-4141	15	15	x	x	x	x	x	
40. Podunk Cross Country Center, Trumansburg, NY 14886		(607)387-6716	12	5	x	x	x			
41. Saratoga Mountain Ski Touring Center, Saratoga Springs, NY 12866		(518)584-2008	20	20	x			x	x	x
42. Skaneateles Rossignol Touring Center, Skaneateles, NY 13152		(315)685-7558	7	7	x	x	x			
43. Snow Ridge Ski Area, Turin, NY 13473		(315)348-3456	10	10	x	x	x	x	x	
44. Sojourn Farm Ski Touring Center, Cayuga, NY 13034		(315)252-1902	25	25	x	x	x			
45. Tamarack Ridge, Colden, NY 14033		(716)941-3613	3	3	x	x	x			
46. The Beresford Farms Ski Touring Center, Delanson, NY 12053		(518)895-2483	16	16	x	x	x	x		
47. Titus Mountain, Malone, NY 12953		(518)483-3740		7		x	x	x	x	
48. Trail North, Latham, NY 12110		(518)785-0340	10		x	x	x	x		
49. Villaggio Resort Hotel, Haines Falls, NY 12348		(518)589-5000								
50. Ward Pound Ridge Reservation, Cross River, NY 10518		(914)763-3493	12							x
51. West Mountain, Glen Falls, NY 12801		(518)793-6608	20				x	x		
52. White Birches Ski Touring Center, Windham, NY 12496		(518)734-3266	14	14	x	x	x			
53. Williams Lake Hotel, Rosendale, NY 12472		(914)658-3101	15	15	x	x	x	x	x	
54. Wills Run, Schroon Lake, NY 12870		(518)532-7936	20	30	x	x	x	x	x	

MAINE

NAME OF AREA	LOCATION	TELEPHONE #	TRAIL MILES	MAINTAINED MILES	INSTRUCTION	RENTAL	SNACKS	MEALS	LODGING	CAMP
1. Acadia National Park, Bar Harbor, ME 04609		(207)288-3338	30		x	x	x	x	x	
2. Akers Ski, Andover, ME 04216		(207)392-4682	25	5		x	x			
3. Baxter State Park, Millinocket, ME 04462		(207)723-5140	50							x
4. Camden Snow Bowl, Camden, ME 04843		(207)236-3438	20		x	x				
5. Carrabassett Valley Rec. Ctr., Carrabassett Valley, ME 04947		(207)237-2205	65	40	x	x	x			
6. Chisholm Winter Park, Rumford, ME 04276		(207)364-8977	7		x	x	x	x	x	
7. Deer Farm Touring Center, Kingsfield, ME 04947		(207)265-2241	35	30	x	x	x	x	x	
8. Evergreen Valley Resort Inc., E. Stoneham, ME 04231		(207)928-3300				x	x	x		
9. Little Lyford Pond Camps, Brownville, ME 04414			43		x	x			x	x
10. Lost Valley Ski Area, Auburn, ME 04210		(207)784-1561	4	4	x	x	x	x		
11. Overland Rolls, Brunswick, ME 04011		(207)725-5199			x		x	x		
12. Pleasant Mountain Ski Area, Bridgton, ME 04009		(207)647-8444	5			x	x	x		
13. Saddleback Ski Area, Rangeley, ME 04970		(207)864-3380	25		x	x	x		x	
14. Samoset Resort, Rockport, ME 04856		(207)594-2511	2			x	x	x	x	

continued . . .

NAME OF AREA	LOCATION	TELEPHONE #	TRAIL MILES	MAINTAINED MILES	INSTRUCTION	RENTAL	SNACKS	MEALS	LODGING	CAMPING
15. **Squaw Mountain at Moosehead,** Greenville, ME 04441		(207)695-2272	25	25	x	x				
16. **Sugarloaf Area Association,** Kingfield, ME 04947		(207)237-2861	50		x	x	x	x	x	
17. **Sunday River,** Bethel, ME 04217		(207)824-2410	25	15	x	x	x	x	x	
18. **The Bethel Inn,** Bethel, ME 04217		(207)824-2175	15	15	x	x	x	x	x	
19. **The Birches Cross Country Ski Center,** Rockwood, ME 04478		(207)534-7305	19	8	x	x	x	x	x	
20. **Titcomb Mt. Ski Area,** Farmington, ME 04938		(207)778-9384	30	30	x		x	x	x	

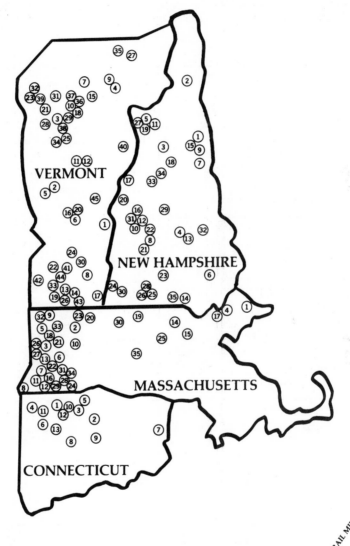

VERMONT

NAME OF AREA	LOCATION	TELEPHONE #	TRAIL MILES	MAINTAINED MILES	INSTRUCTION	RENTAL	SNACKS	MEALS	LODGING	CAMPING
1. **Ascutney Meadows Touring Center,** Brownsville, VT 05037		(802)484-7711								
2. **Blueberry Hill,** Goshen, VT 05477		(802)247-6735	50	30	x	x	x		x	
3. **Bolton Valley Resort,** Bolton, VT 05477		(802)434-2131	29	12	x	x	x	x	x	
4. **Burke Mountain Recreation,** East Burke, VT 05832		(802)626-3305	20	20	x	x	x	x	x	
5. **Churchill House Inn & Ski Touring Center,** Brandon, VT 05733		(802)247-3300	24	12	x	x	x	x	x	
6. **Cortina Inn,** Killington, VT 05751		(802)773-3331	25	15	x		x	x	x	
7. **Craftsbury Ski Touring Center,** Craftsbury Commons, VT 05827		(802)586-2514	25	25	x	x	x	x	x	
8. **Cross Country Ski Shop & Trail System at Grafton,** Grafton, VT 05146		(802)843-2234	18	9	x	x	x	x	x	
9. **Darion Inn,** East Burke, VT 05832		(802)626-5914	15	15	x	x		x	x	
10. **Edson Hill Ski Touring,** Stowe, VT 05672		(802)253-8954	45	25	x	x	x	x	x	

continued . . .

Name of Area	Location	Telephone #	Trail Miles	Maintained Miles	Instruction	Rental	Snacks	Meals	Lodging	Camping
11. Green Mtn. Touring Ctr.,	Green Mtn. Stock Farm, Randolph, VT 05060	(802)728-5575	20	20	x	x	x	x	x	
12. Green Trails Country Inn,	Brookfield, VT 05036	(802)276-2012	25		x	x	x			
13. Haystack,	Wilmington, VT 05477	(802)464-5321	30							
14. Hermitage Touring Center,	Wilmington, VT 05363	(802)464-3579	30	20	x	x	x	x	x	
15. Highland Lodge Ski Touring Ctr.,	Caspian Lake, Greensboro, VT 05841	(802)533-2647	22	15	x	x	x	x	x	
16. Killington Ski Area,	Killington, VT 05751		5			x	x	x	x	
17. Living Memorial Park,	Battleboro, VT 05301	(802)454-5808	1		x					
18. Mount Mansfield Co.,	Stowe, VT 05672	(802)253-7311	30	15	x	x		x	x	
19. Mount Snow Ski Touring Center,	Mount Snow, VT 05356	(802)464-3333	50			x	x	x	x	
20. Mountain Meadows,	Killington, VT 05751	(802)775-7077	40	15	x	x	x	x	x	
21. Mountain Top Ski Touring Center,	Chittenden, VT 05737	(802)483-2311	55	25	x	x	x	x	x	
22. Nordic Inn Ski Touring Center,	Landgrove, VT 05148	(802)824-6444	19	19	x	x	x	x	x	
23. Northland, Inc.,	North Hero, VT 05474	(802)372-8822		6		x	x	x	x	
24. Okemo Mountain Ski Area,	Ludlow, VT 05149	(802)228-4041		8		x	x	x	x	
25. Ole Mosesen,	Warren, VT 05674	(802)496-3430	40	10	x	x	x	x		
26. On The Rocks Lodge,	Wilmington, VT 05363	(802)464-8364	30	18	x	x	x	x	x	
27. Rabbit Hill Inn Ski Touring Center,	Lower Waterford, VT 05848	(802)748-5168	13	3	x	x		x	x	
28. Sherman Hollow Ski Touring Center,	Richmond, VT 05477	(602)735-7540	24	24	x	x	x	x		
29. Ski Hostel Lodge,	Waterbury Center, VT 05677	(802)244-8859					x	x	x	
30. Ski Tours of Vermont,	Chester, VT 05143	(802)875-3631				x	x		x	
31. Smuggler's Notch Ski Area,	Jeffersonville, VT 05464	(802)644-8851	33	33	x	x	x	x	x	
32. Stork's Farm Ski Touring Center,	Westford, VT 05494	(802)878-2282	12	12	x	x	x	x		
33. Stratton Ski Touring Center,	Stratton Mountain, VT 05155	(802)297-1880	16	16	x	x	x	x	x	
34. Sugarbush Inn,	Rossignol Touring Center, Warren, VT 05674	(802)583-2301	35	14	x	x	x	x	x	
35. Sunshine Ski Touring Center,	Jay, VT 05859	(802)988-4459	40		x	x		x	x	
36. Topnotch at Stowe,	Stowe, VT 05672	(802)253-8585	40	25	x	x	x	x	x	
37. Trapp Family Lodge,	Stowe, VT 05672	(802)253-8511	60	36	x	x	x	x	x	
38. Tucker Hill Ski Touring Center,	Waitsfield, VT 05673	(802)496-3203	25	25	x	x		x	x	
39. Tulip Tree Inn,	Chittenden, VT 05737	(802)483-6213					x	x	x	
40. Twin Mount Farm Lodge,	Peacham, VT 05862	(802)592-3579	7	7				x	x	
41. Viking Ski Touring Center,	Londonderry, VT 05148	(802)824-3933	20	18	x	x	x			
42. West Mountain Inn,	Arlington, VT 05250	(802)375-6515	10			x	x	x	x	
43. Whitehouse Ski Touring Center,	Wilmington, VT 05363	(802)464-2135	13	10	x	x		x	x	
44. Wild Wings Ski Touring Center,	Peru, VT 05152	(802)824-6793	10	7	x	x	x			
45. Woodstock Ski Touring Center,	Woodstock, VT 05091	(802)457-2114	47	23	x	x	x	x	x	

NEW HAMPSHIRE

Name of Area	Location	Telephone #	Trail Miles	Maintained Miles	Instruction	Rental	Snacks	Meals	Lodging	Camping
1. Appalachian Mountain Club,	Gorham, NH 03581	(603)466-2727	25		x		x	x	x	
2. Balsams Wilderness,	Dizville Notch, NH 03576	(603)255-3400	25	25	x	x				
3. Bretton Woods Touring Center,	Bretton Woods, NH 03575	(603)278-5000	60	50	x	x	x	x	x	
4. Brickyard Mountain Resort,	Laconia, NH 03246	(603)366-4316	5	5	x	x	x	x	x	
5. Cannon Mountain,	Franconia, NH 03580	(603)823-5563	5			x	x	x		
6. Charmingfare Ski Touring Center,	Candia, NH 03034	(603)483-2307	20	15	x	x	x			
7. Darbyfields Inn,	Conway, NH 03818	(603)447-2181	20	20	x	x	x	x	x	
8. Dexters Inn & Nordic Center,	Sunapee, NH 03782	(603)763-5571	15			x	x	x	x	x
9. Eastern Mountain Sports,	Jackson Village Loop, Jackson, NH 03846	(603)383-9641	75	42	x	x	x	x	x	
10. Eastman Ski Touring Center,	Grantham, NH 03753	(603)863-4240	20	12	x	x	x	x	x	
11. Franconia Inn Ski Touring Center,	Franconia, NH 03580	(603)823-5542	40	40	x	x	x	x	x	
12. Gray Ledges,	Grantham, NH 03753	(603)863-1002	50	25			x	x	x	

continued ...

NAME OF AREA / LOCATION	TELEPHONE #	TRAIL MILES	MAINTAINED MILES	INSTRUCTION	RENTAL	SNACKS	MEALS	LODGING	CAMPING
13. **Gunstock Ski Area**, Laconia, NH 03246	(603)293-4341	15	10	x	x	x	x	x	
14. **Hollis-Hof Ski Touring Center**, Hollis, NH 03049	(603)465-2633	50	10	x	x	x	x		
15. **Jackson Ski Touring Foundation**, Jackson, NH 03846	(603)383-9355	84	42	x	x	x	x	x	
16. **La Salette Ski Touring Center**, Enfield Center, NH 03748	(603)632-4257	25			x	x		x	x
17. **Loch Lyme Lodge**, Lyme, NH 03768	(603)795-2141				x	x		x	x
18. **Loon Mountain Ski Touring**, Lincoln, NH 03251	(603)745-8111	8			x	x	x	x	x
19. **Mitterstill**, Franconia, NH 03580	(603)823-5511	45	15						
20. **Moose Mountain Lodge**, Etna, NH 03750	(603)643-3529	25						x	
21. **Mount Sunapee Ski Area**, Mount Sunapee, NH 03772	(603)763-2356	10			x	x	x	x	
22. **Norsk Ski Touring Center**, New London, NH 03527	(603)526-4685	19	15	x		x	x	x	
23. **Pole And Pedal Ski Touring Center**, Henniker, NH 03242	(603)428-3242	19	19	x	x	x	x		
24. **Roads End Farm Ski Touring Center**, Chesterfield, NH 03443	(603)363-4703	14	14	x	x		x	x	
25. **Sargent Ski Touring Center**, Peterborough, NH 03458	(603)525-3311	15	15	x	x	x	x	x	
26. **Summers Ski Touring Center**, Dublin, NH 03444	(603)563-8556	15	7	x	x	x			
27. **Sunset Hill Touring Center**, Sugar Hill, NH 03585	(603)823-5522	15	12	x	x	x	x	x	
28. **Temple Mountain Ski Center**, Peterborough, NH 03458	(603)424-6949	35	8	x	x	x			
29. **Tenney Mountain**, Plymouth, NH 03264	(603)536-1717	4			x				
30. **The Inn at East Hill Farm**, Troy, NH 03465	(603)242-6495	7	7		x	x	x	x	
31. **The Leages Farm**, Grantham, NH 03753	(603)863-1002	50	35	x	x	x	x	x	
32. **The Nordic Skier**, Wolfboro, NH 03894	(603)569-3151		20	x	x	x	x	x	
33. **Waterville Valley Gateway Condominium Resort**, Campton, NH 03223	(603)726-3724	20	20	x	x	x	x	x	
34. **Waterville Valley Ski Touring Center**, Waterville Valley, NH 03223	(603)236-8311	32	32	x	x	x	x	x	
35. **Windblown Ski Touring**, New Ipswich, NH 03071	(603)878-2869	20	8		x	x		x	

MASSACHUSETTS

NAME OF AREA / LOCATION	TELEPHONE #	TRAIL MILES	MAINTAINED MILES	INSTRUCTION	RENTAL	SNACKS	MEALS	LODGING	CAMPING
1. **All Year Round**, Ipswich, MA 01938	(617)356-0131	100		x	x				
2. **Berkshire East Ski Area**, Charlemont, MA 01339	(413)339-6617			x	x	x	x		
3. **Berkshire Vacation Bureau**, Pittsfield, MA 01201	(413)443-9186								
4. **Boston Hill Ski Area**, North Andover, MA 01845	(617)683-2733							x	
5. **Brodie Mountain X-C Area**, New Ashford, MA 01237	(413)443-4752	12			x	x	x	x	
6. **Bu, steep Manor Ski Touring Center**, Washington, MA 01223	(413)623-5535	18	18	x	x	x	x	x	x
7. **Butternut Ski Touring**, Butternut Basin, Great Barrington, MA 01230	(413)528-0610	12	6	c	c	c			
8. **Catamount**, Hillsdale, NY 12529	(518)325-3200	4							
9. **Clarksburg State Park**, Clarksburg, MA 01247									
10. **Cummington Farm Ski Touring Center**, Cummington, MA 01026	(413)634-2111	27	7	x	x	x	x	x	
11. **Egremont Country Club Ski Touring Ctr.**, South Egremont, MA 01258	(413)528-4222			x		x	x	x	
12. **Egremont Inn**, South Egremont, MA 01258	(413)528-2111			x	x	x	x	x	
13. **Foxhollow Resort**, Lenox, MA 01240	(413)637-2000			x	x	x	x		
14. **Groton Hills Ski Area**, Groton, MA 01450	(617)448-5951	10	10	x	x	x	x	x	x
15. **Hartwell Ski Area**, Littleton, MA 01460	(617)486-9546	6	6			x	x	x	x
16. **Jug End Resort**, South Egremont, MA 01258	(413)528-0434	10							
17. **Merrimac Valley Ski Area**, Methuen, MA 01844	(617)686-6021					x	x		
18. **Mount Greylook State Reservation**, Lanesboro, MA 01237	(413)499-4263								
19. **Mount Watatic Ski Touring Center**, Ashby, MA 01431	(617)386-5680	20	2	x	x	x			
20. **Northfield Mount Ski Touring Center**, Northfield, MA 01360	(413)659-3713	25	25	x	x	x			
21. **Notchview Reservation**, Windsor, MA 01260		25	25						
22. **Oak n' Spruce Resort**, South Lee, MA 01260	(413)243-3500	4	4	x	x			x	x
23. **Oak Ridge Touring Center**, Gill, MA 01376	(413)863-4345	10	10	x	x	x	x		
24. **Otis Ridge Touring Center**, Otis, MA 01253	(413)267-4444	25	5	x	x	x	x	x	x

continued . . .

NAME OF AREA	LOCATION	TELEPHONE #	TRAIL MILES	MAINTAINED MILES	INSTRUCTION	RENTAL	SNACKS	MEALS	LODGING	CAMP
25. Pheasant Run Ski Area,	Leominster, MA 01453	(617)537-9293			x	x	x	x		
26. Pittsfield State Forest,	Pittsfield, MA 01201	(413)442-8992								
27. Pleasant Valley Wildlife Sanctuary,	Lenox, MA 01240	(413)637-0320		14	x					
28. Red Fox Touring Center,	Southfield, MA 01259	(413)229-7790	12	12	x	x	x			
29. Reverrun North,	Sheffield, MA 01257	(413)528-1100	7	5	x	x	x			
30. Riverwood Ski Touring Center,	Wichendon, MA 01475	(617)297-2257	20	15	x	x	x	x	x	
31. Sandisford State Forest,	Sandisford, MA 01255	(413)258-4774	6	2						
32. Savory Mountain State Forest,	North Adams, MA 01247	(413)663-8469	15	15					x	x
33. Stump Sprouts Ski Touring,	West Hawley, MA 01339	(413)339-4265	13	8	x	x	x			
34. The Flying Cloud Inn,	New Marlboro, MA 01230	(413)229-2113	5		x	x	x	x	x	
35. Ward Hill,	Shrewsbury, MA 01545	(617)422-8457	19	6	x	x	x	x		

CONNECTICUT

NAME OF AREA	LOCATION	TELEPHONE #	TRAIL MILES	MAINTAINED MILES	INSTRUCTION	RENTAL	SNACKS	MEALS	LODGING	CAMP
1. Blackberry River Ski Touring Center,	Norfolk, CT 06058	(203)542-5614	20	20	x	x	x	x	x	
2. Connecticut Dept. of Environmental Protection,	Hartford, CT 06115			50		x		x	x	x
3. Great World Touring Center,	West Simsbury, CT 06092	(203)658-4461	13	13	x	x	x	x		
4. Lime Rock Ski Touring Center c/o Village Store,	Salisbury, CT 06068	(203)435-9459				x	x		x	x
5. McLean Sanctuary,	Granby, CT 06035									
6. Mohawk Mountain Ski Area,	Cornwall, CT 06753	(203)627-6100				x	x		x	x
7. Notchang State Forest,	Voluntown, CT 06384	(203)376-2513								
8. Osbornedale State Park,	Middlebury, CT 06072	(203)934-9301								
9. Powder Ridge Ski Area,	Middlefield, CT 06455	(203)349-3454	30	6	x	x	x	x	x	
10. Recreation Specialist,	Pleasant Valley, CT 06063	(203)379-0771								
11. Riverrunning Ski Touring Center,	Falls Village, CT 06031	(203)824-5579	15	15	x	x	x			
12. Topsmeed Forest,	Pleasant Valley, CT 06063	(203)379-0771							x	x
13. White Memorial Foundation, Inc.,	Litchfield, CT 06759	(203)567-8217				x	x			

PENNSYLVANIA

NAME OF AREA	LOCATION	TELEPHONE #	TRAIL MILES	MAINTAINED MILES	INSTRUCTION	RENTAL	SNACKS	MEALS	LODGING	CAMP
1. Apple Valley X-C Ski,	Zionsville, PA 18092	(215)996-5525	7	4	x	x	x			
2. Black Moshannon State Park,	Philipsburg, PA 16866	(814)342-1101		12		x	x		x	
3. Corbrus State Park,	Hanover, PA 17331	(717)637-2816		15		x	x	x		
4. Cross Country Ski Trails,	Gradyville, PA 19039	(215)565-7820	17	2	x	x	x			
5. Crystal Lake Camps,	Hughesville, PA 17737	(717)584-2698	30	15	x	x	x	x	x	
6. Denton Hill Ski Area,	Coudersport, PA 16915	(814)435-6372	85		x	x	x	x	x	
7. Gettysburg National Military Park,	Gettysburg, PA 17325	(717)334-1124								
8. Gifford Pinchot State Park,	Lewisberry, PA 17339	(717)432-5011								
9. Hidden Valley Ski Touring Center,	Somerset, PA 15501	(814)445-6014	40		x	x	x	x	x	
10. The Inn At Starlight Lake,	Starlight, PA 18461	(717)798-2519	18	12	x	x	x	x	x	
11. Kooser State Park,	Somerset, PA 15501	(814)445-8673	3							x
12. Ligonier Mountain Outfitters,	Laughlintown, PA 15655	(412)238-6246	25	25	x	x				
13. Maple Hill Farm,	Starrucca, PA 18462	(717)798-2753	28	28	x	x			x	x
14. Promised Land State Park,	Greentown, PA 18426	(717)676-3428	10				x			
15. Rossignol Nordic Touring Center,	Pocono Manor, PA 18349	(717)839-6964	38		x	x	x		x	
16. Tyler State Park,	Newton Bucks, PA 18940	(215)968-2021	6							

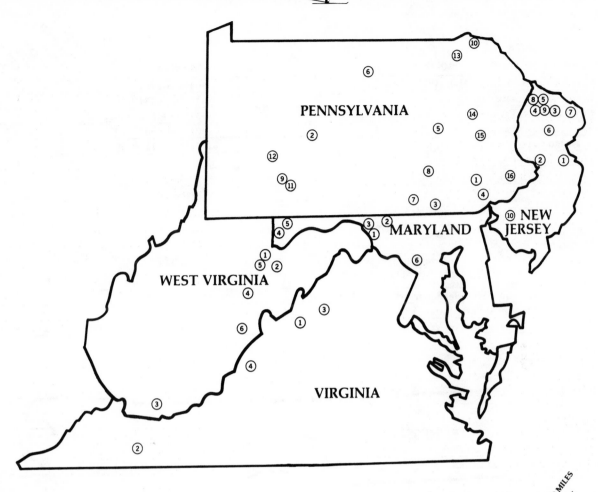

NEW JERSEY

NAME OF AREA	LOCATION	TELEPHONE #	TRAIL MILES	MAINTAINED MILES	INSTRUCTION	RENTAL	SNACKS	MEALS	LODGING	CAMPING
1. Allaire State Park, Farmingdale, NJ 07727										
2. Bureau of Parks, Trenton, NJ 08625										
3. Craigmeur Ski Area, New Foundland, NJ 07435		(603)878-2869	20	8		x	x		x	
4. Fairview Lake Ski Touring Center, Newton, NJ 07860		(201)383-9282	18	9	x	x	x	x	x	
5. Great Gorge/Vernon Valley Ski Areas, McAfee, NJ 07428		(201)827-2000								
6. Morristown National Historical Park, Morristown, NJ 07960		(201)539-2016	19							
7. Ringwood State Park, Ringwood, NJ 07456										
8. Sleepy Hollow Park Kamp Grounds, Sussex, NJ 07826		(201)875-6211	10			x	x			
9. Stokes State Forest, Branchville, NJ 07826				10						
10. The Old Orchard Inn, Greenwich, NJ 08323		(201)542-5751	12	9	x	x	x	x	x	

MARYLAND

NAME OF AREA	LOCATION	TELEPHONE #	TRAIL MILES	MAINTAINED MILES	INSTRUCTION	RENTAL	SNACKS	MEALS	LODGING	CAMPING
1. Antietam National Battlefield Site, Sharpsburg, MD 21782		(301)432-5124								x
2. Catoctin Mountain Park, Thurmont, MD 21788		(301)271-2447	24							
3. Chesapeake & O'Caral National Historical Park, Sharpsburg, MD 21782										x
4. Herrington Manor State Park, Oakland, MD 21550		(301)334-9180	5							x
5. New Germany State Park, Grantsville, MD 21536		(301)895-5453								
6. Trails East, Gaithersburg, MD 20760		(301)840-0650				x	x	x	x	x

WEST VIRGINIA

NAME OF AREA, LOCATION	TELEPHONE #	TRAIL MILES	MAINTAINED MILES	INSTRUCTION	RENTAL	SNACKS	MEALS	LODGING	CAMPING
1. Canaan Valley Resorts, Davis, WV 26260	(304)866-4121				x	x	x	x	
2. Monongahela State Park, Petersburg, WV 26847	(304)257-4484								
3. Pipestem State Park, Pipestem, WV 25979	(304)466-1800	20+	20	x	x	x	x	x	
4. Snowshoe Company, Snowshoe, WV 26209	(304)799-6600	10		x	x	x	x	x	
5. Transmontane Outfitters LTD, Davis, WV 26260	(304)259-5117	50		x	x		x	x	
6. Watoga State Park, Marlington, WV 24954							x	x	

VIRGINIA

NAME OF AREA, LOCATION	TELEPHONE #	TRAIL MILES	MAINTAINED MILES	INSTRUCTION	RENTAL	SNACKS	MEALS	LODGING	CAMPING
1. George Washington National Forest, Harrisonburg, VA 22801									
2. National Recreation Area Headquarters, Marion, VA 24354	(703)783-5196								
3. Shenandoah National Park, Luray, VA 22835	(703)999-2241	95+							
4. The Homestead, Hot Springs, VA 24445	(703)839-5500				x	x	x		

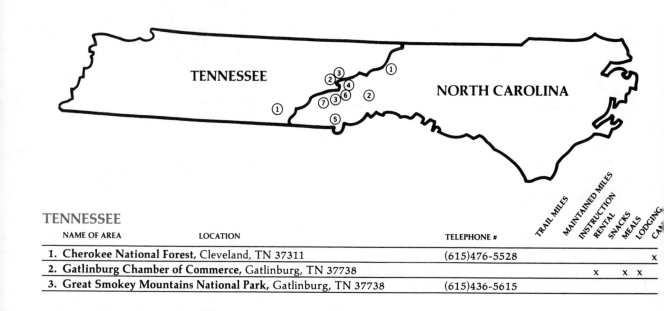

TENNESSEE

NAME OF AREA, LOCATION	TELEPHONE #	TRAIL MILES	MAINTAINED MILES	INSTRUCTION	RENTAL	SNACKS	MEALS	LODGING	CAMPING
1. Cherokee National Forest, Cleveland, TN 37311	(615)476-5528								x
2. Gatlinburg Chamber of Commerce, Gatlinburg, TN 37738					x		x	x	
3. Great Smokey Mountains National Park, Gatlinburg, TN 37738	(615)436-5615								

NORTH CAROLINA

NAME OF AREA, LOCATION	TELEPHONE #	TRAIL MILES	MAINTAINED MILES	INSTRUCTION	RENTAL	SNACKS	MEALS	LODGING	CAMPING
1. Beech Mountain Cross Country Ski Center, Banner Elk, NC 28604	(704)387-4770	6	6	x	x		x	x	
2. Blue Ridge Parkway, Asheville, NC 28801		10							
3. Cataloochee, Maggie Valley, NC 28751	(704)926-0285	5							
4. Great Smokey Mountain National Park, Gatlinburg, TN 37738	(704)497-3081								
5. High Hampton Inn, Cashiers, NC		100					x	x	
6. Mount Mitchell State Park, Burnsville, NC 28714	(704)675-4611								
7. Nantahala Outdoor Center, Bryson City, NC 28713	(704)488-2175				x	x		x	

HAWAII

NAME OF AREA	LOCATION	TELEPHONE #	TRAIL MILES	MAINTAINED MILES	INSTRUCTION	RENTAL	SNACKS	MEALS	LODGING	CAMPING
1. Mauna Kea, Honolulu, HI 96815		(808)537-4065					x	x	x	

SOURCE DEVELOPMENT

Abraham, Horst. *Teaching Concepts ATM.* Boulder, CO: Professional Ski Instructors of America, 1980.

Abraham, Horst. *Skiing Right.* Boulder, CO: Johnson Books, 1983.

Anderson, Bob. *Stretching.* Robert and Jean Anderson, 1975.

Arnold, Arnold. *Teaching Your Child to Learn.* New Jersey: Prentice Hall Inc., 1971.

Caldwell, John. *Caldwell On Cross-Country.* Brattleboro, VT: Stephen Green Press, 1975.

Caldwell, John. *The Cross-Country Ski Book Sixth Edition.* Brattleboro, VT: Stephen Green Press, 1981.

Campbell, Stu. *The American Teaching Method— Methodology.* Denver, CO: The PSIA–Educational Foundation, 1977.

Calhoun, Michael F. *The Parcourse: Guide to Fitness.* San Francisco, CA: Parcourse Ltd.,a 1979.

Cooper, Kenneth H. *The New Aerobics.* New York: Bantam Books, 1970.

Dauer, Victor P. and Pangraze, Robert P. *Dynamic Physical Education.* Minneapolis, MN: Burgess Publishing Co., 1975.

Evans, Harold, Jackman, Brian and Ottaway, Mark. "We Learned to Ski." *The Sunday Times.* New York: St. Martins Press, 1964.

Forsberg, Artur; Grauers, Jan and Haag, Roland. *Langdakning.* Omslagsfoto Roger Kullman, Kaben and Sjogren, 1978.

Flowler, John. *Movement Education.* Colorado: Department of Physical Education, University of Colorado, 1971.

Freeman, Cortland L. and Rieschl, Steve. *Ski Touring For The Fun of It.* Little, Brown and Co., 1974.

Gallwey, Timothy. *Innergame of Tennis.* New York: Random House, 1964.

Fallwey, Timothy. *Innergame of Skiing.* New York: Random House, 1977.

Gilliom, Bonnie and Clerp. *Basic Movement Education for Children.* Reading, MA: Addison-Wesley Publishing Co., 1970.

Hall, Bill. *Teaching Concepts A.T.M.N.* Professional Ski Instructors of America, Boulder, CO, 1983.

Hall, Marty. *One Stride Ahead.* Tulsa, OK: Winchester Press, 1981.

Highet, Gilbery. *The Art of Teaching.* New York: Random House, 1950.

Hilgard, Ernest. *Theories of Learning.* Appleton-Century and Crofts, 1956.

Holden, Michael. *An Instructor's Guide to Ski Mechanics.* Boulder, CO: PSIA Educational Foundation.

Joubert, George. *Teach Yourself To Ski.* Aspen, CO: Aspen Ski Masters, Translation by Sim Thomas, 1970.

Lash, Bill. *American Ski Technique.* Salt Lake City, UT: The Quality Press, 1964.

Maltz, Maxwell. *Psycho-Cybernetics.* New York: Essandess Special Editions. A Division of Simon and Schuster, 1960.

McGlenagham, Bruce A., and Gallhue, David L. *Fundamental Movement.* Philadelphia, PA: W. B. Saunders Co., 1978

Mosston, Muska. *Developmental Movement.* Columbus, OH: Charles E. Merrill Books, 1965.

Ostrander, Sheila, and Lynn Schroeder. *Superlearning.* New York, Dell Publishing Co., 1979.

Postman, Neil and Weingartner, Charles. *Teaching as a Subversive Activity.* New York: Delacorte Press, 1969.

Reifsnyder, William E. *Weathering the Wilderness.* San Francisco: Sierra Club Books, 1980.

Schuster, Werner F. *Risk Awareness and Skiing Safety in the Ski School.* Denver, CO: PSIA Educational Foundation, 1974.

Sharkey, Brian. *Physiology of Fitness.* Champaign, IL: Human Kinetics Publishers, 1979.

Singer, Robert N. *Myths and Truths in Sports Psychology.* New York: Harper and Row.

Strom, Robert D. *Teachers and the Learning Process.* Englewood Cliffs, NJ: Prentice-Hall, Inc., 1971.

Suinn, Richard M. *Psychology in Sports: Methods and Application.* Minneapolis, MN: Burgess Publishing Co., 1980.

Tejada-Flores, Lito. *Backcountry Skiing.* San Francisco, CA: Sierra Club Books, 1981.

Tutko, Thomas and Richards, Jack. *Psychology of Coaching.* Boston: Allyn and Bacon Inc., 1971.

Twardokens, George. *Balance: A Search for Effective Stance.* Boulder, CO: PSIA Educational Foundations, 1979.

United States Ski Team X-C Coaches Manual. Park City, UT: United States Ski Team in Cooperation with Haugen Sports, P.O. Box 100, Park City, UT 84060.

Vagners, Juns Dr. *Biomechanics of Skiing.* Boulder, CO: PSIA Educational Foundation.

Washburn, Bradford. *Frostbite.* Boston, MA: Museum of Science, 1963.

Wiik, Sven and Sumner, David. *Regnery Guide to Ski Touring.* Chicago, IL: Henry Regnery Co., 1964.

Wilkerson, James. *Medicine for Mountaineering.* Seattle, WA: The Mountaineers, 1967.

Witherell, Warren. *How The Racers Ski.* New York: Norton and Co., 1972.

Wollzenmuller, Franz. *Richtig Skilanglaufen 1.* BLV Verlagsgesellschaft, Munich, Wien, Zurich, 1982.